MW00800662

Maximum, Minimum, Medium

MAXIMUM

Julius Melnitzer

MINIMUM

A Journey Through Canadian Prisons

MEDIUM

KEY PORTER BOOKS

To Melissa, my daughter
By loving, you taught me love

Copyright © 1995 Julius Melnitzer

CANADIAN CATALOGUING IN PUBLICATION DATA

Melnitzer, Julius, 1947–
Maximum, medium, minimum: a journey through Canadian prisons

ISBN 1-55013-585-6

1. Melnitzer, Julius, 1947–   Imprisonment.
2. Prisons – Canada.   3. Prisoners – Canada – Biography.

HV9505.M45A3 1995   365'.44'092   C94-932863-4

The publisher gratefully acknowledges the assistance of the Canada Council, the Ontario Arts Council, and the Ontario Publishing Centre.

Distributed to the trade by National Book Network
1-800-462-6420

Key Porter Books Limited
70 The Esplanade
Toronto, Ontario
Canada M5E 1R2

Typesetting: Heidy Lawrance Associates
Printed and bound in Canada

95 96 97 98 99 6 5 4 3 2 1

Contents

Idling Reader, you may believe me when I tell you that I should have liked this book, which is the child of my brain, to be the fairest, the sprightliest, and the cleverest that could be imagined; but I have not been able to contravene the law of nature which would have it that like begets like. And so, what was to be expected of a sterile and uncultivated wit such as that which I possess if not an offspring that was dried up, shrivelled, and eccentric: a story filled with thoughts that never occurred to anyone else, of a sort that might be engendered in a prison where every annoyance has its home and every mournful sound its habitation?...

I, however, have no desire to go with the current of custom, nor would I, dearest reader, beseech you with tears in my eyes as others do to pardon or overlook the faults you discover in this book; you are neither relative nor friend but may call your soul your own and exercise free judgement. You are in your own house where you are master as the king is of his taxes, for you are familiar with the saying, "Under my cloak I kill the king." All of which exempts and frees you from any kind of respect or obligation; you may say of this story whatever you choose without fear of being slandered for an ill opinion any more than you will be rewarded for a good one.

— *Cervantes, Prologue to* Don Quixote

Part One

PUNISHMENT

Tragedies sometimes happen to allow us to get rid of the things we do not have the good sense to get rid of by ourselves.

LAWRENCE J. CRABBE, JR.

Prologue

It had begun as badly as it could
and therefore it must continue.
GENERAL CHARLES DE GAULLE

"Get him, get him, get him, get him!" The chorus, which came from behind a locked steel door on the second floor of the Elgin Middlesex Detention Centre in London, Ontario, was aimed at me, Julius Melnitzer, ex-barrister, by my present community of companions. It was February 10, 1992, my first day in jail: that morning, Mr. Justice Maloney of the Ontario Court, General Division, had sentenced me to nine years for what the media called the "largest bank fraud in Canadian history."

I entered my new world as I had left the old one: an object of derision, hatred, and contempt, all tinged with that most inexorable of human catalysts, envy relieved. My naïveté, however, had allowed me to temper the anticipated hardships of prison by imagining an isolated world where I could escape judgement while serving my punishment.

How wrong I was! As the hoots of murderers, rapists, drug traffickers, paedophiles, bank robbers, and incestuous fathers — in short, fellow criminals — resounded in the ever-present echoes that are so characteristic of houses of detention, I realized the falseness of the instant delusion in a life of illusions: even in jail, in the house of those on whom sentence had been passed, I would not escape judgement; the human condition, it seems, demands judgement as punishment's adjunct, not merely as its prerequisite. As if to emphasize my kismet, prison's echoes never seemed to let me talk without hearing myself speak.

Yet this was my present: here I would learn that while the past may give form to life and the future a reason for its continuance, only the accumulation of the immediate instants we call the present is life itself; here I would learn that the present, anywhere, is most precious because it is most fleeting: even as we contemplate it, it passes. This is the story of the way in, and the way out.

Welcome

I know it's happened, but I don't feel anything yet.
JOHN UPDIKE

The assembly-line efficiency of a much-practised routine belied the chaos of things to come. Selling time and doing time are not all that different. In either case, a superficial and deceptive semblance of discipline and structure is the self-serving casement that governs the lives of both lawyers and convicts; in either case, nothing is what it seems, and the banalities of carefully cultivated public misperceptions fuel and maintain the contradictions.

Without a backward glance at my wife, my daughter, my psychiatrist, my lawyers, Mr. Justice Maloney, or the Crown attorney, I passed through the same door as had many clients who had paid their fee but lost their liberty with nary a further thought from me; my work, I smugly believed, had been done. I was grateful that I was neither handcuffed nor shackled, for it had been some years since I had practised criminal law and I could not, for the life of me, remember whether prisoners were trussed up on leaving the courtroom. The imagery of public bondage had been so terrifying that, at one point, I asked my daughter, Melissa, not to come to the sentencing.

Barely three feet inside this first door to oblivion, the system commenced its torturous striptease of dignity. Three security officers, all officiously self-conscious, stood behind a desk, as if awaiting a convention registrant. They took my tie and my belt, ensuring that I would not die by my own hand and so deprive a contemptuous world of satisfaction by allowing the final act to be one of choice.

Now without power over death, I was equally to have no power over life: away went my wedding ring, my photograph of my daughter, and my watch. God forbid that someone doing time should have the luxury of counting it.

In desperate fear that nothing I could call my own would be left to me, I had smuggled in a token to cling to, a link to the distant warmth of those I loved. Before my arrest, in the summer of 1991, an appreciative guide on a Nile steamer had given my wife, Deena, and me three tiny stone scorpions, good luck charms to an ancient culture. A few days before my sentencing, I gave one to Deena and one to my daughter. The significance of that small act escaped me: my demonstrative opulence was already fading.

As Mr. Justice Maloney pronounced sentence, the scorpion found its way to my mouth, between my upper back teeth and my inner cheek. There it stayed, through numerous checkpoints, metal detectors, pat-downs, and strip searches. It could have been cyanide, drugs, or cash: in their obsession with bureaucracy and symbolic degradation, the system's mandarins could take my clothes, shoes, money, and dignity, but they could not take the symbolic soul I had decided to keep.

A single officer led me from the checkpoint to a cell built to hold prisoners waiting for the courthouse's internal elevator. The lift itself was the tiniest of contraptions, split into two "cages" — one for the prisoners, one for the guards — separated by an iron lattice barrier. Somewhere in the bowels of Correctional Service

Canada (CSC) sits an architect whose devious genius is the pursuit of infinity through the subdivision of minute space. This hidden talent would turn out to be both the perpetrator and the saviour of the overburdened, overcrowded, and sometimes filthy and unsanitary places I passed through.

The elevator took us to the barred "holding cells." These six-foot by three-foot cells accommodate prisoners awaiting their court appearances, house them during recesses, and are the transit points to a real jail. The cells were outfitted with a bench seat and a toilet; only a spanking, surrealistic spotlessness differentiated the scene from the horrors of dirt and grime I had imagined.

I had anticipated panic, but relief came instead. Jail seemed at least momentarily preferable to the alternative of being an outcast in my own world.

The ride from the London Courthouse to the Elgin Middlesex Detention Centre (EMDC) takes about twenty minutes. Too stunned to be anything but philosophical about my handcuffs and shackles, I was separated from the other prisoners and marched to the front of the paddy-wagon, taking momentary heart that my station in life still merited a front-row seat. Indeed it did! But the seat was just behind the front row, in a cage reserved for "PCs," prisoners in "protective custody."

Larry Payne, the head of security, whose acquaintance I had made in my criminal-lawyer days, awaited me.

"Do you want PC?" he asked, with a direct stare.

"No," I insisted.

PC is to prison what open season is to hunting, telling the mainstream penitentiary population that a con is a sex offender or perpetrator of other crimes against women or children; a "rat" (informant); or a member of the establishment, most likely a former cop or prison guard; or that he has broken a fundamental rule of the Prison Code: default on debts, drug rip-offs, and cell thieving are all in this category. Convicts in Millhaven Penitentiary near Kingston are fond of saying that "PCs here would be so full of holes, the only place they could work would be as sprinklers in the yard."

"That's a good choice," Larry agreed. He thought for a moment. "Julius, it's going to be hard. The best thing I can tell you is to be like any other prisoner as much as you can. Good luck."

Larry's kindness unleashed my pent-up emotions. The lump in my throat left me unable to thank him. He spoke to avoid my awkwardness.

"One more thing. They say that you should believe only half of what you see in prison and nothing of what you hear. It's true."

Soon afterwards, I was trundled off to the "bullpen." This barred, filthy, medium-sized cell was my first close contact with other prisoners; most were punks, young hoods disguising their anxieties with bravado, foul language, and callous disdain for civility. The open toilet was fouled with undisguised relish, the garbage can and ashtray ignored, the leftovers and scraps from our institutional meal sprayed around the cell like confetti. I spoke to no one for over two hours, and no one spoke to me.

Doing nothing and being able to do nothing about it were brand new to me. I longed for something to read, to elude the timelessness I couldn't control. When I signed for my property, I had asked Larry whether I could take along my books — and got my first dose of prison's most overused word: Charles de Gaulle's biography and Harvard law professor Alan Dershowitz's best-selling *Chutzpah,* it turned out, were "contraband."

The bullpen was nothing compared to my first strip search. Had I been wearing a tutu, I could have been a ballerina: twirl around, bend over, stand on one foot at a time; ballerinas, of course, don't bend over and "spread their cheeks" on command so a squinty-eyed guard can look up their bum for a "stash," nor are their soles checked for contraband as they lift their feet ever so daintily. The officer looked in my mouth, missing my scorpion.

Dressed in royal blue from head to toe, I sat around for almost an hour in an elevator that served as a holding cell. Finally, a friendly guard, who confided that I was going to the safest "range," or living unit, in the jail, marched me to maximum security. Once there, the hostile chanting made his advice immediately suspect: *"Get him, get him, get him!"*

Judgement, as it had in court that morning, merged with punishment again; only the judges had changed. The shouting didn't stop until the guard unlocked the steel door to the range common area, a desolate stereotype of prisons and mental hospitals, lacking only the wispy haze of filtered camera lenses. The room was twenty feet long by thirty feet wide, ringed around half its perimeter with steel-doored cells; the space was quiet, but the stark walls and furnishings, without acoustical absorbents, fostered a constant, echoing "white noise."

To my right was a cubbyhole the size of a small bedroom where the thirty or so inmates on the range were cloistered during frequent cell searches; farther along the same wall was a pay phone restricted to collect calls, an inaudible and fuzzy TV that was nonetheless constantly on, and a secure glass booth or "cage" through which the guards monitored access to the range.

The bathroom was opposite me. It had no door, and the shower had no curtain. Card players used up the range's seating at picnic-style tables in the middle of the room; the TV watchers sat on the bare floor; the rest of the inmates walked endlessly back and forth along either of the two walls of cells.

Walking is an obsession in prison. Apart from weightlifting, it is by far the most common form of exercise. Inmates walk, usually in pairs, retracing their steps in straight lines or circles: they pace in their tiny cells, shuffle on the ranges, in the exercise yards, on the running tracks, and in the gym. No other activity is as representative of prison's caged bestiality, and nowhere is the frustration more evident than in the local or regional jails — known as buckets — where outdoor access is extremely limited and gyms are not always available.

Buckets are the tensest of institutions. London is hardly the worst of the lot: Toronto's ancient, crumbling Don Jail is the most infamous. As one con put it:

> What can you say about a place with three to a cell where the pigs treat you like shit?... I slept on a mattress on the floor just in front of the cell door and the toilet.
>
> One night I felt a tug on my hair. I thought it was one of the pigs. They're sadists, the coppers in the Don. My case was getting a lot of ugly publicity and I figured they were trying to give me a hard time. I reached out to pull my hair away. Would you believe it, there's a mouse pulling on my hair? There are mice all over the place in the Don. They're almost domesticated.
>
> Stereos and TVs are blasting from five in the morning until one in the morning. Lockup all day with nothing to do. Spaced-out guys all over the place. I've never seen drugs like that anywhere. Not in Millhaven, not in Collins Bay. You can buy drugs in the Don like you buy newspapers on the street. Anything, hash, Vs [Valium], heroin, you name it.
>
> The pigs don't give a damn. Half of them are bringing it in themselves. What do you expect? What kind of person do you think would work in a place like that? The only reason I can think of is to make some money on the side or because they enjoy it.

Toronto East and Toronto West Detention Centres, and the Hamilton, Barrie, and Napanee buckets, are almost on a par with the Don as the most loathed jails in Ontario. The outside world has no idea: some years ago, a sketch of the Barrie jail graced that city's Christmas card.

Generally, bucket populations consist of inmates awaiting trial or sentence or sentenced inmates on their way to a provincial reformatory or the Federal Reception Centre at Millhaven. Uncertainty rules here; for those not yet tried or sentenced, constant remands, unresponsive lawyers, uncooperative witnesses, all add to the tension of waiting on a fate in the hands of others, certain in the knowledge that time in the bucket is "dead time."

Dead time, or time awaiting trial, does not count against a man's sentence, though a judge may take dead time into account when imposing punishment; regardless, dead time, except in the case of life sentences, is never considered in the calculation of parole or statutory release dates. On short sentences, dead time can increase an inmate's stay behind bars by up to fifty percent.

The prisoner doesn't know what these endless days mean to his future until the moment he is sentenced; for first-timers, the unknown also fuels their fear, and the tyranny of dead time may be the most embittering aspect of the prison experience.

For the sentenced, the increasing backlogs in Canada's correctional institutions ensure, for the most part, a stay in the bucket well beyond the fifteen days mandated by law. The bucket has the most rigorous confinement, the tawdriest facilities, the most restrictive rules, and the fewest privileges and programs to pass the long hours. In a twist of irony, cons deeply resent the illegal restraint on their right to move on to the penitentiary; even the most hardened criminals consider one day in the bucket as the equivalent of two days in the penitentiary.

No discernible classification system exists in the buckets. The kids are in with the hard-core cons, the violent with the nonviolent, the impaired drivers with the murderers, the recidivists with the first-timers, the mentally ill with the criminally committed, the accused with the convicted, and the presumed innocent with the admittedly guilty.

Unlike the penitentiaries, particularly the lower-security ones, where inmates have opportunities to be alone, this amalgam of alleged and proven criminality is stuck with one another twenty-four hours a day. Here, the young learn the Prison Code from the indoctrinated; here, false bravado and distrust of the system are infused; here, only the most rigorous, inhumane regimentation prevents more frequent violence. And here, ironically, do we claim to start the path to rehabilitation.

My escort confided that I had been deliberately paired with Spike, who "ran the range" and would ensure that no harm came to me. Spike, an Outlaw biker awaiting trial for attempted murder, stood no more than five feet six inches and weighed about one hundred and forty pounds; his wavy, dark hair and moustache contrasted with a pale complexion whose compensating contortions seemed to cry out, "I am fierce." Spike was the range's "quarterman," his power flowing from his association with the motorcycle gang.

"Quarterman" may be a bastardization of "corridor man" — a trustee of sorts. The quarterman makes sure that the range is clean and quiet and that the free-issue tobacco is distributed fairly; occasionally, as one quarterman eventually told me, "if a guy is giving the guards a hard time, [a quarterman could] arrange for him to have an accident if that's what they want." In return, the quarterman picks the TV channels, makes up the telephone lists, visits other ranges, has his cell door open longer than anyone else, and keeps the extra meals and tobacco issue for himself.

Spike explained the canteen procedure that allowed me to purchase stationery, stamps, newspapers, and snacks out of the $250 account I had brought to jail with me; he described the lockup routine, the meal routine, the shower routine, the laundry routine, and the television routine. He arranged telephone time for me that very night, although all the fifteen-minute slots were pencilled in. When he summarily erased two names, no one so much as raised an eyebrow.

I had arrived on the range after dinner. With nothing to do but watch the blurred TV set, I fought my tension through exercise: pushups, situps, and stretches on the concrete floor sustained me for the next few days. "Jug-up," the evening snack of milk, coffee, and sweets, was served at 8:30 in the common room where I had encountered my ominous welcome. In my phone calls to Deena and Melissa, the reassurance in my tone masked what I felt. The third period of the hockey game rounded out the evening; the guards locked us in our cells at 10:30.

Spike showed me around our small cell with its twin beds; the room was spotlessly clean and meticulously orderly. He delineated his territory; I didn't negotiate.

Following Spike's fastidious example, I scoured the sink after brushing my teeth. A few minutes after I sank into bed, the lights went out, but for one yellow light that stayed on all night, letting the patrolling guards check us out through the small glass panel in the cell door. Despite the pressures of the past six months, I had experienced little trouble sleeping, except in the final days before sentencing. I cherished sleep; for months now, it had been my only refuge.

"You Jewish?" Spike asked, his back to me, in a voice half-asleep and muffled by his blanket pulled high over his head.

"Yes."

"Well," he intoned, "I thought you should know, I'm a White Aryan Supremacist."

I fell off to sleep expecting nightmares. PC was looking good.

Making the grade

Please make sure my son doesn't mix with any undesirables.
JEWISH INMATE'S MOTHER TO KINGSTON PENITENTIARY WARDEN

An unrestrained knock at my cell door woke me, just in time to see Spike hurrying out past a waiting guard.

"You're new, eh?" said the guard. "You've got thirty seconds to dress before you miss breakfast."

As I left, he handed me a knife without meaningful edges, a fork, and a bent spoon. In a tone that left no margin for error, he warned me to return the cutlery with my tray when I finished eating. In the common room, the semblance of a meal was on a cart.

With a good night's sleep behind me, uninterrupted, surprisingly, by nightmares of crosses and white hoods, I had a more clear-headed opportunity to check out my range mates. Collectively, they reminded me of the inhabitants of an alien penal colony on *Star Trek*. "Foreboding" was the best word I could think of: they were coiled, intense, unblinking, methodically sinister in their motion, and affected an abrupt whispering speech that inevitably became a hiss in the rebounding emptiness of the uncarpeted confines.

Most of my second day in jail was taken up by administrative necessities, starting with a mandatory visit to Health Care. Movement within a maximum security facility has decided overtones of cattle herding. The guards collected our group in the common room, shepherding us single file from barrier to barrier, somehow turning all space into compartments; lagging behind or deviating from our position to the right of the hallway brought sharp reproaches verging on threats.

We were inserted into the medical facility's holding cell, taken to see the doctor one at a time, then reinserted until everyone had been examined. This was my first lesson in prison patience: by my third day in jail, I always carried a paperback in my back pocket. Movie and restaurant lines will never bother me again.

A contract doctor obviously wearied by the dull routine of endless cursory examinations was roused from his listless contempt when I told him who I was. He hadn't read the psychiatric report and warrant of committal, which recommended that I continue with the antidepressant Prozac I had been taking for three months. I pointed them out. Fifteen minutes and a quick examination later, I was pronounced fit to be a prisoner, mentally and physically.

That afternoon, Spike acquainted me with the dangers of prison life. He suggested, not too subtly, that a person of station and wealth could not survive in the system without "protection" — and as a Jew, I was in greater danger than most. Spike's Aryan Supremacist affiliations, I suppose, qualified him as an expert on the subject.

Spike went on to describe the power of the Outlaw network, their control of the prisons, and the swiftness and reliability of their grapevine; he showed me pictures of his clubmates partying at various prisons, hinting that their power garnered special privileges.

I told Spike I had no money. He thought it best that "I find a way." I said I'd think about it.

What I thought about was the mentality that had placed me on a maximum security range in a cell with Spike, whose neo-Nazism was no secret to the guards or the inmates. Spike could not let too much happen to me on "his" range, for fear of losing his unspoken privileges and aura of influence. But I wondered how the authorities had overlooked the possibility that a White Aryan Supremacist member of the Outlaws Motorcycle Club just might find a way to garner a little private advantage for himself from my presence. In the entire detention centre, wasn't there a single range that had con artists, impaired drivers, car thieves, fences, small-time losers on temporary absence, or an unfortunate who had failed to pay his parking tickets with whom I could be bunked?

On Tuesday night, I slept very little, and when I did, the nightmares I had anticipated on Monday finally arrived.

Wherever I had been in my life, I tried to fit in, a trait that had contributed considerably to my present predicament. I wanted to fit in here in jail, partly to heal my shattered ego and partly because it made me feel safe. Prison etiquette, however, did not conform to my accustomed methods of getting acquainted. By inclination and training, I was a questioner: I made friends by asking people about themselves. Here, my curiosity provoked suspicion and ostracism.

My social problems were aggravated by other inmates' perceptions of my advantages. I was a lawyer, an integral part of the system that had sent my new *confrères* to jail; I was rich and therefore must think that "my shit didn't stink"; I was clever and educated and therefore must believe that I knew everything; most of all, my background, my associations, and my ability to articulate made me intimidating. That in turn fuelled the anger of unhappiness, despair, and envy that is the driving emotion of so many convicts.

But today was Wednesday, our range's gym day. The Elgin Middlesex Detention Centre, unlike most buckets, boasts a large, well-equipped, staffed gymnasium, including a weight pit. Here — the departure point from prison's deadly routine — things were different: this was cons' territory; here *they* could teach *me* something; here, older, overweight, and tentative in using the equipment, I was not intimidating. My previously silent, brooding companions became helpful, polite, almost concerned. Five minutes did not go by without a voice attached to one Schwarzenegger body or another offering advice on how to avoid injury, use a machine, or exercise efficiently; conversation, built around incredulous questions about my previous workout experience, flowed. Acceptance here, I observed, was deference and humility. I knew what the dictionary said about those words, but nothing about my life had taught me their meaning.

Bodies to kill for abound in the pit: protruding pectorals are paraded as badges of honour, biceps are flexed for maximal exposure, and the earthiest of grunts and groans ensure that stupendous lifts do not go unnoticed. Here, convicts can be yuppies too, pandering to their appearance and their health, and doing it as well as, if not better than, anyone on the street. The pit, in short, is the place where convicts do what convicts do best.

Rarely do guards invade this domain, both because there is a grudging respect for the privacy of the sanctuary and because the convergence of prisoners makes the pit a dangerous place. The more violent and long-term the prisoner, the more likely he is to be a creature of anger and a denizen of the pit.

Tenure rules here. Inmates establish times and patterns for their workouts, maintaining their rights through their stay at the prison. Once the pattern is established, no one intrudes on a prisoner's workout: sets are not interrupted, the efficacy of "pumps" is not endangered, and casual conversation is taboo. Newcomers to the system ease gingerly into the strict regime, earning access to the overcrowded equipment through the constancy of their presence, the passage of time, the meticulousness of their routine, the demonstration of their prowess, and the influence of their friends.

Much of prison's violence transpires in the pit or the yard. If the pit empties early, trouble is coming. The uncanny efficiency of the grapevine and the readily identifiable buildup of special tension that always precedes violence signal that it is time to leave — time to let the protagonists work out their beef, without witnesses.

The rules of the pit, like other precepts of the Prison Code, are exaggerated extensions of societal norms. In a world with little room for individuality, emotion, personal possessions, or intimate contact, where space is at a premium and privacy discouraged, most everything is magnified.

And so, among thieves, it is the gravest of transgressions to steal, because there is so little to have; it is a cardinal sin to ask, because there is so much to hide and precious little room to conceal; toilets are not flushed when the time comes to sleep because there is no choice about bedtime; inmates don't shit in their cells in the presence of their roommates, even if they have to do it in their pants, because the cell is both "house" and "home"; extras aren't taken from the kitchen line until all have eaten, because there are no other times and no other places to eat.

Most importantly, no one talks to "coppers" because the most trivial information can be used by "them" against "us." Us, solid cons, strict adherents to the Prison Code; them, everyone working in the system: coppers, pigs, screws, the Man — and none of them can be trusted. The Code against the Man: everything about the system perpetuates this partition, which is the most insidiously self-defeating feature of the Correctional Service's rehabilitative goals.

The force of the Code was such that Gardiner, an intelligent man in his mid-thirties with no history of substance abuse, refused to implicate his drug-trafficking cellmate when drugs were found in their cell. They were both convicted. Although he was a model inmate serving a twenty-year sentence, Gardiner's conviction led the Parole Board to refuse his pass application. His wife, exasperated by the turn of events, discouraged and lonely, left him; his children's visits became less frequent; the deterioration in family support further jeopardized Gardiner's chances for parole; his offence upgraded his security status throughout his sentence; and CSC wasted time, money, and a scarce space in its substance-abuse programs.

I asked Gardiner whether adherence to the Code was worth it.

"I don't think about it," he replied. "You just don't do that or you're one of them."

Our legislated philosophy of gradual release guides trustworthy prisoners through maximum, medium, and minimum security institutions; on escorted, then unescorted, passes; on limited day parole, day parole to halfway houses, full parole, and statutory release (formerly mandatory release) two-thirds of the way through an inmate's sentence. At each stage, the prisoner earns his passage by the quality of his adjustment to his new freedoms.

On its face, all of this makes sense, but, as Gardiner's experience demonstrates, it fails to address a fundamental problem: throughout, the relationship between the con and his keepers, whether they are prison guards, halfway-house staff, or parole officers, remains one of mistrust. At each step, the inmate remains mired or returns to a home base in which the void between him and society is reinforced by the pervasive psychological separation between them and us.

We assume, mistakenly, that rehabilitation and reintegration can be fostered in an environment of alienation; on warrant expiry day, when the sentence ends, the keepers and restraints disappear, but the gulf between them and us remains firmly entrenched. The con's mistrust and therefore his anger linger and continue to threaten society; too often, precious little has changed from the day of sentencing.

The choices available to a correctional system are either to warehouse or to reintegrate. To the extent that warehousing is the order of the day, them and us is an acceptable and perhaps even an appropriate environment. Those who will never venture beyond the fences have little hope, and their desperation calls for their segregation.

However, virtually all Canadian convicts are released at least once. Accordingly, CSC has reintegration at the forefront of its mission statement. Unfortunately, the process by which reintegration is effected is so adversarial, subjective, arbitrary, frustrating, and secretive that it consistently perpetuates warehouse mentalities that become too entrenched — institutionalized — to give way to successful returns to society.

Occasionally, someone like Sister Margaret, one of the EMDC's chaplains, transcends the chasm. As I approached her in the range's common room, the aura of goodness that radiated from the smallish, greying woman eroded my stoic front with the prospect of warmth and real conversation. Sister Margaret quickly realized that I was unable to speak without crying; she also understood that I could not cry where I might be seen and invited me to her office by the chapel. The casual walk down the now familiar hallways and staircase, by the locked doors, without the admonishments about staying in place, was in itself a much-needed respite from the caged mentality that had overtaken me so quickly: even being *with* another person seemed novel.

Just before we reached the chapel, we passed through the EMDC's large, bright, central vestibule with its huge tree in the centre. I dreaded this place where I had once patiently attended my clients: lawyers; John Howard Society and Salvation Army types; parole, probation, and police officers all awaited their business with the inmates. Either I recognized them or their furtive glances suggested that they knew me. I looked away.

Safely in Sister Margaret's office, I still couldn't speak without tears. Sister Margaret listened, soothed, and reassured me, all with a loving certainty that could only have come from an inner grace. She invited me into the chapel and left me alone there. Despite my Orthodox Jewish upbringing, I had rejected faith many years ago, but could not resist the attraction and peace of this solitary space. I played Schubert's "Moonlight Sonata" on the piano and Peter, Paul, and Mary's "Wedding Song" on Sister Margaret's guitar. Music had always brought me to tears and swept them away. *At least that hasn't changed.* With that thought, I realized that some good remained with me and within me, inkling of a freedom that had nothing to do with bars or their absence. My wonderful psychiatrist, Dr. Hans Arndt, had raised that possibility with me after my arrest; Sister Margaret brought it home.

Spike was unmistakably severe on my return to the range; avoiding him was impossible in a room neither of us could leave.

As usual, he was surrounded by a coterie of two or three ineffectuals, their brains scrambled by a variety of chemicals. One of these fried hangers-on instigated a conversation with me that covered much of the territory Spike had covered the previous day; his task was obviously to lend clout to Spike's threats of danger and his claims of prowess and influence. As I was insisting, again, that I had no money, Spike ambled over.

"You know," he said, "when somebody leaves the bucket with black eyes, he's marked all the way through the system."

"Marked" meant that wherever I went, everyone would assume that I had been beaten up for being a rat or another form of PC. Spike, I was sure, wouldn't hesitate to spread the word, with or without the visual effects.

At suppertime, I made my way to the control booth guarding the common room, ostensibly to mail a letter. The officer was amiable.

"How ya doing?"

"Not great. It's not very safe in there."

"What do you mean? Someone muscling you? Who?"

"If I were you, I'd get me out of there."

An hour later, I was bunked on the transfer range.

The chain

Life is a whole journey of meeting your edge again and again.
PEMA CHODRON

The solitariness of my new cell was liberating. I listened to the radio and read, relieved that I was moving on, unaware that my swift passage from the bucket would mark me as effectively as a black eye — as one of them, someone with "pull."

There were several reasons for the EMDC's haste in getting rid of me. No jail likes to be the centre of attention; it brings on too much "heat" from the media, the public, and the politicians — all of whom were anxious to ensure that I was getting no less than my full due. Paradoxically, the administration was equally concerned that I didn't get too much of what was due: any harm to me could, in that strange pendulum of public empathy, lead to an investigation or, worse, an inquiry. Public opinion, I imagined, would have two schools of thought on the subject: one group would conclude, despite their view of the scum of the earth, that the sentence was nine years and not death, and that, in any event, I would have suffered insufficiently by a demise so early in my punishment; the second school would reason that death was poetic justice for any criminal, but that the public should not be deprived of the satisfaction that comes from the gory details. In either case, it wouldn't have looked good, and the Elgin Middlesex Detention Centre didn't want any part of it.

My track record as a shit-disturbing lawyer also made me potentially troublesome. My specialty had been cases that others laughed at. As a criminal lawyer, I had persuaded the Supreme Court of Canada that the criminal offence of "driving while disqualified" was unconstitutional; thirty thousand criminal charges were annulled by this decision. In 1989, facing the derision and scorn of an always insular London Bar, I convinced Mr. Justice Daniel Chilcott of the Ontario High Court that the Grand Bend Beach near London, the second-largest public beach in Ontario, belonged to my client; the government lost a property that had been used by the public for almost a hundred years.

The prospect of dealing with an informed inmate with access to effective help is reprehensible to most of them. More than once during my incarceration, prison staff who were unfamiliar with my background tried to talk me out of seeking legal help, arguing that "lawyers are useless in here."

I knew my rights and those of my fellow convicts, how to enforce those rights, what made the bureaucracy jump, and how to create expensive and annoying paperwork for the authorities. In short, often I knew the rules and how to use them better than my keepers; what I didn't know, I could learn quickly. By helping other inmates, I could create turmoil in the system.

After a breakfast of indelicacies early the next morning, two semi-jovial officers, to whom the procedure was clearly second nature, strip-searched, handcuffed, and shackled us; again, I successfully hid my friend the scorpion under my tongue. The guards dumped everything but the clothes on our back in small red travel bags: no reading materials, no combs, and no cigarettes until we reached Millhaven the following afternoon.

The "chain" was for real: thirty of us rattled along, one foot at a time, on the inevitable path to the right. Walking in shackles was clearly an art form, and relative grace of manoeuvre easily distinguished the pros from the novices. Those who managed to fake their way down the hallway to the garage were exposed by the steps to the bus.

The "Grey Goose" was not grey, and its squared-off rectangular body bore no resemblance to fowl. I have no idea how the bus got its name, common to several similar vehicles hauling chains of prisoners from local buckets to provincial reformatories in Ontario and the Federal Reception Centre at Millhaven Penitentiary in Kingston. Apart from its uniformly clothed and restrained occupants and two tiny cells up front holding two prisoners each, there wasn't much to distinguish the Goose from its school-bus relatives.

On its route from London to the Toronto East Detention Centre, the Goose alternates between the 401 superhighway and the backroads of southwestern Ontario. Its deviations and stops turn a three-hour, one-hundred-and-thirty-mile drive into a seven-hour journey. There are few extra seats, no room to stretch, no permission to move around, no relief from the handcuffs and shackles, an indescribably inedible box lunch eaten en route, and one five-minute bathroom stop at Guelph Reformatory, the latter thankfully a matter of trust and not of direct observation. Handcuffs stay on for urination and come off for bowel movements, liberties that were a distinct relief to me, as I had spent my first hour on board imagining the various contortions by which I could remove my pants and then wipe my ass while in handcuffs. I conquered the first hurdle conceptually, but the second defied my imagination. The shackles, which stayed on, were another problem: I had never appreciated the connection between the ability to spread my legs more than twelve inches and the resultant relief from constipation. Nonetheless, the brief liberation from the irritating restraint of the cuffs and the momentary privacy of a toilet cubicle contributed to a disproportionate number of alleged bowel movements among my companions.

The hours passed uneventfully, apart from several covert attempts at smoking contraband cigarettes, occasionally eliciting pointed warnings from the guards. Eventually, I noticed the pointy nose, bedroom blue eyes, long white hair, wispy beard, and wistful gaze of the apparition across the aisle: over six feet tall, he seemed an amalgam of Jesus Christ and Bullwinkle.

"How'd you like the reception?" he asked as he caught my eye.

"What reception?"

"When you first got up to the range. I was the quarterman in the range where the guys were shouting at you. I made them stop. You'll notice it never happened again."

It had never happened again. Forty-year-old Kevin had been deliberately placed among the young punks; his previous turns in the penitentiary gave him quarterman status, effectively stabilizing a raucous range.

Detroit was home to Kevin, but his dual citizenship brought him to Canada. Though lacking in formal education, he was intelligent and articulate. He clung to his adolescence as a flower child of the sixties: his hatred of Republicans was easily evoked by the suggestion that George Bush would prevail that election year, and his passion for politics was exceeded only by his love of sports, particularly the Detroit Tigers, Pistons, and Wings; the Toronto Blue Jays and Maple Leafs evoked harsh invective.

Kevin's occupational history was varied and a touch obscure. He had spent some time as a gun-toting Teamsters Union employee in Detroit; most recently he had outraged the legal community in Timmins, Ontario, by stretching his budding paralegal practice into areas of the law traditionally reserved for lawyers, including sentencing hearings. Kevin had spent a total of nine years in

Canadian penitentiaries spread over three fraud "bits" ten years apart. Whenever his personal life became a little hectic, Kevin indulged himself, initially by partying off the fruits of his illegal exploits, followed by what he regarded as a leisurely sabbatical. The prison lifestyle, he explained, left him free to pursue his well-defined goals and interests without intrusion or distraction; this time around, he planned to get a university degree at society's expense.

Initially incredulous at Kevin's breezy approach to incarceration, I became a believer when he refused to apply for parole on his eligibility date in June 1992. And the law afforded the Correctional Service no avenue to throw him out. Kevin represented one of the best arguments I ever encountered against jail for nonviolent offenders.

But Kevin knew how to do time; his calculated *ennui* and good humour made the long bus ride much less trying than it might have been.

When we finally arrived at Toronto East Detention Centre, the chain link fence that incongruously surrounded its apartment building–like exterior induced a foreboding very different from the relief I had initially felt in London; the exactitude of the vehicle check in the jail's sally port, it seemed, put the last set of locks on my doors to the world.

The burly, brusque guards did little to dispel my feelings, throwing our red property bags to the ground in the deliberately careless way that is the signature greeting card of most jails, disdainfully telling the new inmate where he stands and what he has to say about it — as if the offender's property is an inanimate extension of the criminal soul, entitled to the same treatment.

The scene inside suggested a Third World immigration office: uniformly dressed scruffy men stood in line with their uniform baggage, which was unmistakably all they owned. Green-garbed officers went slothfully about their business: for each doing something, another watched. A photographer stood near the doorway, taking our pictures with a Polaroid camera; beyond him, against a choral background of ceaseless hollow chatter, a narrow passageway bathed half-naked prisoners in a dull glow reminiscent of the Turkish prison in the film *Midnight Express.*

If the alcove where the strip searches were conducted was intended for privacy, it failed miserably, lacking a door or partition. The guards delighted in having two prisoners undress in a single space, orchestrating the search so that, as the prisoners bent over, their yawning cheeks graced the passageway.

The Elgin Middlesex Detention Centre had been Eden by comparison, clean and tidy, its staff professional in their treatment of dignity and property. The East was squalid, dirty, and undermaintained, living up to its reputation as one of the worst jails in Ontario; its staff was high-handed, crude, and macho — but not thorough enough to find my scorpion.

After we got some toiletries from an adjacent storeroom, the staff crammed over twenty prisoners into holding cells designed to seat no more than eight. Prisoners from London and points west had been unable to smoke for eight to ten hours, and cigarettes would be unavailable until we cleared Millhaven admissions twenty-four hours hence. With barely enough room to turn around, we waited.

Two hours after our arrival, I stared beyond a barred gateway to a bare space that may have been intended as a storehouse for bodies, but not for the living. At its best, our L-shaped range resembled a crypt; at its worst, its dismal bleakness, accentuated by fluorescent lighting harsh enough to make me squint, reminded me of the photographs of empty chambers that I had seen at the Holocaust Memorial in Jerusalem the previous summer.

Two picnic-type tables, a television set, and two telephones constituted the room's furniture; white noise screamed off chipped walls and floors sprinkled with graffiti and food remnants. The bathroom and shower area to the right was partitioned by a wall that housed the TV and went only halfway to the ceiling, ensuring, as if by macabre design, a total absence of privacy. Typically, the cells, closed off by heavy metal doors, ringed half the perimeter, opposite the bathroom.

We had nothing to read, and neither the TV nor the telephones were working. Thirty minutes later, a pair of desultory guards dispensed us to our cells with affected efficiency. The sound of the key in the cell door was familiar, but now it rang with particular flourish.

Our new premises were standard issue: two inmates, fifty-five square feet of space, bunk beds, open toilet, remains of a mirror, sink, shelf, towel bar, and an open steel closet for hanging clothing. My cell, and as I later learned from my range mates, most of the cells, was full of dead flies and assorted insects (which must have been there for a long time as it was February 13), soiled and torn mattresses, unwashed floors, cracked faucets and basins, all sprinkled with a gentle cover of grime, dust, dirt, and bits of food. The cell's lighting was dim and inadequate, as if to compensate for the range's equatorial brightness.

My roommate, Al, was a career criminal who had spent much of his first fifty years in prison for assorted crimes. Now in his mid-sixties, slim, with a swath of white hair on his head and a neatly trimmed beard, he had stayed out of trouble for over ten years. He lived in Windsor, had thirteen children from various wives whose number he couldn't remember precisely, and prided himself on his good relationships with all his offspring. Al had lost his job in the flagging economy, turned to petty crime to support himself, and was starting a two-year sentence for his latest caper.

"Severance pay — only I'm paying," he griped. "They offered me eighteen months, but then I'd have had to go to Guelph with the punks."

A solid con who swore by the Code, Al was disinclined to vent his emotions, particularly to a stranger like me. But he unleashed a litany of expletives directed at the East, swearing that he had been in every penitentiary in Ontario and many in Quebec. Nothing, he cursed, was as dirty or run down as the East; nowhere else did guards treat prisoners with such disrespect; in any other joint, there would have been a riot. Al went on and on until his aggravations and the long day finally got the better of his senior's body, and he fell asleep on the lower bunk.

The old man slept until dinner, cold goo with gravy and a carton of milk. The food was served grudgingly, with so much hostility that it might as well have been thrown at the recipient.

After dinner, the seasoned prisoners walked out their tension in pairs, back and forth along the two walls of cell doors opposite the bathroom. Before long, however, the punks started bitching, blaming the staff for everything from the food to the score in the hockey game. Soon, every passing guard faced a barrage of verbal abuse and toothpaste projectiles, powered by the full weight of grown men jumping on tiny tubes. Before long, toiletries became footballs, tables became trampolines, and conversations became confrontations.

Professional approaches to maintaining order were away for the evening: so long as there was no bloodshed, the staff stayed safely out of our cage, contenting themselves with occasional threats and taunts. I had visited the Metro Zoo and can say unequivocally that it was better run, cleaner, more sanitary, the food for the animals was better, and I felt decidedly safer than I did in the East — although I'm not sure to this day which zoo was a better show. Locked out of our cells until bedtime, Kevin and I paced back and forth along the back wall, avoiding the tumult as best we could. Luckily, I managed to get the overused collect telephone for a few minutes. I called my family, who, until then, had no idea I was being moved.

Lockup was at the usual time, around 10:30. Once I settled into my top bunk, I drew solace from the relative familiarity of the surroundings. Even the melancholy glow of the yellowish night light was comforting, and I fell asleep in its embrace.

Down under

What did you expect ... we should supply you with Reeboks?
JEAN CUMMING

Early next morning, as we gathered in the hallway, the guards advised alleged leaders of the evening's frolic that their conduct had been "noted." Protestations by the innocent were a waste of time. The notes would stay in the prisoner's file and mark him forever as a troublemaker, potentially affecting his penitentiary placement, his security level, his treatment by the staff, his privileges, his choice of jobs, and his chances of parole. Few of the prisoners ever saw these "activity entries"; by the time an inmate discovered what had been written about him, refutation was a practical impossibility — in a system where accusation routinely amounts to proof.

Chained and shackled, we marched out to the Goose. Most of the excited chatter was about the conditions "Down Under." The prospect of indefinite confinement in Millhaven Reception had haunted me since my arrest: its lengthy backlog, double-bunking, and twenty-four-hour lockup were legend. Although the Commissioner of Penitentiaries had issued directives, known as "CDs," stipulating that no prisoner was to remain in Reception more than six weeks, the average wait was nine to twelve weeks, and some inmates were stuck in Millhaven for more than eight months.

Kevin and I rushed to the head of the line, anxious for good seats, unaware that first arrivals were locked in the cages at the front of the bus. We had barely enough room to get our knees and elbows to ninety-degree angles; the bench was so shallow we sat on the edge of our tailbones and so narrow that our squashed bodies risked becoming the first manifestation of Siamese twins artificially joined in adulthood.

Two hours later the high fences, barbed wire, and tinted glass towers of Millhaven Penitentiary, located just west of Kingston in the village of Bath, were surprisingly, if ominously, welcome.

Millhaven and adjacent minimum security Bath Institution are, like most penitentiaries, set on flat plots of land. From the outside, Millhaven is an unimposing, sterile, two-storey structure, with several wings emanating from a central rotunda, like an airport terminal. Inside, I had expected a corridor of dull concrete touched up with cobwebs and a long check-in line edging by a robotic officer checking off names with clipped disdain behind a standard issue desk; instead, we entered a large, yellow room with a bright linoleum floor. Our driver guided us to two bullpens along the wall to our left.

Three guards, perched on stools next to structural columns, faced the bullpens; each had a clipboard, writing materials, and a sheaf of files in front of him. In the centre of the room lay our red bags, next to plastic sacks filled with basics.

The bullpens' insufficient seating, to which I had become accustomed, was augmented by inadequate standing room. Each bullpen had a toilet surrounded by a three-foot partition that was more symbolic than effective; unimpeded were the fragrances to be expected from forty men who had been hustled out of Toronto East immediately after breakfast without access to a toilet for three hours. The sink by the partition was seldom used, its proximity to the overworked toilet too much even for hardened cons.

An owlish, greying figure about fifty years old dominated the scene. A protrusive beer belly hung from Bruce's portly frame; ill-fitting jeans and a skin-tight dark turtleneck highlighted his drinking habits; what looked like a whistle around his neck accentuated his obvious authority, as did the rapt attention of his underlings. Bruce seemed oblivious to the presence of others even when communicating with them, and his dehumanizing bearing set the tone for the afternoon.

The rote efficiency of the routine that was to terrorize me for the next five hours was testimony to Bruce's twenty years in Admissions and Discharge — the prison department known throughout the system as "A & D." Six CSC androids were engrossed in the admissions procedure, but they had raised serial indifference to a science so precise that neither their tone nor their responses could be differentiated one from another: our questions were answered generically, dismissively, or apathetically — or just ignored.

Three hours later, following the customary box lunch of sandwiches, milk, and an apple, I heard the shrill bark of my name. After pushing my way out of the bullpen, I tried to find out which of the three seated uniformed officers wanted me. A hostile, unrecognizable distortion of my surname brought me to heel. In the confusion, I forgot to bring over my red bag as instructed; at that, my tormentor shook his head so violently, I momentarily considered the onset of apoplexy in the poor man.

Each of the red bags still remaining in the pile bore only a tiny name tag to identify its owner. I must have taken too long; when I returned, the guard had recovered sufficiently from his peculiar tremors to ask whether I had trouble reading my own name. I was tempted to reply that my difficulty was in searching for a spelling that approximated his pronunciation, but I bit my tongue.

Self-importantly, Shakes delved through my property. He let

me keep my gloves, my sunglasses, my address book, and, to my glee, the books that were contraband at the EMDC. Then he dispatched me to an office beyond the last bullpen, where a shy young woman awaited me, her soul seemingly sedated by life. I could reconcile the speedy medical examination she gave me with her lethargy only when I remembered that it was late on a Friday afternoon: she apparently had something to go to that alleviated the paralytic effect of her grim working conditions.

A classification officer (CO) who evidenced no qualifications in the mental health field set out to assess my state of my mind — with two questions: did I want to see a psychologist, and was I suicidal?

"No, but I've been seeing a psychiatrist and taking medication." My lawyers, as well as the white-collar ex-cons I had visited, had warned me to present the most stable front possible; anything else was subject to distortion by untrained personnel desperate for meat to put in their endless reports.

Nonetheless, I had been diagnosed as suffering from thirty years of depression; I had been arrested and publicly, if justifiably, ridiculed; I had been hounded by the press, lost my home and my profession of seventeen years, was cut off from my wife and loving daughter, had recently enjoyed two nights locked up in the company of a racist gangster by whom I had been threatened in no uncertain terms, and just spent two days manacled and shackled. All of this, with my recent history of extensive therapy and my reliance on Prozac, was documented and presumably in my file. Looking at it as objectively as I could, I thought that at least one or two of the above pointed to the need for a psychologist and the potential for suicide.

I cannot to this day imagine that the CO could not see that I was in severe shock. Down Under's cruel admissions procedure had produced the most serious emotional trauma I had ever felt:

I shook, my eyes were red from rubbing away tears of loneliness and fear, and I could barely speak above a whisper; I couldn't sit or stand still, desperate to talk to anyone who would listen.

I asked for help. No dice: "Well, you've been seeing someone so you don't need to talk to anyone now." The approaching weekend had overtaken this man too; further shakiness might put me in a straitjacket on a suicide watch until help arrived Monday morning.

My feelings touched a Saturday afternoon in late January 1992, some two weeks before my sentencing. Deena was hurt and angry over the general dissolution of our lives, the realization that much of our eleven years together were a web of deceit, and the humiliation brought on by the media's disclosure of my affair with another woman. Publicly, she hung tough; privately, we grew apart and fought often.

On this bright afternoon, in our condo overlooking trendy Yorkville in the élitist heart of Toronto, I was again overcome by the years of suppressed rage that had been surfacing since my arrest as life's layers eroded and exploded. In the way of couples, I took it out on Deena.

"You're just like your father, and you'll never change," she screamed.

Deena was frighteningly close to a mark I suddenly couldn't live with. I rushed to the bathroom and methodically swallowed eighty 222s. Over the next few hours, I became nauseated, my vision blurred, and a continuous ringing in my ears disoriented me terribly. When evening came around, I was still conscious, but very weak.

Deena, unaware of my overdose, had no time for my dilemma, going about her Saturday chores with purposeful concentration; to her mind, I was playing up a little stomach upset for all it was worth in an infantile attempt at attention-getting.

By 7 P.M., it was almost impossible to fight off sleep and, I suspected, unconsciousness. I still wasn't prepared to vouch for the fact that life was worth living — but the prospect of a final solitude frightened me even more. The result was near panic, the product of my unresolved, competing fears. Sensing that survival depended on getting up and moving around, I dressed for our dinner date at the Annapurna Restaurant with our friend Joan.

The Annapurna, named for a region of Nepal not far from Mount Everest, where we had trekked during Christmas 1987, is a nonprofit vegetarian Indian restaurant situated near the corner of Dupont and Bathurst streets. Its out-of-the-way location, fresh food, uncluttered docility, unworldly clientele, and volunteer employees dressed in white cotton Indian-style robes had made the Annapurna a haven since my arrest.

I tried to be sociable, bearing, as I had for some time, Deena's affected nonchalance and silent accusations that my crimes, my deceit, and my dalliance disentitled me to depression or discomfort. Finally, unable to defeat the nausea, the dizziness, and the ringing in my ears, I excused myself and began walking home.

The early movies were nearing their end on a Saturday night in Toronto; lines of Torontonians formed on the sidewalks of the city, obsessively assuring their seats for the late show. The second period of the Maple Leaf game was about to start; in the restaurants and residential dining rooms, dinner was hitting its conversational apex as the evening's cocktails and wine filtered silently and effectively through the unsuspecting bloodstreams of society's self-avowed social drinkers. The rest of the city gathered to smoke, snort, gawk, and exchange the socially accepted lies that are the forerunners to lust in the guise of romance.

As I walked, a gentle drizzle softened the steady glow of headlights as daytime traffic gave way to an orderly, rhythmic flow of freely moving vehicles. Time and my sense of it were disengaged, but I guessed that the walk home would take about twenty-five minutes. I had never done much walking on my own; like writing, it requires an equanimity that is largely incompatible with the quest for worldly success; and success, for me, did not exist in the absence of applause.

To overachievers like myself, distraction is essential: it is both opportunity and escape; without it, the mind might turn on itself and its spirit, allowing a glimpse of the barrenness within to induce a fatal hesitation in the always fluttering heartbeat of earthly advancement. My infrequent walks, then, were opportunities for observation, not introspection — sightseeing tours, as it were, to reignite the calculations of the intellect.

Instead of the fastest routes that I normally preferred along the busy arteries of Dupont, Davenport, and Avenue Road, I picked my way through the old residential streets nestled in the quadrant bounded by Bathurst, Dupont, St. George, and Bloor. As long as I stayed west of St. George, I could avoid the gaudiness of Avenue Road, the swagger of the Four Seasons Hotel, the exclusive shops of Hazelton Lanes, and the glitzy boutiques of Cumberland and Yorkville. This had been my territory, this was where I purchased the artefacts that deflected self-scrutiny and attracted the adoration of my circle of friends, acquaintances, business associates, and hangers-on. Now that my fantasy life had shattered, their oohing and ahing had merely turned to its disruption.

The crisp January air was invigorating. Nausea and dizziness gave way to an oddly confident detachment from my turmoil. There were only a few passers-by; no longer evaluating, I opened myself to the beauty of our shared humanity in their faces and glances.

My old world returned as I walked east on Prince Arthur, lined with fancy restaurants with French names, chic art galleries, and oh so precious professional offices in renovated old houses. Near Avenue Road, an ungainly white high-rise signals the glitter and bustle around the corner; the imposing shadow of the Prince Arthur Towers apartments protects the innocuously situated Rendezvous restaurant, which earns its name by subtle panderings to the discreet needs of its patrons. As the elegant building that housed our condo came into view, I fought the inclination to mourn my ouster from this charmed world.

Both sadness and shame pervaded my walk. The shame, strangely, did not come from my cowardly attempt at avoiding the consequences of my actions: I still hadn't grown up enough to realize that surrender to reality was preferable to death by avoidance; rather, I feared humiliation — that others would laugh at my ineptness if I survived. But my sadness was appropriate, for it enshrined a new awareness that the vase must be empty before it could be filled. I no longer wanted to die, but my pride would not let me call a doctor.

By the time I got on the elevator, I felt sicker than ever. Exhausted, I fell onto the couch in our living room overlooking the northernmost lights of the city, turned on the television, and fought the lethal drowsiness.

Deena came home two hours later. She walked Barney and Maude, our bull terriers, and went to sleep. I kept my eyes on the television set as long as I could. Then, I lay down beside Deena in our bedroom, trying hard not to disturb her: blame had become a way of life for both of us. My stillness focused the nausea, and then the retching came; I was up all night with my face in the toilet bowl, falling asleep only with the morning sun.

When I awoke at noon on Sunday, the nausea was back, more mildly, but the ringing in my ears gave me a splitting headache. I dared not take more medication. I went back to the couch, cuddled up with Maude, and tried to stay awake with a disaffected interest in Sunday afternoon football. Deena kept about her business as if the night had not intruded. Melissa dropped by, accepting my explanation that I had eaten something upsetting. By dinnertime, I could take down liquids and plain toast; the nausea stopped, but the headache remained and I was exhausted. I slept well.

Early the next morning, the symptoms were gone. I was disgusted with myself. Substance abuse was foreign to me, and I had never been more than an occasional social drinker. Still, in the month since I had pleaded guilty, as jail's imminence made itself felt, I had taken to combining the Prozac prescribed by Dr. Arndt with Percodan left over from earlier surgery, washing it all down with a healthy shot of Chivas Regal.

I saw Dr. Arndt later that morning. "So how come you're still alive?" he asked. At that moment, I let go of the crutches. One week later, Deena marvelled at the positive change in my attitude and controlling ways.

But only tomorrow, when she comes to visit me in prison, will I tell Melissa this story. This, I will vow again, will be the last broken promise.

The CO's line of questioning, intended to determine what kind of convict I was, brought me back to Millhaven A & D. No, I had no previous record, no history of violence, no drug or alcohol problems, no one I feared. Satisfied, the CO made a note at the bottom of his sheet and sent me on my way.

As I left the CO's office, Jackson, the large black lifer who had taken our measurements while we were in the bullpen, handed me a plastic bag full of "joint greens": one light waist-length jacket, two pairs of green pants, three white T-shirts, three pairs of underwear, three pairs of out-of-place black acrylic dress socks, one pair of practically soleless running shoes, two blue blankets, two white sheets, one pillow, one pillowcase, a toothbrush, toothpaste, a dull razor, sandpaper soap, a shaving brush, shaving cream, and a hairbrush. No shirts or outerwear for a Kingston February —

but then I hadn't imagined prison as an outdoors experience. With my daily pay of $5.25, I could purchase other basics from the canteen.

Clothing issue was the responsibility of SIS, for whom Jackson worked. "What does SIS stand for?" I once asked a guard.

"Institutional Services."

I persisted. "What does the first 'S' stand for?"

The guard thought for a while. "Slow. SIS. Slow Institutional Services."

Jackson told me to change in the now-empty CO's office, and I did so in unaccustomed privacy. The T-shirt and underwear were mouse-sized and the pants giraffe length.

"Make do," said Jackson. "I don't got nothing else. You can put your order in up on the range."

I eventually did put my order in, but discovered that the only assurance of delivery before my nine-year sentence expired was by way of private request to Jackson, accompanied by an appropriate gratuity.

A photographer situated kitty corner to the bullpen took my mug shots. At the EMDC, I had shaved my moustache for the first time in over twenty years. Finally, Bruce, King of the Enclave, fingerprinted me. I was now officially CSC inmate #983280C.

I had been on my feet for over four hours. The bullpen had emptied somewhat, but no seats were available. As inmates who had retrieved their cigarettes fought off those awaiting relief, the tension grew, escalating my sense of panic. Kevin was still in the bullpen, making his share of enemies by refusing to part with his smokes.

"Look at these punks," he complained. "Last time I was here, guys had enough respect to ask for a puff or two. Now, one cigarette isn't enough for the goofs. You can bet your ass they won't be around when I need a smoke. Fuck 'em.... Julius, what range are you on?"

"I don't know."

"What did the CO write down at the bottom of his paper?"

"A or E, I'm not sure."

"Shit, it's probably E. You're so far down the line."

"What's wrong with E?"

"It's seg, man. Segregation. It used to be the hole. It's the armpit of the joint. No TV, no nothing. You can't even get out in the yard with the other inmates."

"Where are they sending you, Kevin?" I asked wretchedly.

"A Unit, pal. Probably won't see you for a while."

To make things worse, a wild-eyed veteran of the Haven was holding court.

I've been here eight months. I just got out for a few days because the damn Crown called me as a witness. What the fuck? Did they think I was going to rat out? I almost jumped him right in court. When I got here, they tell everybody you'll be out of this joint in two months. No fucking chance. They've always got some excuse. Psychological tests or some other bullshit. I'm gonna fuckin' kill somebody soon.

Fighting back the sobs and oblivious to the filth and the odour, I walked to the sink, where I could be alone. There I stood, despondent, until Kevin tapped me gently on the shoulder.

"Time to go inside the Big House," he whispered.

Playing lawyer

Introspection and reasoning is more efficient (for the purpose
of inward awareness) than meditation and prayer.
DALAI LAMA

Except for a few jailhouse interviews, and the odd letter from an incarcerated client, I knew nothing about the workings of penitentiaries; I had no idea that most of my clients' concerns were about what happened to them after sentencing. Over ninety percent of accused plead guilty or are convicted; the art of speaking to sentence, often shoddily practised because it is unglamorous, is therefore of much greater significance than the question of guilt and innocence. From the con's point of view, the length of the sentence is secondary to the proportion of his time that he will actually spend in jail and the conditions and restrictions that will accompany his incarceration and parole.

On a Sunday afternoon not long after my arrest, Deena's uncle, Joe Bloomenfeld, a noted criminal lawyer in Toronto who had been particularly kind to me throughout my ordeal, suggested that I speak to David Cole, the Provincial Court judge who chairs the Ontario government's inquiry into racism in provincial jails.

Before his appointment to the Provincial Court Bench, Cole was the guru of prison law, a legend in the penitentiaries. His tenacity and ability as the foremost advocate of prisoners' rights gave him an awesome reputation he richly deserved. David was still welcome and trusted in the institutions, greeted warmly by everyone from the duty officer to the warden.

When I called David, he reminded me of a professional favour I had done for him long ago and invited me to his home. In his low-key manner, David was the first to tell me what to anticipate and what to do about it; he arranged meetings with white-collar ex-clients who helped prepare me for what was coming.

The judge also unravelled the intricacies of my sentence: I was eligible for day parole after one-sixth of my sentence; while on day parole, I could live in a halfway house during the week, be out all day, and return only to spend the night; I could spend weekends at home. Full parole came after three years: I could live at home, travel relatively freely, and as long as I stayed out of trouble, monthly reporting to a parole officer was the most significant restriction.

It is, however, a long way from parole "eligibility" to freedom. As a first-time white-collar criminal, my chances for early day parole were good except for the National Parole Board's policy of limiting day paroles to six to twelve months. The board reasoned that the "one foot in, one foot out" environment of a halfway house was frustrating and often counterproductive over a longer period.

I had been expecting a sentence in the neighbourhood of eight to ten years. At the midpoint of nine years, day parole eligibility occurred at eighteen months and full parole at three years. If the National Parole Board stuck to its six- to twelve-month guideline, I would spend two years in jail. If a halfway house agreed to take me after eighteen months, my chances of early release would improve considerably. David counselled me to approach halfway houses even before I was sentenced.

David recommended various lawyers to look after me while I was in jail, and I chose Robert Bigelow, who had articled with David and later assumed his practice.

At our first meeting, my inquiries of Bob were basic: How often could I use the phone? Were there any books in Millhaven? Could I bring in any books? Could I wear my wedding ring? What were the visiting privileges? Could I work there? Where would I get stamps? Were the letters censored? Were the telephone calls all monitored? Who could visit me? How soon after I got there could they visit? How long were the visits? What days of the week? Could I bring in any of my own clothes? Could I take my sunglasses? Would I get outside at all? Could I exercise? What, if anything, could I buy in the prison? What does the institution supply? What colour are prison clothes these days? Could I get my medication in Millhaven? Would they allow my psychiatrist to visit?

Throughout, Bob listened quietly and patiently. When he expressed his belief in the strength of the human spirit to cope and renew, his words had the ring of truth. His faith, optimism, decency, and humanity have neither wavered nor waned to this day, and I remain deeply grateful.

I wanted to get to a minimum security camp as quickly as possible. But as my life of respectability had not been what it seemed, CSC would not be relying on it in placing me. In the normal course, a year or so in a medium security institution would allow CSC to assess my suitability for transfer to a minimum security camp. Bob's task was to convince CSC that this vetting was unnecessary.

Echoing David's advice, Bob recommended that any plea bargain I made include letters of support from the prosecutor and the investigating officer. Because so much of the workings of CSC and the Parole Board are in the public eye, Crown and police support buffers these bodies from public criticism.

I well knew that the desired recommendations came only with a guilty plea. Fortunately, from the moment that the RCMP contacted me at 1:30 on a Saturday morning at my suite in the Four Seasons in Montreal, confronting the inevitable was no problem for me. As Deena slept peacefully through the night, I contemplated my options: suicide, flight, or surrender.

I dismissed suicide peremptorily, but flight was realistic. Although I had no "stash," I had little doubt about my resourcefulness; my career as a criminal lawyer had taught me enough about the shady world of phoney passports and extradition havens to give me confidence that I could evade capture. The prospect of "being on the run" did not, on its own, dissuade me, but I couldn't bear to leave my wife or my daughter. I sensed that Deena would not run with me, but I couldn't imagine giving her up; only much later did I realize that my feelings were no more than selfish dependency.

Melissa was another matter: I just couldn't do it to her. There was no question in my mind that she would choose sticking it out together over separation. We were unusually close, from the time I skipped classes to baby-sit her while Cathy, her mother, worked shifts as a nurse to support us. After Cathy and I separated in 1981, I was adamant that the separation would not strain the bonds between us.

In this, I had succeeded splendidly: Melissa was my best friend. As my old life slipped away in the quiet early morning hours of that long weekend in August, my priorities reassembled: I would not leave my daughter to the destiny of mistrust that would inevitably follow her father's desertion.

What, then, was the nature of my surrender to be? Conviction was inevitable, but I could play tough, stretching out the proceedings and the trial itself for years. I had worked entirely alone and had kept very scant records; the multimillion-dollar fraud spanning seven years had victimized numerous banks and individuals to the tune of $30 million in losses; proof of my frauds required an analysis of ten years' records, invoking the meticulous investigation and painstaking testimony of a firm of forensic accountants. If I admitted nothing and refused to co-operate, the case would be excruciatingly difficult, time-consuming, and costly.

A quick resolution of my case, on the other hand, might be seductive: Ontario's courts were hopelessly clogged with unmanageable dockets, and recent decisions of the Supreme Court of Canada mandating a speedy trial had forced the dismissal of thousands of charges; nowadays, Crown attorneys made their name by the speed and cost effectiveness with which they moved their cases through the courts.

I expected to be released on bail upon my arrest. Nonetheless, life's rhythms were already at a standstill, and existence had quickly become a vacuum in the few hours since the fateful phone call from London. Prolonging the agony of my family, my friends, and my victims by denying my crime or hiding anything about it was neither healthy nor right. Getting on with it was the only relief in sight.

Despite haughty platitudes to the contrary, people fare better if they plead guilty; unless someone is innocent or has a good chance to get away with it, it's risky to exercise the presumption of innocence to its fullest. Apart from harsher sentences for obstinate accused who insist on a trial, the Parole Board regards a guilty plea as the most reliable sign of sincere remorse; a not guilty plea, on the other hand, taints subsequent expressions of regret.

I had co-operated with the police and the creditors before ever talking to Cole or Bigelow. Less than twenty-four hours after the police contacted me in Montreal, I surrendered to the RCMP's London office, where I provided details of my activities over the previous ten years, including frauds of which the police were unaware. Three days later, unaccompanied by a lawyer, I attended voluntarily at the Toronto offices of Coopers & Lybrand, the accounting firm representing my creditors. In a lengthy recorded session, working without notes and entirely from memory, I explained the convoluted transactions whose trail resided exclusively in my head.

In the following weeks, I signed consents that eliminated the need for search warrants, admitted forgeries on hundreds of documents, which saved the cost of handwriting experts, and provided dates, names, addresses, correlations, and explanations. By early November, I had struck a deal for a nine-year sentence. On December 19, I pleaded guilty. I was sentenced on February 10, 1992.

Just over six months had gone by since my arrest. Scott Hutchison, the Crown attorney, remarked that six months was a record for a case of this kind. He was obviously relieved: during the half-year that I was on bail, Hutchison had on several occasions expressed his surprise at my failure to disappear.

The Crown had what it wanted: nine years, the "second-longest sentence ever for this type of crime in Ontario," and a compensation order for $20 million, which, in the words of Mr. Justice Maloney, "would hang over your head the rest of your life." Justice had been meted out quickly and inexpensively; Sergeant Ray Porter, the investigating officer, opined that the system had worked as it was meant to.

For my part, nine years under supervision loomed as an eternity. I wondered over and over whether I ought to have hung on longer, put the Crown and the police to work, and held out for a couple of years off the sentence. The prosecutor's worst nightmare, I suspected, was that I would fire my lawyers, Mike Epstein and Brian Greenspan, and conduct the proceedings myself. More than once I wondered whether I would have done better that way.

In the end, I told myself that I would have made the same bargain for a client, after the same risk analysis. I had started that process by pondering my best position, knowing that my sole hope for judicial leniency lay in the psychological origins of the crime.

Unknown to the Crown attorney, I had in hand a detailed report from a respected psychologist, Dr. Al Long, which Dr. Arndt had commissioned for therapeutic purposes. On a frigid, snowy night at the beginning of February, one short week before sentencing, Melissa and I took the long ride from downtown to Rexdale, at the northwestern border of Metro Toronto, where we picked up Dr. Long's report from his typist's home. I parked Deena's Acura down the street, turned on the dome light, and focused on the opening paragraphs of the report.

I cried: tears of fright, desperation, time lost, and a life wasted. Unable to face myself before I faced the consequences, I now admitted to myself what I had sensed for some time: imprisonment would not be the toughest battle.

I am confident that from a psychological point of view Mr. Melnitzer's behaviour was strongly psychologically determined.... On an emotional level and on an interpersonal level, this man although of high intelligence and abilities to learn may be regarded as defective due to the psychological defense of denial which is in him a predominant defense....

The test data indicate a chaotic childhood and severe disruption of ego development such that he well could have suffered a Childhood Psychosis....

He is an extremely sensitive person probably as a result of these problems of rejection with a feeling of sadness again of very early origins....

On a superficial and socially apparent level his need to be aggressive, to demonstrate an intellectual control and superiority, to be above blame and criticism, and to endure the pressures of his life and be consistently in command and to demonstrate these qualities, has been met until recently....

Sadly, he has until recently struggled with the credo that hard work and great accomplishment will bring him love.... He has also suffered the illusion that once he attained satisfaction of his various

immediate goals, that he would no longer be frustrated or tempted to
reach out for further satisfaction: this is impossible of course....

I thought about throwing myself and these devastating revelations on the mercy of the court. In a welter of self-pity, I imagined that any judge would see that I had not intended harm, and that, in the distress of my emotional dungeon, the consequences were beyond me.

My intellect brought me to my senses. If I had not been intentionally malicious, I had been astonishingly reckless. The consequences to my victims were the same in either case: their hurt and their loss were not allayed by any medical interpretation of my conduct. There was no doubt that I had known right from wrong every step of the way, and the choice I had made between them was all that mattered. The explanations that were my blueprint for the future were no excuse for my past.

In this light, the odds for a sentence less than nine years were slight. I would have to draw the perfect judge, hope that he didn't get out of the wrong side of his bed on sentencing morning, get a bravura performance out of my lawyers, trust that all the evidence fell neatly into place, and pray that the shock of listening to my old friends describing the scope of their betrayal did not hit the judge too hard. The downside, I concluded, was great.

Just before the sentencing, the Crown and the RCMP delivered a letter to my lawyers, addressed both to the Parole Board and to Millhaven Penitentiary:

> *Mr. Melnitzer surrendered into custody with no fixed promises of*
> *easy treatment....*
>   *At the time of his surrender and in the intervening period Mr.*
> *Melnitzer was cooperative with the police and with the prosecution....*
> *He provided police with several significant inculpatory statements which*

eliminated or substantially reduced the need for any additional investigation into other offences....

I have no reason to believe that Mr. Melnitzer will pose any sort of security risk to other inmates, members of the Correctional Service, or to the public nor do I have any special reason to believe that he would be a flight risk.

With all these facts in mind I would offer my strong recommendation that Mr. Melnitzer be considered for a minimum security classification and placement as soon as possible, and that he be considered for day parole at the earliest date that this status is available to him....

... I think that ... Mr. Melnitzer would benefit, and his successful return to life outside the institution encouraged, were he allowed to continue with the course of treatment initiated by Dr. Arndt.

I watched Mr. Justice Maloney carefully during the sentencing. During the lunch recess, I whispered to Brian Greenspan: "You guys called it right. Maloney would have given me twelve years on his own."

Maximum

We only have two choices: to live or to die.
ALBERT CAMUS

Millhaven's main corridors, incongruously flooded in natural light from windows on either side, converge on the "Dome," the central rotunda that is the institution's nerve centre. On our way from A & D, we passed through four sliding gates, a security post at the end of each corridor, and, in the Dome itself, the metal detector inmates call a "stool pigeon." These constraints isolate trouble spots, limit communication among inmates, control the flow of contraband, and underscore the strict limitations on movement that dominate maximum security prisons.

As we lined up by the metal detector, I moved the scorpion, secreted in my mouth since early that morning, to my pants pocket.

To my relief, we were led to the barrier marked "A Unit": I wouldn't be in the hole after all. A smaller, yellow, windowless corridor took us by A Unit's duty office and kitchen-servery. Opposite the office, beside the servery, a non-functioning elevator housed the unit's barber shop.

A Unit's ranges consist of eight-foot-wide hallways with cells on each side, built around a glassed-in tower called the "bubble"; each range has its own washer, dryer, and collect telephone. The bubble overlooks the TV lounge, four common rooms, and the canteen; only the cell interiors, the showers, and the utility rooms are beyond the bubble's view: elsewhere, anything that moves is watched. Steel plates with holes in them dot the bubble's perimeter, enabling the guards to point their firearms virtually anywhere in the unit — and chilling me.

In contrast, a grassy yard just outside the canteen features an asphalt walking path around its perimeter and a functional weight pit. The yard, exclusively for A Unit's "work range," is enclosed by the grey concrete walls of various wings of the prison and separated from them by a high chain link fence.

The door to the yard is unguarded, and, by silent agreement, the guards rarely venture there. In the darkness of winter evenings, the yard is one of maximum's few sanctuaries, the favoured place to trade contraband, smoke a little hash, pop a few Valiums, or drink a little homemade brew, concocted by fermenting a mixture of ketchup, sugar, and rice with the aid of yeast pellets smuggled from the kitchen.

Peter, the con who was the unit clerk, led us to the common room adjoining the ground-floor ranges, where dinner, basic but edible in comparison to the culinary abominations of the past few days, was served behind a locked door.

A fifteen-minute orientation followed by a question-and-answer period was our quickie menu to the ins and outs of Millhaven Reception. Most of the time was taken up with inquiries about pay, canteen, and choice of cellmates.

I asked some questions. The ease of my vocabulary, the absence of the vernacular, more than one complete sentence without "fucking" in it, and the uncertain curiosity of my tone provoked a universal reaction: "This guy is not one of us. Who the fuck does he think he is?" I had long refined the art of acquiring and holding attention, and it had been the touchstone of a successful career.

But in prison, being the centre of attention and sticking out like a sore thumb are divided only by a thin line. A general undercurrent of hostility towards me was developing; as Kevin later put it, "For me, there's them and us; for you, it's them, you, and us."

Afterwards, a few of us gathered around Peter, pressing for more answers. Peter's reassurances were tinged with the kind condescension that comes with seasoning, but his best efforts answered my questions without quelling my neuroses. Redoubling my efforts, my voice developed a hostile edge as one leading question after another failed to draw the reply I wanted.

A new voice intruded. "Hi, I'm Perry. You're the lawyer, I hope. Bob Bigelow told me you'd be coming."

"Yes. I'm Julius. Nice to meet you."

The friendly, twinkling eyes of the smiling, cherubic grey-haired man somehow told me that he had never been in jail before either. I had a friend. I thanked a deity I wasn't sure I believed in for Bob Bigelow. And I marvelled, once more, at the grapevine's efficiency.

"Let's get this guy on the work range," Perry said. "I can vouch for him."

"OK," Peter agreed, "but you know the rules. He's got to get classified before he can apply. Then we'll get him moved up the list."

"How long will that take, Peter?" I asked.

"A few weeks," he answered.

"What does 'a few weeks' mean?"

"Hard to tell. Depends on your CO."

My heart fell again. Perry touched my arm and winked.

We were the last cons in the room. "We've got to get you to your cell," Peter said.

Perry and I shook hands. "Don't worry," he said, "we'll look after you." Perry winked again.

Still frustrated, I followed Peter up the stairs past Control to C range, where cell C23 was to be my "drum," my house Down Under.

The cell door was much like the others I had encountered, a heavy steel sliding contraption with a viewing slat eighteen inches wide and three inches high, opened and closed electronically from the bubble. The bars I expected never materialized; in Ontario's federal institutions, only Kingston Penitentiary, the Kingston Prison for Women, and a few ranges in Collins Bay feature that zoological characteristic. A generously sized window opposite the door was secured by horizontal painted metal planks three inches wide and set six inches apart; the grid formed by the bars was barely noticeable, unlike the ominous vertical black iron rails that commonly depict prison settings.

The cell seemed smaller than in the EMDC, where there was enough room for side-by-side twin beds. Here, a bunk bed similar to the one in Toronto East dominated the cell, older and dingier than my previous roosts.

A stifling sense of permanence overwhelmed me.

Carl, a scruffy-looking young man in his mid-twenties, smiled shyly as I walked in. As the newest arrival, I got the top bunk. Unlike Spike, Carl enquired about my needs and moved his belongings around to accommodate me. I unloaded my plastic bag, moved the scorpion from my pants pocket to the buttoned-up breast pocket of my green jacket, made up the bed over the corroded frame and sagging mattress no thicker than four inches, and lay down thankfully without regard to the springs nudging through the thin mattress.

My cell partner had been in Millhaven for the first six months of his four-year term, his first pen bit, having previously served short sentences in provincial reformatories. A long-time member of the drug subculture, his academic level fell short of Grade 8, which he considered a lucky break, as it allowed him to leave the cell each morning to upgrade his schooling. Carl spent his cell time doing a bit of homework, watching television, and writing lengthy, explicitly amorous poems to his girlfriend; he delighted in reading the poems to me, and I delighted in bestowing the superficial approval he sought.

Carl swore that the enforced absence from his love, combined with the horrors of the pen, had motivated him to turn over a new leaf. On his release, he planned to attend community college, marry, and "get straight." I offered to help with his math.

In one of the system's few concessions to the crowded conditions, the cell door stayed open while I organized myself. As I did so, I heard my name and stuck my head out the door. "Somebody looking for me?" I called out. "In here."

A sloppily dressed, dishevelled man of about sixty stuck his head in the room. "Julius? I'm Aaron."

"Pleasure to meet you, Aaron."

"Likewise," he replied. "Bobby told me you'd be coming. He asked me to do what I could for you. Here, I brought you some roast beef." Somehow, Aaron had accumulated what looked like a pound of rare roast beef to which he had added a little creamed horseradish. I put the meat on the desk, without the heart to tell him I was a vegetarian. "That's great. Where did you get it?"

"Boychick, boychick," Aaron rebuked me, "there's so much we'll have to teach you about this way of life." Questioning the source of illicit good fortune is dangerous in prison.

Aaron arched his eyebrows towards Carl, who was feigning nonchalance while sneaking furtive glances at the meat.

"You're on the work range," I asserted. I rationalized putting a question in the form of a statement to end-run the problem of discussing delicate matters in Carl's presence. Aaron didn't seem to mind.

"Yeah, you'll be there soon too. By Monday for sure."

Never one to settle for subtle, I pressed on. "Don't I have to be classified first?"

That brought on another display of arched eyebrows. "Don't worry about that. Just hang on for a few days. And don't ask so many questions. I'll see you later."

Aaron sauntered past Control, waving to the guards as he disappeared down the staircase. Everything about him was smooth and easy: his enormous belly, his double chin, his prominent nose in the best tradition of Jewish caricature, and his waddling gait on his floppy white rubber bath thongs all suggested the blend of a contented bullfrog and a pregnant ostrich.

I was rather smug myself. My spadework before sentencing was paying off; even in prison, influence and preparation had their places. Things were looking good — and, in a nagging way, very familiar. I took the roast beef from the desk and handed it to a grateful Carl.

At 10:45, the range lights went off. In an eerie silence, prison's beat went on.

Aside from the cons on the work range, all prisoners in Reception were double-bunked in standard-sized cells like the one I shared with Carl. The cells were originally designed as living space for one; when the inmate population increased, CSC decided that two could fit in that very same space, possibly on the theory that a convict was less than one human being.

Breakfast was served at 6:15. As most of us did not have alarms, only the unpleasant clank of unlatching doors announced breakfast. The doors stayed open for twenty minutes. In that time, we had to dress, wash, get to the servery, wait in line, bring the meal back to our cell, eat, and return the empty food tray. That made breakfast a race to the wire: dressing hurriedly in space designed for one was a gymnastic experience complicated by the availability of only a single washbasin and toilet in each cell; those unlucky enough to experience the morning urge risked missing breakfast.

We picked up our meals at the servery and ate in our cells. For three of five ranges, this meant that the overloaded trays had to be carried up winding stairs. If the meal made it safely to the cell, the problem was finding room to eat: the desk was the only suitable surface on which to put the tray, but it was often crowded with overflow belongings; in any event, the desktop accommodated only one tray and each cell had only one chair. The shapeless bedding discouraged putting the tray on the top bunk. That left one person to eat on the back end of the lower bunk — the front was inaccessible because the desk chair took up all the floor space at the head of the bed — gingerly balancing his tray on his lap, the springless frames making for contortions worthy of the circus.

After breakfast, we were locked up until lunchtime. We left our cells only for administrative necessities, such as hospital appointments, educational and psychological testing, emergency telephone calls, or lawyers' visits. During the long cell-bound hours, sleeping, reading, watching TV, writing letters, or playing cards represented the range of activities; but playing games was uncomfortable and writing was difficult on the spongy beds.

With only one TV in each room, choosing channels called for delicate negotiation; sleep often gave way to the sound of the television, and reading demanded special concentration. When agreement by negotiation was not achieved, seniority of occupancy prevailed. Terror and brute force also had their place in the close quarters, but, even among societal misfits, most often reason prevailed.

We ate lunch at 11:15, the routine somewhat less hectic than at breakfast, as most of the inmates were up and about. After lunch, they locked us up again until suppertime at 4:00.

"Count," which precedes all meals and bedtime, is part of prisons' daily routine. In maximum and medium, the entire population, with few exceptions, such as inmates on visits, are locked in their cells. The count totals are checked against the census board in each

unit, which reports its numbers to the "keeper," the senior oper-
ational security officer on duty; the count is "cleared" when the
combined sum of the units' individual counts matches the keeper's
grand total. Time in prison revolves around the counts, and time
is the stuff of which prison is made. One of my cell partners, frustrated by a lengthy count that was delaying our meal, acquainted
me with an old prison saying: "They count us like diamonds and
treat us like shit. Ain't that the truth?"

After supper, we alternated five-minute showers and five minutes of telephone time every second day. Even calling a lawyer was
not an easy task at Millhaven, Charter of Rights notwithstanding.
The five-minute evening phone calls we were allowed did not
correspond to business hours. Making things worse, few criminal
lawyers are dedicated enough and imbued with sufficient faith in
rehabilitation to give their home numbers to those from whose
misfortune their substantial incomes are derived.

Business-hours calls to lawyers required permission from a CO.
These requests, as far as I could tell, received no special priority:
if the prisoner was lucky, his request would be granted in two or
three days; if the CO was on holiday, sick, lazy, uninterested, or
didn't like the particular con, the process took much longer. When
a con did manage to find a lawyer in his office, the receptionist
might not accept his collect call.

Each night at seven, and weekend mornings from eight, a
three-hour "rec-up" in the prison's main gym and yard was our
opportunity for exercise and socializing. Thirty yards down the
corridor from the gym's main doors, a grilled barrier guarded the
entrance to the prison hospital. There, a nurse awaited us as we
left the gym, a prescription list and a cart of medication in front
of her and a guard beside her. As I put my hand through the bars
for my medication, neither her hands — nor her eyes — strayed
to my side of the barrier. Back at A Unit, at the gate by the duty

office, another nurse did the same for those inmates who had skipped recreation.

The facelessness of the pill parade characterized Millhaven, and administrative chaos exacerbated it. One poor wretch had not laid eyes on his CO, the person responsible for getting him out of Millhaven, during his entire six-month stay in Reception. Unable to contact a lawyer, Kenny finally filed a grievance; only then did he discover that his file had been lost and, therefore, so had he. For a half-year, his legitimate complaints had been dismissed as another con's groundless grumblings.

Following the delay at the "pill parade," we returned home through the numerous barriers and the stool pigeon in the Dome; the ordeal could take up to twenty minutes. By 10:30, everyone was back on the range.

Bedtime in Millhaven. One fewer day to count.

Heaven in Hell

Hell is just resistance to life.

PEMA CHODRON

On my first morning in Millhaven, Saturday, I filed out to the gym with several hundred others, anxious to keep my prearranged meeting with Kevin. There, and in the yard, guards were nowhere to be seen.

"They're watching," Kevin said, pointing upwards. "There used to be a catwalk up there. The coppers patrolled it with guns. After the riots, they decided that wasn't safe enough for the screws. See the smoked glass. That's the tower. It has gun ports that let them knock off anything in here."

The yard's expanse and dim lighting made it equally dangerous: security there was maintained by armed guards who manned the signature watchtowers and used pickups to patrol the perimeter of the high double fences topped with barbed wire.

It was the dead of winter in eastern Canada. Although Millhaven's huge yard boasted tennis courts, a miniature-golf course, a basketball court, an outdoor weight pit, and a half-mile cinder running track, only the weight pit and the running track were functioning. The pit was unprotected from the elements, but the bodybuilders usually ignored the bitter cold, the slush, and the snow.

The running track wasn't shovelled or salted regularly and was often better suited to skating or swimming. Still, it might have been used more but for the shortage of protective clothing: the waist-length polyester-cotton blend jackets distributed at admission were our only protection from the cold. We could get thermal under-wear at staff's discretion; parkas, however, were dependent on the good graces of Jackson — for the usual price — unless an inmate was lucky enough to move into the cell of a transferee who had left his parka behind. Carl had "scored" two parkas that way and generously parted with the XXL which fit me.

Scrub basketball, soccer, and floor hockey alternated nightly on the gym floor, but four black bullpens, similar to the ones in A & D, were the hub of activity. The cage closest to the entrance housed open toilets and showers; the showers were welcome, but the toilets might as well have been dead centre in Toronto's SkyDome and were rarely used.

The second bullpen functioned as a card room, seating fewer than twenty; the third featured one pool table for the almost five hundred inmates, a Foosball game, and a huge stack of gym mats, far more than could be laid out on the floor.

On a row of low wooden benches outside the bullpens sat the cons who had left their cells simply to escape claustrophobia. These were the quiet, the frightened, and the lonely, enduring their sentences in a timeless void. The socializers, on the other hand, seized on recreation as an opportunity to meet friends and catch up on the grapevine — inveterate gossips for whom information was the sole stimulant. The smokers stood around inside, while the non-smokers, anxious to escape the fumes, alternated between the cold outside and the asphyxiating, sweaty haze of the overcrowded, windowless gym.

The drug dealers, the bookies, and the enforcers out to settle debts, scores, or beefs did what they had to do in the yard, as far away from the towers and as deeply hidden in the night shadows as possible. Much of the drug dealing transpired in the weight pit — curiously distant from the closest watchtower — where the grunts of the bodybuilders helped provide cover.

The gym reflected both the cultural mix and the racial realities of Millhaven. The kaleidoscope included whites, blacks, Hispanics, Asians, and Italians, each group huddled in its own corner; while individual contact was casual and not infrequent, the races did not mix as groups.

The clearest division was between whites and blacks. The blacks played cards at their own table; the pool table and shuffleboard were white territory; basketball was mainly the blacks' game; floor hockey was the province of the whites; and only at indoor soccer did blacks and whites play together regularly. In the yard, walking and weightlifting pairs were like socks — always the same colour.

Two minutes of watching ball hockey, where the rules were non-contact but the game was vicious, convinced me that the gym floor, the easiest place to get away with something you couldn't be blamed for, was an inappropriate setting for a high-profile man my age.

Kevin looked on sceptically. "These goofs think they're all gladiators. Let's go outside."

It was a beautiful, warm weekend morning. The track was slushy with melting snow, but that was no distraction from the exhilaration of an unconstrained walk in the open air. Since my sentencing early in the week, I hadn't been outside apart from short hobbles in handcuffs and shackles to and from the Grey Goose.

"There's no respect," Kevin grumbled. "The joints are full of pukes and rats. Nobody's solid any more."

"Are you trying to tell me that jail's not the right place for a decent criminal?" I laughed.

"Fucking A. I've seen enough. I'm not coming back."

"Me either," I said.

Kevin and I met regularly at evening rec and on weekend mornings. I usually managed a few situps, pushups, and stretches on the mats in the back cage; then we walked as long as we could stand the cold, five to ten times around the half-mile track. I think I asked more questions in four weeks than I had during my entire career in court.

My friend revelled in the teacher–student dependency, giving me advice on marriage ("Let her have her space. It's tougher for her than for you"), visits ("They're a double-edged sword"), sports ("Blow Jays"), and the Code ("Don't stand in a copper's office with the door closed. Everybody will think you're ratting out").

I took it all in with a grain of salt: Kevin improvised when in doubt, but that flaw usually arose with his insistence that his version of the current grapevine rumour was the correct one; his observations about the way the system worked were steeped in experience spanning two decades, and his casual way with the details faded in the depth of his understanding of the overall scheme of things. Kevin was an endless but intelligent and astute talker; he kept to himself, did his own time, honoured confidences, and valued loyalty.

The key to doing time, Kevin said, was to accept it totally:

> Forget about the outside. Write only when you have to, phone only when you have to, don't ask any questions unless you have to. Anything that reminds you about the outside makes the time go slower and harder. It'll all be there when you get out, and if it isn't, there's nothing you can do about it.
>
> Visits are bummers. They treat your visitor like shit. They search them like they've been sentenced themselves and talk to them like they're as bad as you are. And there's no privacy. You're all sitting in a room with some copper watching you and the place is bugged. Kids are

screaming all over the place. The punks are just about sticking their women in front of you. People from the outside never get used to it. So you're making it hard on them too, especially your family, by asking them to visit. Do you really want your kids to remember you in greens, behind fences? Not me.

The worst thing is they leave. You come back to your house and you think about them. All of a sudden, you hate your house, you hate yourself, you hate your cellmate, you hate your situation. You see the Man everywhere.

My first bit, I had visits and calls and letters all the time. It was the hardest time I ever did. The second time, I told everybody to stay away. My kids, my wife, my friends. If they cared, they'd be there when I walked out the gates. That's when you need friends. They can't help you in here.

Only a few weeks into my sentence, I couldn't relate to Kevin's portrayal: loving, if apprehensive, visits from Melissa and Deena and letters and phone calls to and from my family and friends were the scarce interruptions of my despair. But Kevin's advice stayed with me, and a modified version was to serve me well when disappointments overtook me in the months to come.

The unmodified version of Kevin's advice, I suspected, was a front, the lowest common denominator to many who exhibited criminal behaviour. I speculated that Kevin was lonely, unhappy, and not quite as smug, secure, and content in jail as he made himself out to be; I wondered if his stomach cancer was really in remission.

As I got to know Kevin, the cracks showed: before meals, he regularly headed for the mailbox with letters in hand; in the morning, he anxiously awaited his mail with the rest of us; pictures of an ex–common-law wife and a couple of kids appeared in his cell; his daughter wrote of her impending marriage and Kevin proudly spread the word.

With the exception of those with no one to contact, there was no unmodified version of how to do your time, not even for stoical, experienced old Kevin. So long as the hope of returning to the street endured, he, like the rest of us, held to its vestiges.

I drifted absentmindedly through lunch and a quiet Saturday afternoon helping Carl with his math; his short attention span spoke poignantly to the gulf between resolve and action among our outcasts.

Bob Bigelow had promised to speak to a CO named Sharon, in the hope that she would put my file on her caseload. As luck would have it, Sharon was indeed my CO. On the way to supper, I stopped at the duty office, hoping to meet her and get my transfer underway.

"I'm Sharon, Melnitzer," said the pleasantly full-figured, bespectacled woman in civilian clothes who was joking with two male guards.

"How did you know who I was?" I asked, not without a touch of pride at the recognition.

"You're raw, very raw." She laughed. The two guards erupted in laughter.

The blush crawled up my face. "What do you mean?"

"Lawyers aren't the only ones who can read, you know." She chortled, tapping her finger on my name tag. "Bob Bigelow called and we talked about your case."

"Did you get the letters from the Crown and the police that he was supposed to send?" I asked.

"I'm not sure. I haven't had time to look at the file, but he did say something about them."

"Great. When do you think we'll have a chance to talk?"

"I'm trying to do two jobs at once," Sharon replied. "Two or three weeks maybe."

It didn't occur to me that the rule against believing what you heard in prison wasn't aimed solely at the cons. For now, though, things were off to a good start; Bob's spadework had laid a solid basis for his eventual argument to Sharon that medium security was an unnecessary stop on the way to minimum.

"Can I get my name on the list for the work range?" I asked, somewhat coyly. In my previous life, things worked best when I took them into my own hands.

"No way. I have to classify you first." Big-wheel ex-lawyer or not, Bigelow or no Bigelow, interesting case or not, Sharon's message was clear: in here, everybody plays by the same rules.

I was sure the two guards sitting in the office wouldn't forget the exchange. I shuddered. Bob had warned me against coming across as a manipulator.

"Melnitzer, you fucking Jew, where the fuck are you?"

I had finished my less than memorable Saturday night dinner. Carl was asleep. I poked my head out the doorway, expecting to see an old client welcoming me to his digs. Instead, off to my right, a short, squat, uniformed figure was making his way down the range, sticking a head without a neck into each cell, screaming my name louder and louder with each failure in the manifest hope that the din would flush the quarry. I wondered what I had done wrong.

"I'm Melnitzer," I admitted. His name tag read, "Connelly R."

"Are you deaf?" he bellowed.

"Actually, I am a little."

"Actually, actually," he mocked as he stuck his nose in the air. "You goddamn cocksucking Jewish lawyers always have excuses. I suppose you're going to tell me your ancestors didn't rub out Jesus. Where have you got all the dough stashed?"

"I don't have any money."

"And I don't have any balls," Connelly mimicked. "You'll remember your stash when you see the bat in my office. Get the fuck out of that cell."

"Why, what did I do?"

"You're just a low-life con, Melnitzer. Don't ask any questions, because you're not entitled to any answers. Get your stuff and get out of there, like I told you, and then come on down to the office. I'll give you five minutes."

Connelly turned and walked away. Hoping that promptness would mollify him, I packed all my belongings into plastic bags in less than three minutes. I hurried down the stairs to the door of the duty office.

Connelly was hunched over his desk, on the telephone, with his back to me. I didn't have the assurance to interrupt him by announcing myself. Ten minutes later, he put the phone down, pivoted in his swivel chair, and glared at me.

"I gave you five minutes. Do you think I've got nothing to do but look after you wimpy-eyed lawyers?"

"I came down right away," I said, mustering as much meekness as I could — meekness which suddenly came quite naturally. "I didn't want to interrupt while you were on the phone. Sorry."

"You're not fucking sorry, you low-life con. Don't wimp out on me or I'll make sure you do every minute of your nine years in seg with the diddlers and the Rastafarians. They're not too fond of Jews, you know."

This was one of the few times in my life that I didn't know what to say or do.

Connelly wasn't finished. "Cat got your tongue? Where's the old gift of gab? This joint must be half full of your old clients doing double life for shoplifting. If I were a criminal, I'd consider myself lucky they took your licence and threw you off the street. What do you think about that, sonny?"

I shrugged. Connelly looked me right in the eye. "It's about time you did an honest day's work. I'm putting you on the work range."

"The work range," I mumbled.

Connelly pursed his lips in the thin inkling of a smile. And it dawned on me. *The work range. Heaven. Thank you again, Bob Bigelow! Thank you, Aaron! Thank you, Perry!*

Connelly's eyes danced as his smile became an uproarious laugh; he pounded his desk in glee at the success of his ruse; his five-foot-four, three-hundred-fifty-pound body shook as his short, stubby legs came off the ground; the red of his bulbous nose, which had lit his way through many a dark tavern, spread to his cheeks, his forehead, and his ears, all obscured by his mouth as he opened it wide to catch his breath. Connelly wiped away the tears forming around his eyes.

"You see, Melnitzer," he called as I stepped back to pick up my plastic bags, "I can make you laugh or I can make you cry. It just depends what side of bed I got out of in the morning. So don't ever forget who's boss while you're on my unit."

Too overjoyed to ponder the price of getting to the work range, I headed to the unit clerk's cell at the far end of the range.

"What are you doing here?" Peter cried. "If the sixes catch you, you're in all kinds of shit. Me too, if they find you in my house."

"Sixes?" I asked.

"Sixes. Guards." Peter replied. "Comes from CX, maybe, that's how CSC classifies security people."

Then he noticed my belongings. "Oh, I get it. Plug must have come on shift. As usual, he didn't bother telling me that you were coming. One night double-bunked. That's a record in here."

Notice of transfers was important to Peter, whose job it was to organize new arrivals on the range, to complete the endless paperwork that accompanies administrative change, and to ensure that cell doors were properly labelled with their occupants' names for the edification of the patrolling guards. Peter was also the liaison between inmates and staff — the complaint department for two hundred and fifty inmates, most of whom led lives of chronic complaint.

Quiet and easygoing in his relationships, serious and organized in his work, Peter was perfect for the job.

My new cell was towards the middle of the range, smaller than the others and less private. Over my protestations, Peter promised better soon; but three jails and five cells in six days made another move unthinkable.

I wandered into the hallway, too excited to set up my cell, but hesitating to ensure that the freedom was permissible. After walking back to Peter's end of the range, I turned around and strolled all the way back to the other end and looked up at the bubble, feeling stealthy as I passed the TV room and approached the duty office. Plug was still there, regaling his co-workers with tales of my humiliation and gullibility.

Although I had seen all there was to see, I retraced my route, inhaling the luxury of movement without escort or authorization. I explored every nook and cranny of the range, the utility rooms, and the yard. The entire space was probably not much bigger than either of the houses that had been taken from me on my arrest, but I revelled in the unfamiliar and unregulated exercise of curiosity. On my second pass by the duty office, I had recovered from my trials sufficiently to share Plug's humour.

Intermittently, I entered and left my cell at will, simply for the experience of an open door. Only Control could shut cell doors; inmates strung blankets and sheets over their doorways for privacy, the obstructions tolerated if the viewing slats were uncovered for count.

Back on the range again, I grabbed the telephone, impulsively dialling Melissa's number with the urgency that bursts from the need to share joy. I hadn't spoken to her since the East. My daughter's relief at my good fortune sparkled over the line. The relative quiet of the work range and the absence of inmates tensely awaiting their turn on the phone allowed us a half hour of renewed intimacy. I lost myself in those precious moments, until I focused on the warning posted at all joint telephones:

ALL ACTIVITIES, INCLUDING CONVERSATIONS
AND TELEPHONE COMMUNICATIONS IN THIS
AREA, ARE SUBJECT TO MONITORING AND
MAY BE RECORDED

The cold reminder broke the spell without interrupting the conversation, and I said goodbye before my sinking feelings polluted our happiness.

My open cell door restored my good mood. As I lay on my bed, Aaron's grinning face intruded on my weary blankness.

"Did I tell you or what? Everything all right?" he beamed.

"Yes. Thanks a lot. This is great. How'd you pull it off?"

"We Jews have to stick together. Come on by my house. It's just across from Pete's. We'll talk a while and then have a little dinner."

"I ate already," I said.

"Not like we're going to eat. Just rest up and come by at eight."

"Will the cell doors be open then?"

"*Boychick,* the cell doors are open all the time, except during count and at night."

"You're kidding!"

"No, my friend. This is Heaven in Hell. Enjoy!"

Heaven in Hell. "Fascinating," as Spock would say, and complex — but agreeable fodder for pleasant dreams.

Forgetting I had no watch, I checked my wrist when I awoke; disoriented, I rushed to Aaron's cell.

"You'll find him in the kitchen. He's in there kissing ass and stuffing his fat face," said a rough voice behind me. The muscle-bound body looked at me sternly. "You're the lawyer, aren't you?

Just came into the joint, eh? I'd stay away from that rat if you know what's good for you."

"Well, I have to talk to him," I apologized, taken aback.

"It's your choice, man," was the retort, "but cop lovers ain't good friends to have in here."

More than a little unnerved, I arrived in the servery just as Aaron was spooning sauce out of a dish on the grill directly into the mouths of Plug and a companion guard. Their incongruous, exaggerated indulgences brought on memories of *La Dolce Vita,* the hedonistic movie classic of my youth.

The clock on the wall said 8:45. "Sleazy lawyer like you wouldn't sleep through a party," Plug said. "I suppose you want some of our food."

"There's plenty for everyone," Aaron insisted. "Julie, don't pay any attention to this guy. He's half-loaded when he's not asleep."

The other guard, pleasant-faced, spoke up. "That's why I have to do all the work when we're on together. Hi, I'm Neil."

Guards as people. What a strange sensation.

Stranger still was the next hour. Dinner consisted of pasta in a seafood sauce with a side salad, freshly prepared by Aaron with the panache of a master chef. The well-equipped kitchen included an adequate spice rack, which Aaron supplemented with his personal supply of ingredients. I could barely keep myself from asking where the goodies came from.

After ordering me to sit down, Aaron snapped at Plug and Neil, insisting that they set the Arborite table just so, clean the grill thoroughly, and load the pots and pans in the kitchen's commercial dishwasher. Only then did he pronounce his masterpiece ready for consumption. It was delicious.

The guards left after a leisurely dinner. Aaron and I cleaned up, as fastidiously as we might have in our own homes — perhaps more so.

"The last thing I expected was a spotless kitchen," I remarked.

"The last thing you expected was a gourmet Saturday night dinner," Aaron replied, capturing the evening's essence.

"You're right," I admitted. "But look at this kitchen."

"Don't underestimate the Fat Man," Aaron explained, using Plug's other nickname. "He runs a tight ship. Drinks like a fish, but it never affects his work. And he's always here — comes in on his days off. He hates going home. This is his home."

"Is he in charge of the range?" I asked, pouncing on potentially useful information.

"Well, there are three senior guards — ICs they call them — and an acting unit manager who's supposed to be in charge. But he's just a kid. His father's a warden or some kind of pooh-bah in the system. Plug's been here for twenty-five years and he knows all the skeletons in the closet, so they leave him alone."

"He's been in Millhaven for a quarter of a century?"

"Almost. Since it opened, anyway. He set up the work range. It's his baby. They say this is one of the best-run units in the country. Did you notice how clean it is?"

I had noticed. Some ranges had been painted recently. The cells on the work range were the best kept I had seen, though my impressions were doubtlessly influenced by the open doors and the orderliness and personal care that is a natural outgrowth of space people could call their own.

Aaron went on. "By the way, the less you say about this the better. The guys on the range are already jealous enough. I pass a few of them a little food here and there to keep them quiet."

Mr. Muscles' remarks came to mind as I poured myself some orange juice from the refrigerator. The television on top of the fridge was tuned to CMT, Country Music Television; Hank Williams, Jr., was belting out "Hotel Whisky."

"How long have you been here, Aaron?" I asked.

"About six months."

"All on the work range?"

"No, I spent two months locked up."

"How was that?"

"Don't ask," Aaron replied, with a wave of his hand.

"How'd you get down here? Pull?"

"No such luck," he explained, "or I wouldn't have been locked up for two months. It started off when they needed a guy to fix the TVs and converters. I've got an electronic engineering degree from MIT, so I heard about it and volunteered. Then they found out I was pretty good on computers and they sent me down to the school. I work as an assistant to the education director."

"Is it a good job?"

"Great." He giggled. "I run the place down there. It's not hard. Ken, my boss, owes me big. He's taking upgrading university courses from Queen's. I write his papers. He'll do anything I ask."

I was impressed. "What are the other good jobs around here?"

"Plug told me he's going to put you here, in the kitchen. You're a high-profile guy and he wants you right under his nose. The servery's a good job. No guards watching over you."

I cringed at the thought of kitchen work, forgetting that choice was no longer in my repertoire. "Anything else you'd recommend?"

"Well, Pete has the run of the prison. I think he showers down in the hospital. But he has to put up with a lot of whining. If the cons aren't at him, the guards are."

"He seems like a good guy," I probed.

"You can't trust anyone in here," Aaron warned. "But he's OK. You'll hear a lot of guys say he's a rat because of his job, but most of the time they don't know what they're talking about. He's a little jealous of me. He doesn't get along with Plug and I do."

I nodded. "I can see why he's jealous. How do you manage all this?"

Aaron put an index finger to his mouth. He whispered as he pointed to a grate just above the table.

"The other side is the hall just outside the duty office. Plug sits there and listens in once in a while. Anything you don't want heard, don't say in here. For now, let's just say that certain people around here like their comforts and they're willing to barter."

"OK," I agreed.

"Come on to my house. We can talk there," Aaron urged.

I begged off; the idea of sitting alone in the empty servery appealed to me. I flipped the TV tuner to *Hockey Night in Canada*: Don Cherry was berating Ron MacLean. Here and now, fulfilment was watching the hockey game in a real chair at a real table. As far as I was concerned, if this wasn't Heaven, it was at least Paradise.

Paradise lost

I got so fuckin' tied up all I could see was a big arse in frunna me, so I takes a bite out of it, and Christ, it was me own arse.
FROM A STORY TOLD BY NORTHROP FRYE

On the work range, we could do as we pleased when we weren't working. We showered privately, laundered at our convenience, used the telephone at will, watched television, and played cards or any variety of board games; we read, wrote, listened to music in the privacy of our cells, exercised in the weight pit or on the range's exercise bike, jogged in the yard, or hung around the office trading insults with Plug and his cronies. Access to the kitchen, staffed by our range mates, was limited only at mealtimes, and culinary perks were regular.

Working hours were eight to four, but few of the jobs exacted a full day's work; those that did offered a benign flexibility. In the unusual prison environment, however, most of the jobs made hidden demands on their holders. Plug's ability to mix and match his charges to these special requirements was testimony to his astuteness and experience; his talent was most evident in his choices for rec cleaner, kitchen supervisor, and canteen clerk.

The rec cleaner's job was a plum, requiring only a half-hour's work every evening, and on weekend mornings setting up and cleaning the gym before and after A Unit's recreation periods. But the rec cleaner was really an enforcer, responsible for ensuring that Reception inmates did not misuse the gym they shared with J Unit, Millhaven's permanent population of one hundred and twenty-five of Canada's most violent criminals.

Before Millhaven became a Regional Reception Centre, its permanent population occupied the entire prison. Now J Unit resented the intruders for their imposition on gym space and time; making things worse, Reception's transient population was lax in cleaning and maintaining the gym, and the sports equipment habitually disappeared during recreation. A disgruntled J Unit was prone to rioting.

Jason was six foot one and two hundred and twenty pounds of muscle; his dark, swarthy looks were entirely suited to the grim double-breasted suits and matching fedoras of Chicago gangland days; his build exuded strength in its natural cast, without the cuts and bulges of dedicated narcissists trying to make a point; the absence of restraining bulk allowed him to move as effortlessly and elegantly as a stalking tiger, and his history was no less imposing.

Now thirty-seven, Jason was a fabled bank robber in the seventies. He snickered at today's variety-store bandits — amateurs who, in his opinion, demeaned an honourable and demanding profession. The law caught up to Jason in a big way in 1977, when he earned a ten-year sentence after several spectacular and successful gun-wielding attacks on financial institutions.

By 1981, Jason, who was clever, polite, and erudite in spite of his limited education, had manoeuvred his way to Bath, the minimum security camp located beside Millhaven. While there, he extended a temporary absence pass into a permanent truancy in the United States, where he continued his career until the FBI caught up with him.

Jason served most of a decade in Marion and Leavenworth, two of the toughest prisons in the United States. On his release, he stopped in Toronto on his way to Europe; there the RCMP, tipped off by the FBI, arrested him. Plug knew Jason from years gone by, and it wasn't long before Jason turned up on the work range as the rec cleaner.

As a legendary armed robber, Jason was at the top of Millhaven's criminal hierarchy. His tendency to keep to himself, following his own schedule at his own pace through a disciplined routine, was evidence of his many solitary years in one joint or another. He slept until noon, except on weekends, spending the afternoon pumping iron in the range's weight pit and voraciously reading newspapers and magazines, which he scavenged wherever he could. In the pit, Jason's effortless lifts perpetuated his stature among witnesses, who quickly embellished his reputation as it swept along the grapevine. When he quietly let it be known that a dirty gym and damaged or stolen equipment were personal affronts, acts of disrespect, no one challenged him.

Jason never joined the hordes at yard-up until it was time to go to work, preferring to spend his evenings watching sports on TV. His distaste for the decline of the Prison Code in Reception was well known, and he preferred not to mix with most other inmates. Jason was the classic prison loner, doing his own time, left alone to do it out of fear and respect.

Rock, two years into a life term for a passion killing, his first prison experience, was a tall, good-looking tennis pro in his early thirties. Adept at manipulation through his exposure to the club crowd, he manoeuvred his way into the canteen manager's job by ingratiating himself to Plug and the rest of the staff.

In doing so, Rock made himself quite unpopular — with the wrong people. His predecessor at the canteen was Butch, a veteran weapons and drug dealer who was well connected to J Unit. Butch kept those connections smoothly oiled, enriching himself by funnelling A Unit canteen stock to his friends in the permanent population. When he was eventually caught and fired, the beneficiary of his misfortune, the aloof and occasionally abrupt Rock, was blamed for "putting it on" Butch.

Somebody in J Unit decided to get rid of Rock. Candidates were not hard to find, either among the old-timers who would not blink at avenging Butch or the surfeit of punks anxious to make a lasting name for themselves with the powers in J.

Fortunately for Rock, he had a good friend in Dick, a fifty-year-old bull of a man who weighed in at three hundred pounds. While Dick had pretensions to white-collar status, the extensive tattoos on his arms and three missing front teeth were ineradicable signs of his violent, drunken past, including a mid-seventies stint in Millhaven's Special Handling Unit, or "SHU," which is reserved for the most violent offenders, those who kill or maim in prison.

Dick's solid history made him privy to the goings-on in J Unit; he intervened on Rock's behalf, and, for good measure, became Rock's bodyguard — Rock never went to the yard or gym without Dick in tow. By the time Dick left for Warkworth a few months later, things had settled down. But the point had been made: from then on, only J Unit favourites took the canteen manager's job.

Apart from the unit clerk, the remaining jobs were in the barber shop, maintenance, cleaning, and in the kitchen.

To some, the lack of staff supervision was the outstanding benefit of toiling in the servery. On the other hand, workers in the servery were always pressured by dissatisfied meal lines. As well, the absence of a clear division of labour, the need for benign co-operation in a habitually distrustful group, and the dull repetitive nature of the work made for constant bickering. Part of the problem arose from the servery's departure from the Prison Code's rule against inmate hierarchies. Absent staff supervision, someone was needed to run the operation.

While I was there, Bryce, a hardworking lifer whom Plug took under his wing, had the job. His history as a prosecution witness meant that his safety was best ensured by keeping him in Reception. Bryce gratefully took on the thankless task of managing other inmates; lacking personal authority, he managed with a self-effacing nature and an acquired and sometimes forced tolerance. In the background, a lurking awareness that Plug was Bryce's sponsor, that Plug had an abiding interest in a smoothly running kitchen, and that an unkind word from Bryce to Plug made for a quick exit from the work range played no small part in keeping things under control. Unfortunately, Bryce's position isolated him further; he was a friendly but lonely and sad man doing what he could to survive his next twenty-five years.

The "V & C" cleaner looked after the visiting and administration area. "V & C" stood for "Visiting and Correspondence," not, as many surmised, "Visitors and Convicts." The work included maintenance of the reception area and administrative wing, the visiting room, and the warden's office. On my first Sunday on the work range, Plug explained that I was the only inmate available who met the security requirements for the V & C job; warning me of its difficulties, he promised to move me to the kitchen as soon as a replacement appeared.

According to Plug, the staff in the V & C area considered themselves the *crème de la crème* of Millhaven staff. Each employee there, from the warden to the file clerk, exercised his *de facto* prerogative to organize the cleaner's day, vying with the others for the cleaner's attention to his office, his bathroom, the bins in his photocopy machine, and the trash in his wastebaskets.

As in any case where the chiefs grossly outnumbered the Indians (in this case, the sole Indian), the job was highly political. The situation was worsened by CSC's distrust of anyone wearing green, which was more acute among staff unaccustomed to mixing with the animals in the body of the prison. Because cons could not retaliate or withdraw, a certain passive astuteness was required to keep everyone happy.

To me, the job seemed perfect: I was being recognized as low risk and worthy of trust, and I would be among the powers, who would probably be delighted to have a person of my standing around. Even as Plug was warning me, I resolved to make the most of this opportunity to extend my influence. I couldn't wait to go to work the next morning.

But the job was a nightmare. I was never outside the scrutiny of the staff, all of whom regarded me as their personal valet. Their knowledge of my background, which was evident, served only to whet their appetite for service and servility. My inability to be present without presence was taken as arrogance. To be sure, I met the warden, but he was rarely in his office; the real power there was the warden's secretary, Diane, whose demands could not have been satisfied by a crew of cleaning professionals on twenty-four-hour call.

For three mornings, I managed. On the fourth morning, I was cleaning the cubicles used for closed, non-contact visits when a disapproving guard came by.

"We're moving some prisoners down here. Aren't you finished yet?" he demanded.

"They asked me to do a few extra things on the other side, so I'm running a little late," I explained.

"Don't let it happen again. Get out," was the curt reply.

The high-handed dismissal didn't sit well with me. "What the hell am I supposed to do?" I retorted. "The vacuum cleaner doesn't work and everybody wants things done at the same time. It's fucking impossible."

"You're not doing a very good job, anyway," the guard screamed, "and you're pretty mouthy. You're fired. Get back to your range."

I was stunned. "Why? I'm doing the best —"

"Get back on your range. You're fired. We'll get someone who can do the job. This is going on your record,... counsellor."

I reported to A Unit's IC, confused.

"Pack up your stuff," he said quietly. "You're moving upstairs."

"Why? I didn't do anything wrong."

"Grieve it if you want, but I doubt that it'll do you any good. When you're fired, you're off the work range. That applies to everybody."

"When do I have to move?" I asked, manoeuvring for a reprieve.

"Right now. Another inmate's on the way down to take your cell."

I rushed onto the range, looking for Plug and Aaron, but neither was around. Frightened, dispirited, and alone, unable to phone anyone until the evening, I packed up and moved back to a double-bunked cell on C2 range.

In tears, I sat on my bed and wrote letters: to my daughter, to my wife, to my friends. They were brave letters. How does a proud man explain that he's been fired from a job as a cleaner?

Predictably, I was humiliated, not humbled — extending the chaos of a lifetime.

Part Two

REASONS

The past has a vote, but it does not have a veto.

RABBI MORDECAI KAPLAN

Shadows

I am an adult and I do not think I am merely the sum of my past.
I can make choices and I suffer the consequences....
MARGARET ATWOOD

The parochial Jewish school on the border of the affluent Outremont district of Montreal was housed on the second floor of an old Orthodox synagogue. In 1953, sports and recreation were not an integral part of a Jewish upbringing, and the rabbis gave no thought to gymnasiums. Recess was a time for touch football in the yard or snowball fights in the cold Montreal winters.

When the weather was bad, the boys played soccer with a pop bottle cap in the vestibule outside the chapel. The playing area wasn't large, and though there were only a dozen boys in the class, not everyone could play. Most often I watched. It was hard. I loved team sports because they let me escape my estrangement and pretend I was part of the group, but I was rarely picked to play. I was painfully shy and a little chubby; for years, the two would go hand in hand.

When you don't feel wanted, "yes" becomes a way of life; "no" is too risky. Ingratiation and approval become the means of communication, the arteries of love and friendship, and the touchstones of social survival. Of course, if nobody notices you and nobody asks, you don't get a chance to say yes. Then, the only choice is to make an offer. After a few weeks of watching the soccer games, I made mine: I promised candy bars, player cards, comics, marbles, and money; I learned that if I gave others what they wanted, they would play with me and I could pretend that they liked me. I never outgrew the lesson, and, over the years, pretence became substance. At the age of six, I found myself under financial pressure. It would never leave me. No matter how successful I became, I could never earn enough to buy the love of the whole world: some crimes start when kids don't get to play.

Eventually, I learned to pander to adults' needs as I had to children's wants. Maybe the awful pain of having so little love of myself gave me my understanding of others' vulnerability. There was a time when I thought this comprehension bestowed both sensitivity and power. That was a rationalization; with few exceptions, even when my understanding soothed others' pain, my reward was in their gratitude and not in their solace. Gratitude was both a bond and a debt, and, to the needy like myself, could pass for love.

At home, I always felt loved, in the sense that I could count on shelter, material needs, and affection. My brother and sister and I knew that, no matter what we did, we wouldn't be thrown out on the street. That feeling, I suppose, with the conservative middle-class company in which I grew up, kept my loneliness from tossing me on the trash heap of drugs, alcohol, or street crime. Expectations, not rejection, fashioned my future, as fear, rather than ambition, later drove it.

My father, a Holocaust survivor, loved as best he could, but his love for his family was etched in pain, in loss, in guilt, and in fear. It was a love that sought to do what love cannot do: erase the past and safeguard the future. It ignored the present, and so it was joyless.

On the Russian Army's victory drive to Berlin, my father's regiment passed through his home town in Ukraine. There, he found the bodies of his mother, his father, his three brothers, his three sisters, his wife, and his twin children in the same grave. On the walls of the synagogue, his sister had scrawled "Remember Revenge" — in her own blood. My father's hair turned grey overnight. He never overcame the guilt of survival; his guilt became his God and his God became his tormentor.

In 1946, he met and married my mother in Munich, where I was born a year later. He lived for his wife and child, but could not separate his self from theirs, nor from the separate identities of my brother and sister, who were born in 1949 and 1953. The reconstruction of my father's life became a sin for which he could repent only by the consecration of his family to the ghosts of the past. To the moment of his death at the age of seventy-eight in November 1990, and beyond, he was a constant presence: my phone call from the RCMP came on the morning of the ceremonial unveiling of his tombstone in a Montreal cemetery just nine months after he died.

My father's terrible loss at the hands of the Nazis kindled a pathological fear that provoked a sense of unworthiness; convinced that, at any moment, all would be lost again, he elicited interminable demands for attention and reassurance. Love did not exist for my father without its expression every waking hour; he would rather fight, and sometimes hate, than be alone. Stillness did not exist in our home; it was as if my father feared that his loved ones would die again if the noise was not there to keep us alive.

None of us, of course, could rise to his level of intensity. His anguish became anger, and he railed at us every day of our lives; he imagined slights, turned harmless oversights into personal affronts, and made differences of opinion into acts of treachery. His disproportionate reactions to trifling behaviour taught me to avoid admissions of failure, error, or wrongdoing at any cost. Once, when I was ten, he kept me up for hours well into the night explaining, in anger, how to properly fold my pants over a hanger; I listened dutifully, silently. My father never tired of saying that his great love for me hinged on the cherished "respect" that my silence meant to him.

Respect. Fear. Indistinguishable to my father. I could never risk disappointing or confronting him or anyone else; instead, anticipation, evasiveness, and manipulation became my tools of survival. What I couldn't face directly, I did indirectly.

As the firstborn, I was the repository of my father's fears and of his worst memories. I was also his favourite by far, the object of his dreams, his expectations, and his needs. His needs were unquenchable so I set out to fulfil his dreams.

My father's dreams filtered through a tortured ego that defined accomplishment and happiness through the eyes of others: their respect, their admiration, their envy. Self-respect, self-esteem, and self-love were only subsets of the regard in which a person was held. Although he spoke often of his deserved reputation as a family man, a businessman, a pillar of the Jewish community, and a philanthropist, I never heard my father say that he was happy, even momentarily. I wish I had known that chasing his dreams would take me on the same endless hunt.

Dreams of my own were not allowed. Love as my father saw it brooked no competition: independence was treason, time away from his needs, and my father drove away its traces by denigrating our feelings of regard, admiration, gratitude, or loyalty towards anyone he did not embrace in his sheltered circle of tolerance; in the same way, he banished ideas and ideals he didn't understand or that challenged his narrow focus. "Only family can be trusted," he told us. "Friends are there for the good times." Life itself threatened him.

So I lived my dreams in hiding. When my dreams became my life, I lived my life in hiding, unable to trust my father to be happy for me; perhaps his guilt was triggered by the joy of those he had lived to spawn. My spurts of happiness, my delights, and my satisfactions were sheltered, protected, tucked away. I have never escaped the dread that the things that mattered to me weren't important; at the age of forty, I had difficulty telling anyone about my day or admitting that I had a nice vacation. Simple pleasures, simple moments, and ninety-nine percent were not good enough: embellishment waxed the floors of all my relationships. In my home, there was no other way to survive.

Consequences were everywhere, and I dealt with them in the only way I knew how: I became an excellent liar, bearing only the corporeal trademarks of life, my reality twisted like the strands of a pretzel, distinct but interwoven, around an empty core.

My father did not live in the real world. No one could live up to standards of complete honesty, perfect ethics, total unselfishness, unremitting compassion, and blind love. Unable to reconcile his words with his actions, he denied his shortfalls, rationalizing his shortcomings and self-betrayals, calling up necessity, God, the protection of the family, an imperfect world, and the comparative sins of others as justification. He went to delusional lengths to avoid admitting to inconsistency, mistake, or misapprehension. In his eyes, these normal human frailties were tragic failures; unable to admit them in himself, he could not tolerate them in his children. Values and images became indistinguishable to me.

Images sustained my father. His public charm masked his private gloom; he was successful and well-off, but encouraged the notion that he ranked among the wealthy; he promoted his philanthropy even when his generosity was self-serving; he advocated unwavering honesty, but compromised as we all do; he basked in the glory of his family, but denied them a sense of worth; he lived for his children, but loved them in bondage; he professed faith and practised fear; he hoarded an estate but left no heritage.

My father's inability to approach his own absolutes fatally diluted them, and his near-psychotic incapacity to come to terms with the imperfections of his flawed humanity robbed his values of their meaning. I longed to embrace the honesty, ethics, and compassion that my father preached day after day; but without a model to differentiate the rest of the world from my first experiences, I pretended to adopt my father's values by learning their utility without knowing what they meant. Soon after my arrest, I told Dr. Arndt that what bothered me most about my crimes was the absence of values they reflected. He reassured me: "You're not lacking values. You could never live up to the ones you were told to have. So you rejected them."

That my father loved me in his own way, I am sure: but both a dandelion and a rose are flowers. Did I love him? Do I love him? I'm not sure: I don't know enough about love yet. I know that I go on. Maybe his love has something to do with it.

Lest anyone misunderstand, I do not suggest that my life is the sum of my past. I made my own choices and accept responsibility for them. My father did not steal, nor would it ever have crossed his mind to do so. Instead, unable to speak a word of English, he overcame his personal tragedies and started life over in Canada in October 1950, at the age of thirty-eight, with his wife and two young children. Tirelessly, he and his partners built a multimillion-dollar meat-packing business on the principles of commerce he had learned from his father and grandfather in their *shtetl* in Ukraine. As his fortunes grew, his friends never changed: "Just because you trade in your Duster for a Cadillac," he once told me, "you don't change the passengers."

My mother was beautiful, vivacious, loving, and tolerant; the children were healthy, intelligent, capable, and charismatic. But homage to the guilt of survival led my father to an invisible force field, a one-way mirror that forever separated him from what he had built and from those who mattered to him. Through this shield, he could indulge in and call to his loved ones, but never reach out and touch them. Nor could anything touch him. His love, his pain, and his anger converged in a pervasive throb, filling him to the brim with the agony of survival. His eyes did not observe, his ears did not listen, and his heart did not respond. He could not react, except in a preprogrammed burst. The ache that flowed from him in waves immersed the energy of all his senses, an offensive force and a defensive stratagem. In its aggressive form, the ache sought, demanded, postured, and postulated, grasping for an unattainable warmth and closeness, for the potential oneness with life that the Nazis had wrested. At the same time, the cacophony of his demands formed an impenetrable barrier, deliberately obscuring the fact of his survival and ensconcing the loneliness he had unwittingly chosen as his penance.

My own successes did not come without hard work or genuine ability. The tragedy of my life, as that of my father's, was that its very real achievements were not good enough for me. They could not be: they were not my choice of achievements and had no meaning in themselves. Satisfaction was in glory, in image, in recognition rather than in accomplishment; it could be but fleeting and frail. All it took was an unkind word from an irrelevant stranger to cast a bittersweet pall over moments of exhilaration or happiness, turning confidence to self-doubt.

My father revelled in the adulation I earned, which he could not distinguish from my accomplishments. In company, he praised me to the point of embarrassment; alone, he competed with me. Although my mother told me he hung on my every word of advice, I never noticed; instead, he frequently derided my opinions, often, I thought, out of an irrational fear that his own would be displaced.

Even at the peak of my career, my father reminded me of my place — always in Yiddish, the language of the ghosts, of the memories, a dialect in danger of extinction, paradoxically giving life to the past. My father never learned to use English fluently. To do so would have been a confrontation of the present, an admission of survival. His frenzy still haunts me. I remember the words in Yiddish as I write them in English:

> *What do you know about life or business? You're just a lawyer. Everything you've learned you've read in books. You may think you're a big shot, but it's a good thing your father was born before you. I came here without a cent. Where would you be if I hadn't worked so hard? I sacrificed my life for you, and what do I get for it? I've been alone all my life. If my father was alive, I'd be a lawyer, too. I'd have time for my father, I can tell you that.*

Was it my fault that my father's family had perished? To a child, it seemed that way. How could I make it up to him? By producing a properly wrapped package, perhaps, to take to the rest of the world, an enhanced repertoire for his unrelenting image building. He seemed happy when he boasted of my accomplishments. For a moment or two, it was quiet, no demands.

I couldn't provide an image without having one. What they see is what I am. Integrity and fair play became the truest arrows in my quiver of deception. I learned to shout honesty, show it, peddle it, barter it, everything but be it. In my profession, in my friendships, in my legitimate investments, everywhere but on the dark side, the reality, my word was my bond. I promised the unexpected and did what I said I would do, always with a flourish that guaranteed the deed would not be forgotten. Nobody questioned how I did it, preferring to savour the expectation for their own reasons.

In my law practice, I revelled in cases no one else would take, worked while the sceptics laughed, and won when I had to. Cohen, Melnitzer grew from two founding partners to become the fourth-largest firm in London in less than fifteen years. As my legal and organizational reputation outgrew London, I associated with a firm in Toronto, built one of the two largest rent-review practices in the province, and ultimately chaired the Fair Rental Policy Organization, Ontario's powerful apartment industry lobby. When the Law Society permitted lawyers to advertise in the mid-1980s, Cohen, Melnitzer launched an innovative marketing campaign that drew the attention of the *Financial Post*. I wrote legal texts, lectured tirelessly at professional and trade conferences, and cultivated a résumé that was thirty-two pages long when it all ended in August 1991.

I accomplished this working only nine months a year in my last ten years of practice, putting in longer hours than most of my partners and associates managed full time. I coped with these pressures as I coped with living: I called for another world every few months and spent the rest of the year travelling. *Escaping. Not escape. Compartments. Sanity and insanity? Maybe. Sanity in insanity? More likely. Two separate worlds. No link. No reality.*

To my admirers, I seemed to have time for everything and time enough to do it well. Every year, three months of mysterious, exotic trips encouraged my air of resplendent wealth, handily promoting the myth of the global businessman. I coated it all with a calculated and selective arrogance, an acceptable match to a marvellous résumé.

My destructiveness lay in a Machiavellian awareness of three related assumptions: first, in understanding that many people, especially those with credentials themselves, believe that proper credentials justify the most extraordinary extrapolations about their bearer;

second, in taking advantage of the common conjecture that the advice a man gives to others is a reliable reflection of the adviser's personal convictions; and third, utilizing the misperception that displays of fairness and unselfishness are good indicators of a man's inner character. None of the above is true. All are rooted in our desire to believe that what makes us feel good is good or at least not bad. All three ignore the role of personal motivation. All are synergistically powerful. Allied with the proper credentials, these assumptions beget a dependent trust.

I abused that trust. Born a marketer, I played my legitimate credentials to the hilt, luring many to seek my advice beyond the range of my professional or other expertise. Where I had nothing at stake, I gave sincere, solid, sensible, and, above all, decent advice to others. I had no difficulty with values when I didn't have to live up to them.

When something was at stake, I exuded purposeful generosity. I never drove a hard financial bargain with my business or professional partners; I loaned money to anyone who asked, without interest; I invested in projects against my better judgement because refusing was an admission of financial shortcomings or fear of risk; I picked up the tab; I bought lavish gifts and left lavish tips, whatever the service; I bought airline tickets and paid hotel bills for friends who couldn't otherwise afford to accompany me — to salvage their pride, I shrugged off my generosity as mileage points, business favours, or special connections; I made large charitable donations without attending the thank-you functions.

The beneficiaries of my excesses praised my magnanimity and fairness. Why look a gift horse in the mouth? That's not a fair question. How could anyone imagine that, as a child of forty, I was still unable to say no? If anyone suspected the enormous gap between my professional affect and my personal feelings, no one spoke up.

As these images were my weapons, they were also my captors:

I overstated my assets during the divorce proceedings with my first wife to cover up the lies I had told her, laying the groundwork for the lies in my future. I secretly enriched my law partners by paying off $6 million of clients' accounts myself; it was crazy, but I was incapable of confronting my partners' disappointment or wrath about our receivables. A voracious financial chasm opened wider.

Cracks in the armour

He has perfected a way of leaning on his cane
without appearing weak.

ARTHUR MILLER

Long before the frauds began, catastrophic thinking dominated my life. I never did come around to understanding that it was OK to spill the milk accidentally, OK to bash up the car, OK to lose at squash, OK to forget to pick up the newspaper once in a while, OK to be out with a woman who didn't look like Cheryl Tiegs. I was long since the master of the cover-up.

There's not much sense detailing the daily practice sessions as I grew up. Simply put, what I thought I lacked, I invented. The tales did little but fill in the emptiness with a momentary sense of belonging. They didn't make me popular, part of the group, or get me laid. They might have made me a curiosity. At the time, that was good enough; any attention was better than indifference.

The stories were harmless enough in high school and my undergraduate years, and I don't know whether anyone believed them. It didn't matter. It felt better to tell them than to have nothing to say. And I always believed I had nothing worthwhile to say, for my father lectured, he never listened; my mother did her best to balance things out, but her best could not cope with my father's compulsive dominance.

In high school, the social insecurity of a lonely teenager ravaged me, making my academic performance spotty and inconsistent. I was suspended for the last three months of my senior year after playing hookey at the pool hall and was allowed to return only to write matriculation exams at year's end. Despite a respectable but unremarkable overall graduation average of seventy-seven percent, I managed to get the highest marks in the province of Quebec in the History final. The vice-principal who had ejected me suffered the ignominy of presenting my medal; the cheer from the partisan students at graduation polished the myth of academic brilliance.

Later that year, I felt more lost than ever in the unstructured environment of McGill University's General Arts program; I had trouble attending classes or studying and almost failed first year. As I adjusted socially, my marks improved, and by my third year, I was in the Honours Philosophy program, with an eye on becoming a trial lawyer. Despite personal problems that plagued my senior year, I graduated with honours from the Philosophy program. That was good enough to get me into the finest law school in the country at the University of Toronto.

I married in February 1968: I was twenty; Cathy, a high school acquaintance, was twenty-one.

Marriage got me out of the house, but didn't change anything else. Cathy had no idea whom she was marrying. Had I had the good judgement to appreciate her or at least see the sense in her ways, she might have turned me from my self-destructive course. Bright, sensible, pretty, and fanatically loyal, Cathy could have been the model I needed for the values I lacked. Image didn't count with Cathy; she loved me for what I meant to her. Lacking the maturity to see it that way, I insisted on a lifestyle that perpetuated the past as it shaped the future.

Partially freed from my loneliness, I could concentrate on my studies. Sometimes clichés say it perfectly: I took to law school like a fish to water — in my own sea, naturally. My academic habits were unorthodox. Throughout law school, I rarely attended lectures, substituting disciplined study habits that later governed my professional life.

My new sense of commitment paid off: I stood third in a class of one hundred and fifty. In an enduring emotional pattern, I took as much pride in the notoriety of "beating the system" through my nonattendance at class as I did in the accomplishment itself. *If no one notices, what's the point?*

Melissa was born in January 1970, during my second year of law school. I was twenty-two. In those days, fathers were unheard of in delivery rooms; for five days, I stared solemnly through the glass of the hospital's nursery, unable to relate to this new complication in my life. I first held my baby girl on the sixth day, lifting her from Cathy's hospital bed where she lay clad in a pink and white knit outfit and bonnet, arms and legs defiantly askew, her cheeky face puckered in insolence. I was hooked on her, hooked on being her dad.

Cathy's staggered nursing shifts left me with an equal role in raising the baby, and my inclination to study at home rather than attend classes or go to the library worked well. Diapering Melissa, feeding her, dealing with diarrhoea and painful new teeth, and keeping an infant amused forged a fierce bond; I took Melissa everywhere, even letting her sleep under my table at the pool hall in the removable crib I lifted from her pram. I felt maternal, and loved it. My relationship with my daughter is the pride of my life today, the hand-in-hand strength that motivates me to continue.

On a different level, in the dichotomy of spirit that has plagued my life, the birth of a child contributed to my sense of isolation. I felt different, older, burdened, and excluded from the milieu of my classmates. Walking down the street pushing a baby carriage gave me a sense that life, youth, independence, and fun had all passed me by; there was no money for free-wheeling weekends or vacations and no time for the lolling hours of university years. I drifted from sadness to resentment to a sulking anger at the undefined conspiracy that had locked me in and locked me out. But those feelings never intruded on my love for or commitment to Melissa: in my fragmented psyche, the fury was between myself and the rest of the world.

At the end of my second year, I stood fifth, winning the Company Law prize; in my third year, I represented the school in national and international moot court competitions.

Harvard offered a scholarship for LL.M. studies, but the flattering demand for my services as an articling student enticed me. Despite my craving for prestige, in a decision that presaged my move to London four years later, I spurned offers from the very top firms, suspicious that an ingrained hierarchy would not tolerate my impatient, rebellious discomfort with the norms of legal practice: those were places, I surmised, where boys who play hookey do not belong. I preferred to enter the Establishment by tearing at it; what I overlooked was that, with this strategy, I could occupy space in the structure, but I would never be welcome.

In August 1971, I began my articles at Miller, Thomson, an old, established, medium-sized Toronto law firm. My interests lay solely in courtroom work, "litigation," another of the incomprehensible terms lawyers perpetuate to emphasize the mysterious in justification of their fees.

I set out to make myself invaluable. Nothing remained on my desk for more than twenty-four hours. For two months, I worked round the clock, leaving the office only for minimal sleep and when no other arrangements could be made for Melissa's care. I completed memorandums of law overnight — to the consternation of the students' secretary and the delight of Brian Kelsey, the head of the litigation department. The lawyers attributed the quick turnover to my very visible long hours, but my ability to speed-read, a virtually photographic memory, a capacity for organization and working quickly with few outlines and few drafts, and the confidence to cut corners when necessary, all contributed to my efficiency. My childhood habit of withdrawing to shut out the din and the demands left me with inordinate powers of concentration. In November, Brian sent me to court to defend two impaired driving charges; when I unexpectedly won both cases, my place in the firm was secure.

I quickly lost interest in the grind of regular articles; the meagre salary and limited educational returns derived from the repetitive tasks that make up much of the articling experience weren't worth it. Because I turned work over so fast, the impression that I was busy persisted.

With free time on my hands, another pattern, which was to last for twenty years, began. "Womanizing," the conventional expression describing males looking for something that can't be found, filled the empty hours of my articling and bar admission course periods. My new status as a Bay Street lawyer and the confidence that came with my academic success motivated me to seek free-wheeling female companionship, and with it, the macho status I had lacked as a student. Uncommitted as I was to anything but the self-glorification that I equated with self-esteem, marriage did not stand in my way. In this way, by recalling that most encounters were a fruitless, momentary search for Hollywood fantasies that do not exist, do I inaccurately explain away lust by telling why I *acted* on that lust. What was real, however, was the self-estrangement my double life created, an alienation that ingrained my drift from reality.

Still, I couldn't have been happier with my articles. Brian and I were both academic, both wedded to an appreciation of language and a passion for articulation, both fiercely competitive, and both mavericks who preferred to do things our own way. Our relation-ship transcended the workplace; we became fast friends and remain so today.

Brian shaped my professional attitudes and work habits. He taught me careful preparation as an instrument of tenacity, the pri-macy of the right question over the right answer in the context of legal issues, the need for courage — taking on unpopular causes and being unafraid of losing — and the importance of keeping an eye to an opponent's strengths even in the glare of his weaknesses. Ultimately, I am grateful to Brian for instilling the pride in my work that survived my greed, my machinations, and my turmoil. I cling to what I can.

When Brian abruptly left Miller, Thomson, I decided to seek employment elsewhere and completed my articles at Blaney, Pasternak, an up-and-coming first-generation Bay Street firm, to whom I returned after graduating from the bar admission course with honours in April 1973.

I worked hard, my billings were good, and, even in my first year, I was drawing attention from the partners by attracting busi-ness as friends referred cases to me. But working for others wasn't for me, and the firm's institutional approach to compensation hastened my desire to leave.

In March 1974, my law school buddy Harris Cohen announced that he was leaving his Bay Street firm, getting married, and returning home to London, Ontario. Would I join him in partnership?

I had been considering professional alternatives for some time: I turned down an opportunity at a dynamic young firm because I feared subservience to the senior partners; I considered opening my own criminal practice in Toronto, but that seemed lonely and risky. And Harris's offer had many attractions: I liked the idea of being a big fish in a small pond, confident that I could spread my reputation from London back to Toronto; Harris was the well-known eldest son of a prominent merchant family, ensuring bread and butter business until we built our reputations; he was trustworthy, decent, and a very competent solicitor, specializing in real estate and business law. We complemented each other personally and professionally. The more I thought about it, the more I liked the idea of practising law with my best friend.

As I think back on the decision to leave Toronto, I belatedly appreciate that the association with Harris gave me the presentability I was convinced I lacked, the external image I believed was vital to success. Practising law, I thought, was about being good; attracting clients, however, was about looking good. Harris may not have been quite as proficient or dynamic as a lawyer, but he looked a whole lot better than me. I needed another mask, and Harris was perfect.

A scouting trip to London turned up a lovely, if staid "forest city," a spacious, green campus, cheap housing, an excellent day-care centre, a fine Jewish school, and an active Jewish community; the reassuring warmth of Harris's large family eased the unfamiliarity.

In June 1974, Cathy, Melissa, and I moved to London. Cathy enrolled in the Bachelor of Science nursing program at the University of Western Ontario. Cohen, Melnitzer opened its doors on August 12, 1974, on the second floor of an elegantly renovated old house on the perimeter of Victoria Park in the centre of the city.

At the outset, Harris's connections did not pay off in real estate and corporate work, although his friends referred important litigation clients who became the backbone of my reputation. The most significant was the London Property Management Association, whose patronage led me to the prestigious environs of constitutional cases, appearances in the Supreme Court of Canada, counsel work at the Thom Commission into Residential Housing following the Crown Trust–Greymac scandal in the early 1980s, and the chair of the Fair Rental Policy Organization of Ontario.

When we started out in London, the legal community was in need of a shakeup. I was interested in criminal law, a good place for a maverick to be. Unlike any other area of the law in which I practised, I believed in criminal law. I valued procedural justice in a meaningful, passionate, and substantive way that filled an inner vacuum. The strong civil libertarian tendencies endemic to children of Holocaust survivors, the streak of antiauthoritarianism that got me tossed out of high school, my internal sense of not belonging, and my own victim mentality gave me the perfect psychological makeup for a specialty that pitted the outcasts against the State. I read and summarized law reports avidly and constantly attended continuing education conferences to keep up on novel approaches to my work.

The London legal community didn't take to me very well. A handful of lawyers maintained a stranglehold on the criminal cases in London, referring cases to one another and discouraging newcomers in a not-so-silent conspiracy that perpetuated their monopoly. Acclimatized to the gentlemanly courtship of plea bargaining and joint submissions that allowed early retirement to the London Club for lunch or the Hunt Club for a round of golf, many of London's criminal lawyers frowned on courtroom free-for-alls, technicalities, and appeals. I had no patience for their stubborn adherence to form, no respect for customs legitimized only by their repetition over time, and no desire to fade into the inbred clubiness that permeated the London criminal bar as it had atrophied the social structure of the city.

In retaliation, my losses in court were occasions for mirth. I was accused of "milking Legal Aid" by stretching out trials and contesting seemingly hopeless cases, stealing clients from other lawyers, abusing my stints as duty counsel at the courthouse to refer clients to myself, and being a general repository of harebrained ideas conceived to garner attention from the media. When my first murder client fired her lawyer, she retained me at the suggestion of a sympathetic detective. Her former lawyer, who was senior and well established and had more work than he could handle, threatened to report me to the Law Society and Legal Aid for my "unethical conduct." Publicly, my arrogance effectively masked my pain, and an acquittal in my first big case dulled its symptoms.

I could think of no other way to succeed than to work hard and fight the system. Success was the avoidance of mediocrity; fading in the crowd was my nightmare. What better way to avoid that fate than to stir things up, particularly when I had the talent and discipline to make the commotion meaningful?

At considerable emotional toll, I overcame the clawing, the infighting, and the politics with hard work and clever marketing. A few against-the-odds victories in the Court of Appeal brought me the reputation I wanted; eventually, sixty of my precedent-setting cases found their way to the law reports. The *London Free Press* publicized many of my successes, and early on, I warmed to the relationship between an attentive media and a successful practice. The Establishment doubters were muted, but their silence was loud.

Fighting the system also protected me from the threat of rejection. While remaining on the outside suited me intellectually and professionally, it tore me apart inside. True crusaders and rebels welcome rejection as the reason for their existence — but I did not: I wished to be admired by those I had beaten and found myself opposing them largely to avoid their rebuff.

But it was self-rebuff that was my demon. Even as I worked seven days a week, without a holiday for years, I considered myself lazy. While my courtroom victories were acclaimed, I pored over my notes long after cases had ended, agonizing over my mistakes. Appeals of my own trials were exercises in distress, as I dreaded the review of my transcripts — and my abilities — by the appellate judges whom I so admired. As I became more experienced, preparation quite properly gave way to accumulated knowledge, but if I lost a case, I blamed myself for taking things for granted. I attributed success to good fortune or being in the right place, never to hard work or talent.

Instead of seeking help for my inner dilemma, I wasted my energy with constant, angry resentment of the easy path I imagined for those who "fit in" and "looked good" — including Harris. On the rare occasions when I reached out, I did so tentatively and halfheartedly, hoping the listener would read my mind, but my practised front prevented anyone from taking me seriously.

As accomplishment and acclaim proved to be salves, not antidotes, my irrationality grew and provoked a consuming ascent, motivated by the belief that the higher I climbed, the safer I would be. In the end, as my sense of unworthiness took a drastic turn, it made for a longer fall. It wasn't a long way from feeling like a fraud to becoming one.

The 1980s began auspiciously, but misleadingly. Business was good, and I was a provincial director of the Ontario Criminal Lawyers' Association. The glow of achievement cast a shadow that hid my sense of inadequacy without tempering it. Growth in confidence and growth in self-esteem did not coincide: sadly, the whole of my self remained the sum of the incremental recognition of my achievements. Because confidence and self-esteem are inextricably associated in most human judgements, they are regularly mistaken for each other. I, for one, recognized and orchestrated their interaction, which became the dynamic sword of my duplicity.

In the formative years of my career, I had little interest in personal wealth or comforts; after eight years of practice, in 1981, Cathy, Melissa, and I hadn't moved from our rent-controlled four-bedroom house in London North, where the bargain rent of $350 monthly kept our personal expenses well within our means; for transportation, Cathy and I alternated between our Cutlass and aging yellow Gremlin. If I made a personal show, it was over my simple lifestyle and lack of materialism.

Professional appearances were a different matter. Harris and I spent lavishly on a large law library before we opened our first file. A few years later, when we moved downtown, I reiterated my philosophy: "We can't look like we're trying to make it; we've got to look like we've made it" — emphasis on "look"; consequently, we spent a fortune on furnishings. Whenever the firm made money, I wanted to move on, grow, outstrip ourselves and everybody else; even when life's reservoir was full, I was running on empty.

I was thirty-two years old as the decade began, and felt, after seven years of constant toil and personal sacrifice, that my career should have been further along. The five-member firm that started the eighties was not, to my mind, reflective of our efforts or abilities. I felt overburdened, overworked, and occasionally resentful of Harris for not performing to my expectations.

The addition of new partners to our firm created more problems for me. The spectacular evolution of the litigation practice dwarfed Harris's corporate department, though we remained equal financial beneficiaries; our new partners would eventually become dissatisfied unless my production grew to levels compensating them for Harris's disproportionate share of the profits. The situation worsened when the recession of the early eighties wiped out Harris's budding client base of small entrepreneurs. Each year, as budget time rolled around, I set increasingly difficult billings targets for myself; finally, when those targets became impossible in the mid-eighties, I drew up phoney accounts, never sent them to clients, and paid the bills myself — at first from my own pocket, eventually from the fruits of my frauds.

In 1981, at the height of my reputation as a criminal lawyer, my biggest victory, the *Boggs* decision, was just around the corner.

Fletcher Dawson, our newest partner, resented my appropriation of challenging, high-profile criminal cases. Foolishly, I promised him that I would give up criminal law and concentrate on building a corporate litigation practice. For I was afraid of losing Fletcher, as I was afraid of losing Harris: people of character were buffers against the insecurity within.

The decision to leave criminal law was a terrible personal choice, made for all the wrong reasons: I gave up passion for recognition, interest for appearance, value for size, commitment for success, professional pride for societal acclaim, and satisfaction in simplicity for insatiable acquisitiveness. If the powers-that-be in London wouldn't accept me, I'd outstrip them: I would build a larger, more diverse firm than any of them, beat them at their own haughty game of business litigation, and contemptuously leave them behind in their insular oasis as I marched off to Toronto to meet my reputation.

Fear drove me, breeding mistrust of time and its ally, patience. The world rushed by, leaving me without a sense of time or place, and my goals became way-station grab bags, where anything that shone sufficed as fuel for the continuance of the journey.

The Supreme Court of Canada announced its decision in the *Boggs* case during the first week of March 1981. Quietly, Cathy and I celebrated the happiest moment of my career with Wally Libis, a local criminal lawyer who had become my best friend, and his wife, Linda, over a candlelit chocolate cake and a bottle of champagne in their modest home.

As we raised our glasses in triumph, I should have been waving goodbye — to many things, but mostly to myself. Earlier that evening, I had been judging the Moot Court Competition at the University of Western Ontario Law School. One of the black-robed finalists was an attractive second-year law student named Deena Baltman.

Part Three

RESPITE

Depression is a luxury that someone in my situation can't afford.
SORIN HIRSHKO

Trouble in paradise

*In the game of life, it's a good idea to have
a few early losses, which relieves you of the pressure
of trying to maintain an undefeated season.*

BILL VAUGHAN

Both Deena and freedom seemed remote from my perch on the stone floor outside my new cell on C range, its door inexplicably open at mid-morning. In our daily telephone conversations during my two weeks of incarceration, I had not again heard the "I love you" of our parting at the London courthouse; yet I clung to the notion that my wife's duplicate of the scorpion in my left hand somehow bound us.

My sprawling, self-absorbed roost was an uncommon sight in the hallways of maximum security, especially in an inmate just fired and banished from the loftier comforts of the work range; obliviously, I poured out the morning's travails in my semi-legible handwriting. Since my arrival at Millhaven, correspondence with Deena, Melissa, and the many friends who remained supportive was my vehicle through the difficult process of withdrawal and renewal that was yet in its formative stages — a digression inward, healthy and soothing.

Suddenly, the loudspeaker boomed out. "You're not in your office, Melnitzer, get inside your cell and lock the door."

A Unit's routine had not changed from the time of my short

stay with Carl; the surroundings were familiar, the shock no longer heightened by apprehension. My roommate, Monte, a black man in his mid-twenties, made no secret of his displeasure at a white cell partner. As the senior occupant of the cell, he controlled the television that was on all day, taxing the concentrative powers I needed for reading and writing. This was the low point of prison so far. I was sad, not despairing, as if naked solitude was allowing me to meet myself after years of elusiveness.

An awakening knock on my cell door in the early afternoon renewed prison's pervasiveness.

"I told you to watch it in V & C," Aaron whispered through the door, in the aggravating tone of those who know it all.

"I couldn't do anything. The screw had it in for me."

"The story is you couldn't keep your mouth shut, Julius. I heard you told off the copper."

"Fuck him," I retorted, defiant as usual when backed into a corner. "I'll get his ass sooner or later."

"You're in prison, my friend. You better learn to eat it. Next time I won't be able to do anything for you."

My defiance sensibly gave way to supplication. "Can you get me back on the work range?"

"Plug's off for a couple of days, but he'll come in tomorrow and put his ass on the line because I asked him to. So don't screw up again."

"I'll be out of here tomorrow?"

"In a day or two," Aaron reassured me. "Take it easy."

I was relieved, but not convinced. For all that had happened, it was hard for me to believe that influence went as far in the penitentiary as it had in society; notwithstanding Aaron's unusual relationship with Plug, I doubted that I could rely on his grandiose boasts. Peter's assurance at recreation that night that "we're working on things" didn't bolster my confidence.

On our nightly walk around the dark track, Kevin tried to help. "You got out of the bucket in record time, they broke all the rules to get you to the work range, and they'll break them again to get you back."

Why did I keep coming up smelling like a rose in this god-forsaken garden? My mind, energized by disquiet as it had been on the street, sought information to feed control. Kevin, true to form, seized the opportunity to theorize, lighting up yet another cigarette in his yellowed fingers, protecting his match from the winter wind with his other hand.

"Either they don't want you hurt, or your pal Aaron's paying off the Man," Kevin theorized.

"No way." I laughed. "You've been watching too many videos."

"Trust me. It happens all the time."

"You're full of shit, Kevin, and if you're not, I don't want any part of it."

"*You're* full of shit," Kevin responded. "And you're a strange one to write off corruption."

That hurt.

By my third day on C range, I had settled in. I missed my daily chats with Melissa, and the sparseness of shower and telephone time irritated; but in short order, I became accustomed to, even enjoyed, the quiet sameness of the passing hours. The consequences of being alone with little to do were not cataclysmic, as I had imagined them. There were few necessities and no demands; survival was not the obstacle course of magical thinking it had always seemed to be. Tucked away as I was in a corner of oblivion, with little to distinguish night and day, and with no one to please, I found time to visit with myself. I enjoyed the conversation, one of my first clues that happiness was self-sustainable.

It was peculiar, I told myself, that silence breaks us down while the sensory influences we arrange to avoid silence keep us going. Perhaps the paradox arises because we associate the breakdown we call death with stillness and the vitality of life with activity. Why, though, do we measure the quality of life and the quality of death by the same standards? Is it because we are afraid that death is the end and so spend our lives avoiding the stillness we believe death brings? Was my father's turbulence, his way of staying alive, also my way?

At 1:30 P.M., the cell door slid open. Plug had returned to work, and Peter was there to take me back to the work range. I hesitated, momentarily unsure, then went with Peter, as yet unequipped to forsake the lures of the work range for the peace I was discovering. But I had tasted the silence, and savoured it.

The inmates on the work range gaped at me in disbelief; no one had ever returned after being fired. Soon, puzzlement turned to jealousy. Rumours circulated that my quick passage through the bucket, my immediate transfer to the work range, and my unprecedented return were the result of "pull": judges had called, hit men had threatened the warden, and huge sums of money had changed hands. There was some truth in the general suggestion: my careful advance planning had in fact connected with influence.

Then the stories turned ugly and dangerous. No amount of money, it was said, could have bought so much favoured treatment: "ratting out" must have been part of the deal. Kevin passed on rumours of my previous life as a Crown attorney gone bad, of the two accomplices I had allegedly betrayed, of the cocaine suppliers who got life because of my testimony, and of the nine-year sentence that was a ruse to protect me from vengeful *Mafioso*; other inmates empathized with the widows and orphans I had embezzled money from or speculated about the "big sex beef" that forced me to become a rat to protect myself. My remoteness from the drug and alcohol subculture was proof of my treason: "Who ever heard of a lawyer who doesn't drink or do dope?" When I started work in the kitchen, bypassing the dishwasher's job that normally fell to the junior worker, Plug was said to be treating me with "kid gloves"; in truth, Joe, the dishwasher, liked his job.

By comparison, London, Ontario, cliquishness was a pale joke. On the work range, the ostracism was rarely overt, but its undercurrents were always there, in endless complaints about favouritism, pointed barbs, and mirth over any accident, misfortune, or confusion that came my way. In the gym I could hear the hushed whispers, feel the distance of avoidance, and sense the rancour when I placed my name on the pool table list. When Kevin warned of threats of violence against me, I stopped going to the gym, working out instead on the range exercise bike and with long walks in A Unit's yard. The separation from Kevin and his joint-wise ways, until he made it to the work range a few weeks later, made things harder — as did my job as a server on the meal line.

Serving was a difficult job; the server was invariably blamed for the frequent shortages caused largely by kitchen workers eating as it suited them and for the flagrant inadequacies of the fare; he was constantly harassed for white meat, brown bread, darker toast, larger portions, and extras. Darryl, the psychopathic brush-cut contract killer who was our coffee man, had the special kind of personality to be a server: nightly, he exhibited the tools of his trade by kick-boxing the bag in the gym, ensuring that he was rarely bothered at his work station. Without Darryl's martial skills, I didn't have the right disposition for the job, which required the diffidence of a regretful, solid con reluctantly refusing the legitimate needs of his own kind; nor did I have the good sense to avoid the job — having learned little, it seemed, from my experience in V & C.

The first few days went smoothly, apart from the odd troublemaker whom I deflected with style — at least in my own mind.

The brooders bothered me most, as I couldn't gauge their speechless malice. Sean, the most prominent among them, no older than twenty-five, short and stubby, gave off violence as a kettle gives off steam. His face looked bloodied without a mark on it but for the crooked shadow of a nose broken more than once.

For three days, the emphatic thud of Sean's tray on the stainless steel counter delivered his demands. He communicated his wants with a finger thrust at eye level through the opening in the wall. Accommodating him or refusing him made no difference to the way he left, somehow lifting his tray from the counter more loudly than he had put it down.

On my fourth day at the job, the kitchen was short of everything, including bread. The bread man, who toasted and stacked the slices of white and brown plastic-bagged bread that CSC buys, had let the pile beside me run low while he chased down the steward to ask him for a few more loaves. As Sean came along, I reached for the four slices of brown bread he preferred — two extra, he wasn't the kind of person whose order I forgot — and found only four cold end pieces. I hesitated before putting them on Sean's tray.

"What the fuck is this?" he boomed.

"Sorry, that's all I've got. We're out of bread," I said, referring to our supply of brown bread.

Sean grimaced, sticking his twisted face forward to the serving area of the counter. With two fingers, he pointed to the small pile of white bread and, in the same motion, upended his tray, dumping its contents over the dozen plates of food in front of me.

"Asshole," I screamed, inviting Sean to lose it — which he did, without hesitation.

"You fucking goof, I'm gonna kill you. You better be in the yard tonight or I'll come and get you, you goof."

"Fuck *you*," I replied, "I'll be there right when it opens — and

I don't like to wait around for assholes I'm going to kill."

Sean danced up and down, pounding his left fist into his right palm, repeating, "You goof, you fucking goof, you fucking goof, you're dead meat, you're dead meat." A curious guard approached. "You better be there," Sean threatened, without moving his lips.

Bryce served the last few inmates.

"What happens now?" I asked.

"No choice. A guy calls you a goof, you kill him or he kills you," chimed Bryce's second-in-command, Fred, the grill man and self-professed keeper of the Code.

"Fine," I said, "I'm sick and tired of putting up with all you guys. Just because a guy's got a little more education, you think all he can do is sit behind a desk. Where's a fucking shiv?" I asked, more interested in the symbolism than the weapon.

"Take it easy, Mel, this is no time to make more enemies," Bryce muttered, using my prison nickname.

"Just leave me alone. I can take care of myself." By now, I was trembling — which doubtless reflected on my credibility.

"What's going on?" Rod, a tough middle-aged recidivist who had made a life out of robbery and assault, had come into the kitchen for a late lunch on his day off. "I heard that punk Sean's been making trouble."

"I'll have to look after this myself, Rod. You've got no beef with him." My joint jargon was insincere, aimed solely at restoring my honour.

"No, this is my concern. The way I hear it, that punk had no business throwing food back in the kitchen. Anyone who does that is an asshole. That's what you called him, isn't it?"

"Yes."

"That ain't like calling him a goof."

"He called me a goof."

"He'll apologize. I don't like his attitude. He never says please or thank you, like he's better than we are. Who does he think he is?"

Bryce agreed. "Rod's right. This isn't between Mel and the kid. It could have been anybody at the counter. The kid's got no respect for us."

"Respect" is a magic word in prison, ringing a bell with the other old cons in the kitchen, particularly Fred — though his interpretations of the Code wavered with the exigencies of the day.

"You got a point there, Rod. Let's the three of us go talk to the kid. We'll get the two of them to shake hands, like it was a misunderstanding, or else he'll have to answer to us." Fred was a prison tough guy — but only, I suspected, at odds of three-to-one.

"It's not a misunderstanding," Rod said. "I told you, that punk's got no respect. We'll go and see him, and he'll apologize to us for the guys in the kitchen. Then he can apologize to Mel for calling him a goof. After that, they can shake hands, if they want."

Darryl, the psycho, jumped at the opportunity. "Rod's right. I haven't kicked butt in a while."

"When?" I prodded. "At yard tonight?"

"No," Rod answered. "By then the beef's on. It'll have to be this afternoon, so you two can shake hands at supper."

"OK," Rod agreed, "Fred and I will go. I'll talk to Jason. He'll go too. He's got no use for punks. You just talk to the screw, Bryce, and tell him what's going on. You're good at that."

I stayed behind in the empty kitchen, positive that the incident was now the talk of the unit, if not of the prison. Being peeked at, talked about, and taunted was getting to me; alone in the kitchen, I could collect myself.

I was now in the most acute danger I had faced since my encounter with Spike in London. Psychologically, I was unarmed: I had no idea whether Rod was serious, whether my co-workers would be successful in their one-sided negotiation with Sean, whether Sean would nod acceptance or seek retaliation. I had size,

Sean had experience — in a fair fight.

No way. Sean was as likely to take to a pipe or a shiv as to his fists. I searched the utensil rack for a weapon and came upon a large, double-pronged fork with a Bakelite handle, the kind used for managing slabs of meat. I could get my parka from my cell, go for a walk in the yard, and on the way back stop in the kitchen for a coffee, tucking the fork in my parka. Jason or Darryl would know how to get it past the stool pigeon at rec-up.

My contingency plan in place, I took a deep breath, braced myself for the afternoon's furore of asked and unasked inquiries, and started out of the servery. At the dishwasher, I ran into Plug, coming around the corner with a purpose.

"What's this I hear about a fight? You're more trouble than the rest of the unit put together, Melnitzer."

"I'm sorry, Plug, it wasn't my fault."

"Don't start that again. What were you doing at the counter? Haven't you learned to lay low like I keep telling you?"

"It's nothing. The guys are taking care of it. I don't want to get anybody in trouble."

"Don't play the solid con with me, you Jew. I know everything that's going on around here before it happens. If that jerk-off kid doesn't come across by dinner, he'll do the rest of his sentence in the hole."

That would make me a rat. *On the other hand, I'm not that interested in this fight.* With my life at stake, I could overlook due process.

Plug screwed up his lips and nose. "Don't worry," he reassured me, "I've been around long enough to know how to do this."

I had no idea what Plug meant, but I didn't doubt its effectiveness.

"It would be better for the boys to straighten this out," he explained, "then we can ship that little fucker out of here and nobody'll know any better."

Unnerved, I returned to the kitchen to settle my synapses with a cup of tea. Rod walked in before the hot water had cooled sufficiently to drink.

"It's done. You wait outside in the hall after Sean's range comes by. Bryce knows to relieve you. He'll apologize for calling you a goof and shake your hand. Short and sweet. If you want, tell him you didn't mean nothing."

"That's great. Thanks. What about his apologizing to the rest of the kitchen workers?"

"He did what he had to do up there," Rod said mysteriously. "That's between him and us. No reason to humiliate the kid. He's got to live in here."

At close range, Sean's demeanour confirmed my feelings about his basic instincts. I tried to look as contrite as I felt.

"Shouldn't have called you a goof," Sean muttered sullenly.

"I'm sorry about the end pieces. They were the only brown I had."

Sean didn't extend his hand. I extended mine. He took it, briefly, and left.

I went to Rod's cell after dinner. He didn't look up from his TV.

"Can I talk to you a minute?"

"What about?"

"I just —"

"The business with Sean is over. Forget it. Do your time."

"I just wanted to say thanks. I'm new at this. I really didn't know what to do. You've been a real friend."

Rod's eyes flared in the TV's glow; he looked at me for a moment, rising from his prone position on the bed.

"Come in, kid, and sit down." Rod motioned me to the chair by the desk, turning it around for me as he did so. I sat down and looked up at him. He put his hand over his mouth, thoughtfully, as matter-of-fact menacing as anyone I had ever seen.

"You still don't understand, eh? There are no friends and no enemies in the joint. I'm not your friend. Don't call me that. Don't call anyone that. We're acquaintances. We get along. That's as far as it goes in here."

"OK, but —"

"Shut up and listen. Maybe this will straighten you out. If I knew you had ten thousand bucks, or five thousand bucks, and I could get away with it, I'd kill you for it and never think about it. You know why? Better my kid should have it than yours. You understand?"

"I think so."

"Good. See you later."

Violence

Every animal leaves traces of what it was;
man alone leaves traces of what he created.
JACOB BRONOWSKI

Spanking, screaming, shoving my fist through the odd wall, and a few athletic curses were as close as I had come to real violence before my incarceration. That stuff on TV wasn't in my world and couldn't happen to me. All violent people must be crazy, look crazy, and act crazy, I believed.

My image of violent criminals was cast by the public's steady diet of movies, TV, and Grade B thrillers. In truth, killers, rapists, and other violent criminals look and act normally most of the time, more so in the penitentiary, where they are at home. I have vivid memories of a triple murderer, in jail for twenty-one years, collecting all the kids in V & C on weekday afternoons, playing Sesame Street games with them, like a marvellous kindergarten teacher.

Our criminals eat, sleep at night, love, have visitors, play with their kids in the visiting room, watch television, cheer the Blue Jays, hate Brian Mulroney and Bob Rae, write letters, talk on the phone, wash their clothes, dress up for special occasions, worry about their weight, and complain about their jobs and their bosses. Some are educated and articulate, and many are talented. Most have lives, like the rest of us. We build prisons so we can ignore that fact, punishing them and theirs by taking most of their real life away. Then we pretend they don't have one, and that makes us feel civilized.

It is at the margin that the violent explode. As one guard said to me, "Just watch them when anybody says no to them. Then watch them when they hear no a second time." We all have buttons that can be pushed; the difference with the violent is that their buttons can be pushed more easily and detonate more explosively. My pleasant surprise at the politeness, geniality, generosity, and concern of much of the criminal element soon gave way to a realization that prison was always a dangerous place, exceptionally hazardous for me because I had no experience with the underlying nature of my neighbours.

At first, I dismissed much of the macho banter as the exaggerated swagger of the prison environment. It was difficult, I reasoned, to be proud of much in prison, so the best thing to do was to glorify it; even the guards required justification for their danger pay. In reality, many of the tough-guy braggarts, none of whom had ever lost a fight, were transparent cowards. Besides, it was beyond my experience that someone might maim or kill another human being for an insult, a bad debt, or nondelivery of last Saturday night's hash — despite my experiences with Spike and Sean. Even when I decided to quit my nightly outings to the gym at Millhaven, precaution and a desire to keep the resentment to a minimum, rather than fear of violence, motivated me. I felt like a reporter on the police beat: immersed in the violence, but detached from it.

What I did understand was that, with few exceptions, my fellow cons and I shared a devastating lack of self-esteem. On the street, I dealt with the problem by using the advantages of my upbringing and my abilities to take society's games beyond their moral limits. My crimes were controlled, crimes of choice explained (not excused) by psychological factors and greed. By contrast, the crimes of the violent are often uncontrolled and rarely crimes of choice; for the most part, violent criminals have little, if any, idea what their problems and choices are. They are unable to recognize their needs, their patterns, or the situations that cause them to explode. Their psyches often turn on a dime, and the prison environment that, through maximum, medium, and minimum, rewards violence as the ultimate source of power is the mint for their coin.

Time after time, I observed pleasant, passive personalities erupt under the strain of prison debts, institutional pressures, marital problems, or just plain loneliness. I watched ferocity at basketball and floor hockey that reminded me of the instinctually savage rituals of dominance I had seen among wild animals on my trips to Kenya, Tanzania, and South Africa. These were not simple outbursts of anger, but frenzies of rage, sometimes only a sentence long, unmistakably conveying barely contained hatred, accompanied by a tortured struggle for control that separates minimum and medium from maximum and the SHU, the Special Handling Units also known as "Super Max," reserved only for killers or near-killers of guards or other inmates. In the end, the shift from good inmate to bad citizen occurs in an instant, without warning.

My own behaviour was not unaffected by the atmosphere of savagery. After just a short time in prison, I found myself using my size as an advantage, not hesitating to threaten others whom I found offensive, nor refraining from the odd shove when tempers rose. It was always a fine and very trying line between not being pushed around and not pushing back too hard. Perhaps I was just fitting into my environment, trying to make do where reason would not, but my behaviour was a radical departure from the norms of my first forty-five years.

I wondered how the young coped. Did they have any choice but to make violence their credo?

"The people coming in the system now have an identity crisis," a seasoned con nicknamed Lucifer told me at Millhaven. "In the old days, everyone was solid. The rules were the rules, and the punishment was the same for everybody. Rats and hounds were in PC or they didn't survive. Everybody had respect. Now the kids come in, they don't know who's solid and who's not. There aren't any rules. They don't know what to be, so they try to be tough guys."

"When's the last time you saw anybody killed?" I asked Lucifer.

"About a year ago, in the upholstery shop in Kingston. Some young guy out to make his name put a pair of shears right through that diddler Fredericks' back in the upholstery shop."

At forty years old, Lucifer looked menacing. No taller than five foot eight, he carried one hundred and eighty muscular pounds carefully crafted over fifteen years of his life sentence. Two shocks of hair on the sides of his head framed his baldness; his thinning moustache seemed deliberately organized in an alternating pattern of hair and skin; and the shape of his piercing eyes hinted at the Oriental villains in James Bond movies; the sudden squints of his bushy right eyebrow and the simultaneous flinch of his curling upper lip revealed two missing front teeth that made both his laughter and his frequent scowls repulsively alluring. At the time, my wariness had not yet set in, and Lucifer didn't frighten me; he seemed, like many prison characters, more a caricature than a threat.

"Are you dangerous?" I asked Lucifer.

"Here's how it is," he replied. "When I get up in the mornin' and I get a little time to open my eyes, sit on the edge of the bed, and have a cup of coffee, it's OK. Man, but if I get shook, rrrrrr, look out!"

Lucifer's offhand way with the language of violence told me much more about him than his stories:

> One Saturday mornin', I'm in Kingston, I'm sleepin', and some fuckin' jerk has his stereo goin' real loud. I jump out of bed, kick the cell door right open and run down the range. It's this huge French guy

I never seen before. I'm so riled I'm heaving. Man, this motherfucker was huge, but I get right in his face. "I got the fucking stereo on and it's gonna stay this way," he says to me in that faggot frog accent. So I put up my mitts and he says, "Bring a blade to the yard tonight and we'll settle it there." Now I'm scared, I mean, I got my fists up and all of a sudden we're talkin' knives. I go back to my cell wonderin' what I'm gonna do.

At lunch this French goof comes by callin' me a yellowbelly and a chickenheart. All his goof friends are laughin' at me and my friends, they aren't lookin' at me. Everybody in the joint knows what's goin' down. I mean I'm a lifer, I gotta live with these guys for a long time.

I'm scared shitless, but I know I'm going to have to do somethin' or there ain't gonna be no peace never. I'm heaving, man, but I got no choice, so I go to his cell and tell him we'll settle it in the yard tonight. I'm gonna kill him, I tell him. "You gonna kill me, you piece of shit?" he says to me. "I gone spill your guts from one end of the yard to the other. The pigs, they take a week to collect you." He's wearin' a coat, he pulls it back and I can see the longest fuckin' blade you've ever seen.

After lunch my buddy Andy gives me a blade. Aluminum, about two inches wide and nine inches long. I'm hopin' Frenchy'll just forget it but I stick the knife in my coat. Then I go to the shop and I steal some turpentine and hide it in a tobacco can. I go back to my cell and get one of those spray bottles, you know, atomizers, the stuff they use for cleaning and for watering plants. I fix it so it shoots out straight but sprays when it hits you, then I tape the nozzle in place. I fill the thing with the tobacco can of turp and use the tape to make sure the top stays put. I stick the bottle in my coat pocket and the blade inside my coat. My buddy Andy, he gives me a new lighter. I turn the flame up so you could light a bonfire with it.

You know, when you're scared, you gotta breathe deep. You do it easy so the other guy don't know you're scared. At rec-up, I walk up to Frenchy in the weight pit and look him straight in the eye. If I wasn't

*breathin' so deep, I'd be shakin'. "Let's go," I tell him. He stops laughin'
at me, cause, like I said, I'm lookin' him straight in the eye and he's
surprised. I shove him and I say, "Let's do it, motherfucker!" He pulls out
his knife, and starts swingin' at me. I got the lighter in my right hand.
I get the bottle out of my pocket and start goin' at him and sprayin' him.
He puts his hand up to cover his eyes and he keeps sayin' to me, "What
you got?" He doesn't twig to the lighter. I keep sprayin' him with the
turp, all over his jacket, the side of his face, his hands, his eyes. He
can't figure out what the fuck's going on. Then like a shot, he smells the
turp and he goes bug-eyed. "Hey, man, take it easy, it's all right," he
says to me. "I was just kiddin'. Take it easy. Take it easy. Here, shake
hands." Man, he was snivelling. But I wasn't breathing deep no more. I'd
killed a guy before and I was so hyped up it didn't matter none to kill
this frog. But my buddy Andy says to me, "The copper in the tower's got
you in his sights. Don't be nuts." At KP, they shoot you. So I walk away.*

*Every time I seen Frenchy since, all he does is jerk his fuckin' neck
and say, "Uh huh, uh huh." Never bothered me no more. Hardly ever
came out of his cell. Just sat there with his kid.*

"You'd kill me too, wouldn't you, Lucifer, even though you
go around patting me on the back," I teased — but I was serious.

"Only if I had to. I don't do that shit for fun any more. You're
only on top in here till you get old. I wanna get out." Hopefully, I
prayed, Lucifer did not represent the outer limits of rehabilitation.

Things are a little better in the medium security institutions. Of
the three in Ontario, Collins Bay, one-quarter black and teeming
with racial problems, is reputedly the most violent, with Joyceville
not far behind. Whiff, who rarely bathed and supported his drug
habit with armed robberies, had been around the system more than
once; he described the difference between the potential for violence
in maximums and mediums:

In max, it can happen to anyone. You get a nice quiet guy, next day, boom, he's gone. You never know what's going to happen. You could get into trouble for anything. Let's say you're walking down the range, and you say, "Hello" or "Good morning," the guy could be some-body's kid. Next thing you know someone's accusing you of putting the make on his kid. In medium, there's usually a reason — like a drug beef or a debt or something like that. In maximum, it's shivs or pipes. In medium, shivs are pretty rare. A lot of fist fights and kicking there.

I witnessed only six or seven fights with my own eyes, none involving weapons, but another "pal" erased my doubts about the violence of my surroundings.

Mex, who was fifty-six, had not a single grey hair and the body of a triathlete; his friendly, diffident manner, the charming hint of a French-Canadian accent, and his schoolmarmish glasses, left no clue to the "dangerous offender" status that had kept him in prison for twenty-two years, with no prospects for release on his inde-terminate sentence. Mex had spent seven of those years in the SHU for killing another prisoner.

"Do you ever think about the guys you killed?" I asked him one day.

"Yeah, I do," Mex replied, with chilling satisfaction. "I'm glad I did it. They deserved it."

"Why do you say they deserved it, Mex?"

"Who, the guy outside or the guy in the joint?"

"The guy outside."

Mex stroked his chin, like a professor contemplating a stu-dent's probing question. "I really can't remember. It was so long ago. I don't kill people for nothing, you know. I'm telling you he deserved it."

"What about the guy in jail?"

"What would you do? The guy ratted me out for some dope.

Can't let him get away with that. Eh, what do you think? I'm right, aren't I?"

"How'd you kill these guys? With a knife?"

Mex turned his palms over, studied them, and, with a cruelly delicate smile, slowly lifted them to my face. "With these hands. Always with my hands. That's the only way to do it. You can feel the sucker dying that way."

Quite apart from my run-in with Sean, I sensed an undercurrent of violence directed at me. Presence, charisma, and verbal skills complicated my problems. Keeping a low profile was difficult: I asked questions, offered opinions, spent more time with Aaron, and eventually resorted to unprovoked sarcasm as the outlet for my frustration. On the telephone, Deena was impatient but noncommittal; I complained to Bob Bigelow, Dr. Arndt, and Melissa about my tension and isolation.

Two weeks into my stay at Millhaven, the strain became unbearable. I contemplated a transfer back to C range again, but Aaron wisely talked me out of it.

"Believe me," he warned, "you don't want to do that. Plug'll have to do a report on you. They think someone's muscling you. You'll be a PC and they'll never send you to camp."

Aaron and I would have been in greater danger had the thirty inmates on the work range not been the envy — often the spiteful envy — of the deprived majority. Our range mates were, to varying degrees, in the same position as Aaron and myself, and so unlikely to carry through with threats that might put them back among the jealous.

Much of the anger of the double-bunked and the work range's reputation as a "rat haven" sprang from the partiality and arbitrariness that governed work range selections; the prescribed procedure was usually an exercise in futility.

Freedom to work, in a prison setting, involves serious security considerations, including freedom of movement and access to potentially dangerous tools and confidential material. Until an inmate is assessed, his trustworthiness is unknown. But the rule requiring classification as a prerequisite to the work range was selectively employed: what it amounted to was a handy excuse to mollify those whom the staff, and Plug in particular, didn't want.

What Plug wanted on the work range were hardened cons, bikers, and recidivists, people who had been through the system and knew how it worked; he boasted that some of Canada's most heinous offenders had been on "my range" without incident. Apart from those preferences, if Plug liked you, you were in; if you were a buddy of one of his favourites, you would as likely as not also find yourself on easy street. Kevin made it to the work range by this route, at my request. If you didn't meet either of those criteria, you were out.

Day after day, Plug stood by the servery watching the line, joking, questioning, insulting, and threatening, all devices in an instinctual scanner, honed by years of experience and polished with Plug's unabashed humanity. He was searching for cons with the old values or for prisoners who would forever be grateful for relief: inmates like Bryce, the servery chief, whose dilemmas Plug could exploit. Occasionally, for variety, Plug chose personalities who interested him or tugged at his considerable heartstrings.

Although he worked with the rest of the staff well enough, Plug had no real use for them. They were company men and he was his own man, a maverick through and through. The dislike was mutual, solidified by Plug's animosity to the powerful public service union, which he regarded as a useless bureaucracy. Plug had sealed his social fate among his peers when he crossed picket lines early in his career.

The two other ICs on A Unit, Plug's equals in rank, were only a minor nuisance to Plug. Once in a while, another IC might post his own choice to the work range. It didn't happen often. Plug was either more clever or more persistent. He made it a point to be at work when departures begot vacancies; even in his absence, Plug prearranged the placement of his favourites.

The favouritism was plain and led to much grumbling. Yet Millhaven was an old-style maximum security prison where, even in Reception, the griping gave way to the Code: no matter how much a prisoner was wronged by the Man, it was semi-suicidal to right the wrong by pointing a finger at a fellow con.

Still, Plug's domination endowed the work range with a beneficial homogeneity; the preponderance of old cons, the absence of punks, and the unspoken fealty to Plug ensured a quiet order disturbed only by the petty bickering that is a mainstay of confinement for all species. Plug's habit of spending many hours at the prison, frequently showing up unscheduled, encouraged an admirable uniformity of atmosphere and administration. His raspy drill sergeant's voice, his indiscriminate sarcasm, his instantly recognizable step, and his romps down the work range throwing punches at anyone in his way were constant reminders of his mastery, but the eccentric humour that accompanied his shenanigans kept the mood light and the cons loose.

What Plug didn't say outright was that he harboured a special empathy for many of his "low-life cons." Beneath the blustery exterior was a pussycat with a big heart. Older cons, even ones whom he did not know, but who were having a hard time double-bunked, could find themselves in a soft job on the work range. Plug regularly interrupted his rampages through the range to enquire after cons whom his practised eye told him were not quite right.

All this was a huge turnaround for Plug: he had, various old-timers told me, been the "meanest pig of them all." Stories abounded of Plug leading his distinctive version of *The Charge of the Light*

Brigade into the thick of various riots and brawls, brandishing a billy stick and a shotgun and howling imaginative blasphemies as his battle cry.

When CSC gave Plug the work range, it became this lonely man's baby and the inmates his people. After a quarter century in the Service, Plug's charges had become his kind, and Plug was proud of it. His bosom buddy was the inmate baker at nearby Pittsburgh minimum security camp, and his drinking cronies were all ex-cons.

Three heart attacks likely hastened the transformation — not that heart disease should have been any surprise to an alcoholic chain smoker who was at least one hundred and fifty pounds overweight and, undeterred, ate four meals on each eight-hour shift. Plug's long hours elevated the stress, leaving his marriage on the rocks. His obstinate fantasy was to shuck his financial problems long enough to take a year off work and spend it in a bar.

> *That's all it would take to make me happy. I just want to sit around with the old cons in downtown Kingston, drink, and talk about the old days. I'd go there when it opened and stay till it closed. I'd stay drunk for a year.*
>
> *Those people are my friends, you know. I don't have any other friends. Even your enemies, they become your friends. That's what happened when the system changed, when they decided the guards and the cons should talk. You can't be a hard-ass any more. You don't ask what they're doing when they're not drinking with you. You drink with them, you talk, you have a good time. A year in a bar with my friends. Drunk with enough money to stay drunk. Drunk enough not to worry. That's all I want out of life. That's my dream.*

Plug may have mellowed, but the two baseball bats he kept in the duty office were grim reminders that he was still the boss. Plug bristled when I asked him about the weapons.

"I don't give a shit what those goddamn higher-ups think about you cons getting to those bats. I'll be damned if some snot-nosed warden with fancy letters after his name who's never seen the inside of a cell is gonna tell me how to protect myself in here. No inmate's ever tried to get near those bats, 'cause they're not stupid enough to take their life in their hands."

With that, Plug grabbed a bat and chased me all the way to my cell, flailing it wildly and screaming as we both ran down the range to the chortling of the onlookers, who welcomed the relief Plug's regular histrionics brought to the monotony of their days.

Eventually, the screaming, the kidding, the drinking, the smoking, and the overeating would not be enough to contain the simmering desperation of this unhappy man. He would bring it home. I lived at his home, and watched him unravel.

Black and white

*The truth you believe in and cling to makes you
unavailable to hear anything new.*

PEMA CHODRON

Plug had no use for blacks; to him, they were unclean punks, drug
traffickers, and pimps — newcomers with no respect for the Code,
usurpers trying to remake the system to their detested ways. Peter
told me that he had never seen a black on the work range in his
twelve months as unit clerk. Although I estimated that fifteen percent of Reception's population was black, only one black, Marshall,
made it to the work range while I was there.

On the afternoon of Marshall's first day in the servery, Bryce
and I were alone in the kitchen when Plug, who had been off for
a couple of days, roared in.

"How did that fucking nigger get on this range?"

"I don't know," Bryce said. "He came on the range yesterday."

"Well, he isn't going to be here long. No nigger's going to
touch my unit's food."

At dawn, Marshall, who had been pleading for a transfer for
months, was on his way to Collins Bay.

Security staff at Millhaven Reception, to whom stereotyping came
as naturally as putting on the uniform, constantly derogated their
black charges: blacks were dirty troublemakers, mistreated women,

lacked values, inspired the deteriorative changes in the system, and were unworthy of privilege. Whites dominated the work range and manned the servery: extras from the meal line and goodies smuggled out of the kitchen found their way to white cells. The range cleaners, on whom confined inmates depended to communicate their needs, pass messages to friends, do laundry, and trade contraband, were all white — and so were their buddies.

The racial problems are not confined to Millhaven. Stories of racial unrest at Collins Bay are rampant. A recent staff transfer from the Bay to Millhaven Reception confirmed the problem by the way he denied it: "We didn't have any problem with the blacks. If they stepped out of line, the whites called them down to the gym and dummied them. There was never any racial trouble."

I never saw a black guard or classification officer at Millhaven. At most, three black guards work at Collins Bay and three at Kingston Penitentiary. Warkworth, Canada's largest prison, lists six or seven black security officers, one black CO and one black teacher, but their numbers are still disproportionate to the black population. Despite the presence of many blacks at Beaver Creek, there is no black staff there.

Perhaps CSC is doing its best; its policies have long condemned discrimination while heralding equality and the preservation of inmate's cultural ties. The Jamaican community newspaper in Toronto carries want ads for federal correctional officers, and the service has made impressive inroads in employment equity for women and native Canadians. But blacks see few of their own among the Man, none at the management level, causing alienation even greater than that which normally comes with prison territory.

If staff were sarcastic, demeaning, or indifferent when it came to blacks, the inmates were downright hateful. They blamed blacks for the extended double-bunking and for the breakdown of the Prison Code; blacks were unsanitary and disreputable, moochers who couldn't be trusted to pay their debts, resorted to cell thievery as a way of surviving, and played their rap music too loudly. A white heroin trafficker distinguished himself from black drug dealers by explaining that his customers were "grown men, forty-, fifty-, sixty-year-olds, buying at the office or in bars; those niggers sell crack to ten- and twelve-year-olds right on the street."

Millhaven Reception is many convicts' first point of contact with the penitentiary system. Once the herd mentality forms, it follows inmates to other institutions. The anger against authority, represented by the white man, grows and grows; eventually, the most violent segment of an embittered minority goes back on the street with more hatred than ever.

The almost constant lockup kept the festering racial rivalry under control in Reception. The close conditions on J Unit, however, magnified the bigotry there. As one con put it, "J Unit was the worst. The type of people there, nothing matters to them. I seen pencils broken in guys' eyes. I seen them tie cons to the bed and pour boiling water over them."

On a weekday in early March, the barriers at the end of the work range were uncharacteristically closed and recreation was delayed. In prison, a change in routine usually signals trouble somewhere in the institution, often followed by an unexplained "lockdown." Sometimes, inmates are confined to their cells for weeks or months — experienced cons can be quickly identified by the oversupply of toilet paper in their cells. With a lockdown, the grapevine takes over: whispered truths and rumours shuttle from cell to cell, transcending the quarantine through the cracks between the sliding doors and the walls.

Word spread that J Unit was locked down; a white con had stabbed a black, and the blacks had sworn revenge. Suddenly, the inmates from J Unit who frequented Reception, like Jackson, were nowhere to be seen; the grapevine buzzed with stories of cell searches turning up as many as seventy knives in J Unit; and Reception's recreation was changed from 7:30 to 5:30, an indication that J Unit was not using the gym. Personnel in the Dome increased as movement and activity in the prison decreased; as things slowed down, tension went up. No one thought of quelling our anxiety by keeping us informed.

Plug reported two stabbings and three shootings when armed guards invaded J Unit. Other sources claimed at least one death by stabbing, but Kingston television evening news made no mention of Millhaven. Fatalities are the one thing that media-shy CSC cannot keep from the press; anything short of death, other than a prolonged full-scale riot, is hushed up with the skill of Madison Avenue professionals.

Lockdowns disrupt routine, but convicts, who must march to the drummer, become wedded to the beat and so have little tolerance for change in the rhythm. Delays of any kind induce pounding on cell doors and cursing at staff; even the silent gather at the narrow slats in the cell doors, exuding malice with their eyes alone.

A Unit was never locked down during the disturbance in J Unit. Plug understood that confinement would exacerbate the pressure; cleverly, he distanced Reception from the problems in J Unit by avoiding disruption on his territory. Still, blacks and whites eyed and sidestepped one another. Plug and other guards exclaimed that things would not get better until the "niggers were shipped home."

On Thursday, the third day of J Unit's lockdown, the authorities, trying to ease the strains of twenty-four-hour lockup, allowed a segregated recreation period for J Unit: blacks got the gym; whites got the yard. An unfortunate inmate of mixed parenthood chose recreation with the whites, who considered him black enough to qualify for retribution.

Standing outside the duty office on Friday evening, I saw black-suited, black-booted men in riot gear sprawled on the floor of the Dome, with revolvers at their hips and automatic weapons on the floor beside them. I couldn't believe it. Here I was in the middle of a full-blown riot, SWAT squad and all. Just like on TV. I used every excuse I could to hang around the duty office until bedtime, when I marched off to my cell in a huff, a petulant child denied the end of his show.

In the morning, the SWAT squad was gone. I longed to get closer to the action, to probe the mysterious J Unit, to separate truth from fiction, and to confront the danger I could only imagine.

My chance came when the confinement of J Unit's inmates created a labour shortage. Plug requested volunteers to clean J Unit's kitchen. To individuals earning $5.25 daily, extra work at overtime rates of $10 makes for a significant increase in the standard of living; Plug sweetened the pie by promising to double the hours actually worked. "His boys" were taking on a dangerous job and making him look good in the process: "What's a few bucks out of the government's pocket?" he proclaimed.

At first, there were no takers. The Code is specially sacrosanct during lockdowns, the ultimate symbol of "pig power": an inmate helping the Man during a lockdown is like a scab in a violent labour dispute, except that in prison, the danger is imminent. It would take only one J unit inmate poking his head in the kitchen to identify the scabs; besides, J Unit's contacts in Reception would not hesitate to name the volunteers, particularly if they came from the privileged environs of the work range; even other work range inmates might rat out the volunteers to divert suspicion from themselves.

Eventually, four prisoners came forward. I was one of them. Our motivations differed, but a quiet desperation was our common bond.

Bryce, the inmate who ran the kitchen, was a family man nearing forty, in the second year of a life term for first-degree murder, which was under appeal. Bryce took on the dangerous work in J

Unit so he could send money home to his family.

"It's hard to be loving from jail," he told me. "We left them." Deena was of the same mind.

Rob, twenty-three, a minor player in a drug conspiracy serving a first-ever sentence of three years, believed every story he had ever heard about the rape of young men in jail. His vacillation between obsequiousness and arrogance brought on the wrath of his servery co-workers, who activated his panicky propensities at every opportunity. Rob was desperate for acceptance, hoping to command respect with this show of courage.

Fred was the servery's grill man, a vociferous pretender to the Code's mantle who, with Rod and Jason, had intervened in my dispute with Sean. When his delusions about his bridge-playing skills combined with his chain smoking, pop guzzling, and pot toking to put him deeply in debt, he was stuck between two Code tenets: one, you pay what you owe, and two, you don't help the Man by working during a lockdown. To a solid con, the principles were not inconsistent: if you couldn't pay what you owed, you stood up and fought.

As one of many prison illiterates I encountered, Fred had asked me to read his mail and write letters to his family and girlfriends. His intimacies revealed a manipulative coward who fashioned his violent history of assaults in a string of drug- and alcohol-induced rages, which he rationalized in the clichés of the criminal subculture: his victims were "goofs or stiffs," they "got what was coming to them" because they "only picked on women and kids," and Fred "wasn't going to be in the same room with them and let them stand up." It didn't surprise me that he took the easy way out of his debts by volunteering to work in J.

I volunteered because I was curious. And desperate in my own way too, stripped of the trappings that had sustained me in society, needing fresh emblems to define myself in this new environment. I would make prison an experience, something to talk about, something to distinguish me, rendering my humiliation a badge of honour by making the most of it. In this way, I could deny prison its immediacy as my life's reality, creating the illusion of meaning where there was none. Working in J Unit in the middle of a riot seemed just the thing.

Two days later, sober, conservative "Clark Julius" resurfaced as "Danger Man," his true identity unknown to the ignorant masses around him. Discrepantly garbed in greens, but with his head held high, Danger Man presented himself to the duty office for his mission. In his mind's eye, he imagined how they marvelled at his steely courage; he stood ready to allay their fears for his safety and graciously acknowledge their anxious wishes for his prompt and uneventful return.

"I'm off to J unit," he announced, as the butterflies in his stomach massaged the stolid front of a fearless man in times of crisis.

A crisis it was. "You're off, all right," shrieked Plug. "Off the face of the fuckin' earth, you mealy-mouthed sniveller. You were probably never there when your clients needed you either."

The wings of the butterflies in Danger Man's stomach promptly fell off. Danger Man became Blubbering Man.

"What do you mean? You told me I could go over there and help with the kitchen cleanup."

"What do you mean 'what do I mean?'" Plug yelled. "We've been looking all over for you for half an hour. The keeper's having a shit fit. I had to send Baby Lee. Dinner'll be half an hour late. It'll cost a fortune in overtime. The warden's gonna have my ass, but not before I eat you up, shit you out, and lance you like the haemorrhoid you are."

"I don't understand," I protested, glancing at the clock on the wall. "It's five to six. You told me to be ready at six."

"Don't you tell me what I told you, you low-life con. I said to be back from J by six. Where the fuck were you?"

Danger Man had fallen asleep in another inmate's cell; the occupant graciously let him sleep and wandered off. Danger Man's failing hearing — an anomaly in the modern equivalent of 007 — had caused him to miss the boat. I was lucky that Plug hadn't locked down the unit looking for me, making Clark Julius the laughing-stock of the work range.

Next evening, I showed up on time and in a different incarnation.

The ominously quiet corridor from the Dome to J Unit, lacking office windows, seemed narrower and dimmer than Reception's passageways; flickering shadows suggested lurking figures around the squared corners where the unit's hallways converged.

The servery's layout was identical to Reception's, but I was repelled by the disgusting conditions: the walls were spotted with dried remains of cooked eggs and chocolate pudding; the service entrance doors were a kaleidoscope of crusty red ketchup, pale yellow mustard, and white sugar crystals; crumpled paper towels, dirty J-cloths, food remnants, fruit peels, and assorted liquids competed for space on the floor; the grime on the windows made them opaque, their sills and frames rust-stained and dusty; the stainless steel hood over the grill was dirty and streaked, the shelves and counters disorganized and grimy; one hundred and fifty used trays rested on the floor at the far end of the kitchen near the dishwasher and sink.

"Holy shit," Bryce exclaimed. "This is worse than yesterday. We'll never get this clean in an hour. What happened?"

"They let the boys out to eat today," the guard replied. "They thanked us by tossing the food back into the kitchen. They'll be in their cells for a while, I'll tell you."

"We'll need some more help if you want this place done right," Bryce insisted.

"You can stay here till lockup," the guard said. "Do the best you can. Just don't go out in the hall. Call if you need anything."

The warning was unnecessary.

After washing the trays, we scrubbed the walls, swept the floors, emptied and cleaned the freezer, dusted the shelves and counters, reorganized the cupboard, wiped down the window sills and frames, and polished the stainless steel. Without industrial cleaning equipment, the years of neglect could not be totally erased, but four hours after we started, the kitchen was clean.

The IC was impressed. "I'm going to write you guys up for this. Make sure they send you guys every night."

With that, he picked up a cardboard carton and sauntered through the kitchen, filling it with coffee, sugar, cartons of cereal, and a selection of fruits, all precious commodities Down Under.

"There's as much of that as you want. I'll call ahead to A Unit and tell them it's OK. Make sure you're here tomorrow," he repeated as he left. "Make yourselves a coffee and take a rest. You've earned it."

"Great," said Fred, conveniently forgetting the Code's sanctions against accepting favours from the Man.

"What about the mess outside on the counters?" Rob asked. "We should clean that up and sweep the floor."

"You go, hero," I said. Danger Man had vanished.

"I'll make the coffee and something to eat," Bryce offered.

"And I'll sit here," I replied. "I'm the oldest."

"Figures," Rob retorted, already on his way out to the hallway.

Bryce grilled three cheese omelettes; I turned on the radio. For almost an hour, we forgot we were in prison as we tapped to the music and laughed ourselves silly each time Rob, red-faced in fear at the faintest sound in the hallway, raced back to the kitchen for cover, taking forty-five minutes to do a fifteen-minute job. We celebrated at his expense over Bryce's cooking and Cokes the guards provided.

As we left, I couldn't resist a peek into the bowels of J Unit. Around the corner, an inmate with his back to me was on J Unit's telephone — a human goldfish in a locked, circular glass booth.

Two weeks later, CSC dispersed the ringleaders throughout the country, ending the siege.

Politics in paradise

... a sideshow got up as major theatre.

JOHN LE CARRÉ

Despite my anguish over my disappearing marriage and the animosity from other inmates in my first four weeks Down Under, I felt lucky.

When melancholy overtook me, as it did almost daily, I could count on Melissa's love, Dr. Arndt's devotion and guidance, and Bob Bigelow's sensible and stoic support. I could reach Hans, as Dr. Arndt insisted I call him, any time of day or night, at his office, his home, his cottage, or in his car; Bob gave me his home phone number. Visits from Melissa, my mother, my faithful friend Joan, and even from Deena, were beacons in a loveless world.

Meanwhile, Aaron's connections ensured a steady flow of ingredients for our nightly feasts. On Saturdays, he invariably showed up with food worthy of a fine restaurant: shrimp, oysters, lobster, prime roast beef and veal, Grade A steaks, assortments of fresh vegetables, and delicate pastries. Take-out pizzas, Chinese food, and Kentucky fried chicken made it onto the range when Aaron wasn't up to cooking. The smokers in our group consummated their meals with contraband cigars or priceless Marlboros or Camels that brought three to five times their value on Millhaven's thriving black market.

In his cell, Aaron habitually relaxed with a few joints. Most guards in maximum security prisons tolerate marijuana, welcoming it as a harmless "downer." Even at that, Aaron was flagrant, leaving joints on his desk and unhesitatingly toking them in staff's presence.

For a few weeks, Aaron coyly played on my curiosity about his standard of living, but his stupendous ego finally succumbed to my calculated lack of inquiry. Aaron, who boasted of great wealth and connections, claimed to own a restaurant in nearby Kingston.

"I told some of the guards about my restaurant and made sure they never paid when they went there. After a while, it was hard for them not to do something for me. I never asked, they offered. First it was a few vegetables, seasonal fruits, a couple of packs of cigarettes, that sort of thing. Now, they get me whatever I want and don't bother me about a few joints. What do you need?"

"Nothing," I insisted, disinclined to be more beholden to Aaron than I already was, worried as well that his incestuous relationship with Plug would backfire, drawing me into a mess. Although proximity to the consequences of criminal behaviour was close at hand as a deterrent to temptation, it was also wrong, just plain wrong, and the simplicity of that proposition made the decision effortless. For once, getting ahead, proving I could beat the system, and making the most of everything paled beside that unadorned axiom. I suppose sceptics would frown on my continued participation in the gourmet dinners: to them I say, I was seeking progress, not perfection.

Aaron, a Canadian citizen, was transferred to Canada from an American prison in mid-1991. He had served almost ten years of a ten- to fifty-year sentence imposed in Detroit after conviction, he asserted, for a several-hundred-million-dollar computer fraud on the Federal Reserve Bank of the United States.

"Just for fun," he said, "I wanted to see if I could do it. That's why you did it, didn't you?"

The personal photographs of celebrities plastered on the walls of Aaron's cell illustrated his anecdotes of wealth, beautiful women, and exploits among the rich and famous. He claimed an engineering degree from the Massachusetts Institute of Technology, but his business was television and movie production; he had earned his spurs in a senior position with ABC's *Wide World of Sports* and moved on to his own company based in New York and Chicago. His wife, twenty years his junior, her beauty prominently displayed among the notables over Aaron's bed, was a Manhattan TV anchorwoman earning $175,000 annually and moonlighting with her own production firm. At Aaron's behest, I could dial a Chicago number collect; "Henry," who answered the phone, call-forwarded anywhere for me.

Aaron was unusually bright, knew the ins and outs of high society, and demonstrated an astonishing aptitude for computers and electronics; he exploited that talent to endear himself to many staff, whose small appliances cluttered his cell awaiting repair. His usefulness engendered a grateful respect, almost a deference, and special favours, including after-hours use of the classification officers' private offices and government telephone lines.

I was impressed but wary: the tip of the iceberg, I knew only too well, tells us little about the rest of the iceberg. I suspected that beneath Aaron's mask was a brilliant, conniving, and creative mind, capable of building an illusory empire on a shallow foundation. I wondered whether Aaron's emotional fate at sixty years of age presaged my own.

Aaron's exposition of his crime made no sense to me. Why was he tried in Detroit for a crime perpetrated in New York? How could theft that approached Michael Milken's Wall Street shenanigans in its enormity escape widespread publicity?

"They've hushed it up," Aaron explained. "If anyone discovered what I did, it would be a disaster to the banking system. The government would have to fire half the Treasury staff."

I had my doubts that the very same media that forced President

Nixon to resign would worry about the lackeys in Treasury. Aaron's sentence was truly lengthy, suggesting a crime of some proportions. On his treaty transfer to Canada, his sentence was recalculated to a definite term of thirty-seven years, of which he had served nine.

Aaron, three years past his day parole, elderly, nonviolent, a first-time offender with clear means of support and stable family roots, seemed inordinately concerned about his prospects for release. Naturally, he had a plausible explanation, which he articulated with sincerity, passion, and a hint of mischievousness. "The Fed is missing a few hundred million bucks, and they're still not sure how I did it. That's how come I got such a long sentence and why it took all this time to be transferred back to Canada. The RCMP is working with the FBI to put the screws to me, trying to keep me in here until I co-operate."

Aaron was right: absence of remorse and refusal to co-operate are assurances of failure at the Parole Board. Yet... *I recognize this. Put the emphasis on the explanation. Make it so logical, so convincing, so fascinating that no one will realize it holds together only if they believe the premise. If possible, make the explanation a little more grandiose than the premise. If your credentials are good enough, the listener will be caught up in them, in you, and will forget the premise.* Aaron's explanation made perfect sense — but only if I accepted his version of his crime.

Searching, I scanned for the subtleties of overwhelming insecurity I knew so well: insignificant lies shoring up chinks in the armour, innocent braggadocio smoothing out the image, genuine achievement buttressed with mantles of hyperbole, and generosity contrived to breed admiration, gratitude, and dependence.

Aaron's secretiveness, his obsession with compartmentalization, was also familiar to me. He claimed that no one, other than his wife and "Henry," the voice in Chicago, knew of his imprisonment: his business associates and friends believed he was recuperating from a serious automobile accident back home in Canada. *For nine years?*

Must have been a hell of an accident. I gave Aaron the benefit of the doubt; after all, my friends believed I was honest for almost as long.

It was Aaron's possessiveness about Plug that sealed my distrust. Plug loved to kid me about the "stash" he was sure I had and was constantly suggesting — only half in jest — that my life in prison could be much improved if I lent him a little money. Although I laughed off his hints, Plug confided in me, seeking my advice on dealing with his creditors and on the financial consequences of the divorce he was contemplating. As my relationship with Plug intensified and I started discussing transfer with him, Aaron grew nervous. He whispered of a financial relationship with Plug that went beyond free restaurant meals.

"Let me deal with Plug about your case. Don't even tell him you talked to me. It'll work out better that way."

I ignored the offer, spending more and more time with Plug as my classification drew near. Aaron's tactics changed. He warned me not to trust Plug, spicing his admonitions with revelations about Plug's instability, his drinking, and his financial straits. Aaron's hushed advice was now frequently accompanied with cautions against "saying a word to Plug." Whenever he could, Aaron joined in my conversations with Plug at the duty office door. I couldn't help but wonder what he was telling each of us that he wasn't telling the other.

Prison was tough enough without the constant, intrusive proximity of my mirror image. Despite the relative comfort, privacy, and freedom of movement on the work range, Millhaven was very depressing. The magnitude of my losses, the harm I had done, the regimentation, the loneliness, and the absence of meaningful choice still drove me to tears and desperation frequently. I fretted about my future, realizing that if Deena left me, I would have no home, no partner, and no income. Even my acknowledged abilities could work against me, as potential employers, friends, and lovers shielded themselves against a recurrence of my abuses.

On my bad days, I functioned in a daze of despondency that distanced me further from my range mates, who interpreted my black moods as an élitist haughtiness: "What's the matter, Melnitzer, you too good to talk to us?" and "Your shit stinks, too, just like mine" were variations of taunts I heard daily.

On the good days, I revelled in new horizons without the responsibilities and bugbears of the past. The disadvantages of my criminal record, I told myself, were merely worldly obstacles to overcome, not nearly as onerous as the awful secrets I had lived with for so many years.

My relationship with Aaron was a barrier to that new life. Aaron was an operator, and I didn't want to be one any more; sharing my days with Aaron drew me away from myself, from my need for solitude and reflection, to a medium of distraction, wily intrigue, material convenience, and temptation. Each moment I spent with Aaron was time in an emotional space I no longer wished to endure.

To Plug's way of thinking, however, Aaron and I were two peas in a pod: a pair of successful wheeler-dealers whose only sin was that we were caught, to whom jail was but a minor detour on the road to full enjoyment of our riches. We were, Plug admitted once, what he aspired to be.

Looking more dishevelled than usual, Plug barged into my cell, waking me from a mid-morning nap.

"Here," he whispered, shoving a brown shopping bag at me. "Hide these somewhere and give them to Aaron when he gets back from work."

"What's the matter?" I murmured, only half-awakened by this strange turn of events.

"That big inspection is today. The office'll be packed with bigwigs and guards. I don't want anyone noticing this stuff. You be quiet about this."

I was mystified, but initially unconcerned, guessing that the bag contained Saturday night's banquet provisions. But Plug's jumpiness had left its mark; I decided to check out the goods.

I stuck my homemade cardboard "ON THE THRONE" sign in the viewing pane of my cell door and drew the makeshift curtain I had fashioned from a bedsheet over the entranceway to my cell. As I reached for the bag, two cartons of American cigarettes fell out; inside, I counted six more cartons. The bag crackled as I handled it; I squirmed, as concerned with discovery by other inmates as I was about the guards. Shortages of staples abounded as we neared the end of the current pay period; the familiar crackling sound could alert the parasites to the availability of cigarettes or other canteen supplies in my cell. And eight cartons of cigarettes were enough to get me thrown in the hole for a month, forever labelled as a merchant, gambler, or drug trafficker. Minimum would be out of the question for a long time.

Why hadn't Plug turned the goods over to Aaron that morning? Or left the package in Aaron's cell? Was Plug setting me up to encourage my co-operation in Aaron's schemes?

The sinking feeling was familiar, reminiscent of the close calls I had dodged to keep my frauds going. But there was no comparison: I had done nothing wrong; I had nothing to hide. All I had to do was march straight to the warden and tell him the truth. Simple enough, if this wasn't prison — but it was. The guards had a code too; wherever I was incarcerated, staff would be looking to get even with me for ratting out one of their own. And the warden might not believe a convicted con artist.

In a convoluted way, I enjoyed the confusion. It was comforting to be innocent. Buoyed, I discarded my paranoia, shoved the cigarettes back under the bed and buried myself in Charles de Gaulle's biography.

At 11:30, Aaron, wearing a big grin, stepped into my house. I handed him the bag without a word.

"Help me look through these," he commanded, taking a carton out of the bag.

"Please, Aaron. Go unpack in your cell. I've had enough hide and seek for one morning."

"I understand, but I want to show you something. Let's take the stuff to my cell."

"You take it. I'll come in a minute."

I waited as long as I politely could. When I arrived in his cell, Aaron was watching *Global News*, an open pack of Marlboros on his desk beside a black institutional ashtray filled with butts and a live smoke. Still grinning broadly, he handed me a carton of cigarettes as he fished out another.

"Open both ends of the carton and take out the pack on each end."

"What's going on here?"

"Don't you like surprises?"

Grudgingly, I opened two cartons and showed the four end packs to Aaron.

"Keep going," he said, casually picking his cigarette out of the ashtray and keeping an eye on the television.

When Aaron removed an end pack from the fifth carton we examined, he smirked as he squinted into it, satisfying himself as to its contents by wiggling his index finger on the surface of the top pack. He held it up to me.

"See!" he exclaimed triumphantly.

"See what?"

"There's no cellophane on the package. Shame on you, my barrister friend. You, of all people, should notice little things like that."

"So what? The cigarette company fucked up."

"You really are a little naïve, you poor thing." Aaron chuckled. Still holding up the package, he opened it and peeled away the foil from its right side, revealing a greyish-brown substance that looked like cork.

"Jesus Christ," I exclaimed. "Hashish. That stuff's worth a fortune in here."

"It's worth five hundred bucks on the street. At least three thousand dollars in here," Aaron gloated.

"Three thousand dollars! Who are you going to sell it to?"

"You should know better than that. The stuff's just for me and my friends. It's cheaper and easier to bring it in in bulk than to buy it in the joint and let everybody know my business. Want some?"

"No, thanks. I don't do any drugs, you know that ... and you had no fucking business leaving that stuff in my room or even having me in here now. Christ, Aaron."

"There's no risk."

"No risk for you, you stupid f—" I cut myself short. *That's what I told my victims. I believed it too.* "Figure it out for yourself," I said in disgust, primarily at myself. "I'll see you later."

I stalked halfway down the hall before I turned around, returning to find Aaron standing over his toilet. Unconcerned. *Pissing on everybody.*

Aaron jumped as I asked without warning, "Did Plug know what was in the packs?"

"Of course not. That would jeopardize him. I wouldn't do that."

I couldn't understand why Aaron was applying for a transfer to Bath, which didn't share Beaver Creek's amenities or its relaxed "country club" atmosphere.

"Plug knows the deputy warden there," he explained. "He'll arrange for us to be out on passes half the week. Plug will come himself and take us, and you know what it'll be like with him. As long as we buy the booze, he won't care what we do. I've got a lot invested in Plug."

That was an invitation to work the system and turn prison to child's play. Without Plug's intervention, the hardships of Joyceville were a more realistic prospect than any minimum security camp. But I knew it was only a question of time before Aaron and Plug called on me to pay the piper, in currency far more expensive than money — a new dance of deceit that could continue long after my release.

My heart pounded as the temptation took. The sensation of choice was novel: since I could remember, I had felt trapped by misperceived necessity. Here was a chance to make a real choice, perhaps the first since I'd bought my way into the soccer games at the age of six. I understood Aaron, even sympathized with him as I saw through his mask. He wasn't my friend, but he couldn't help it; his life, whatever it was, had left him as alone as I had been; he needed me — another distraction to ease his forlorn, calamitous path.

"I'm sorry, Aaron. I'm going to try for Beaver Creek and take my chances."

"Why are you so stubborn?" Aaron protested. "Let me help you. You'll see what Plug can do."

"No, thanks."

"OK, it's your life, but don't tell Plug we talked about this."

Aaron's final words on the subject, echoing his life and mine past, convinced me I was doing the right thing. I set out to distance myself from my benefactor.

Party's over

When you live in secrecy, you think in secrecy.

JOHN LE CARRÉ

Four and a half weeks into my stay at Millhaven, I revelled in a long shower after a Monday evening workout. Twelve restful hours of sleep the previous night suggested an accommodating routine. In the ten days since I decided to dissociate myself from Aaron, I spent more and more time in my cell and with my new friend, Mickey, an architect turned entrepreneur serving three and a half years for cocaine trafficking; he had arrived on the work range about the time I got there. We worked together in the servery, where his quick mind and diverse interests brought welcome relief from the intellectual wasteland of prison kitchen banter.

The detachment from Aaron relieved the pressure from the other prisoners and eased the tension of my own ambivalence about him. For the first time since my arrest, I felt refreshed. The scalding spray wrapped me in a benevolent fog; its needle-point tingle on my skin exorcised the barriers to sensation that crisis had set in my pores. No one was in line for the shower, and I followed the steamy half hour with an icy blast that confirmed the basics of existence.

As I stepped out of the shower, barefoot and clad only in a

towel, Plug came around the corner.

"Julius, do me a favour and come around the duty office after you're dressed."

Plug had never used my first name before, nor was he in the habit of politely requesting an audience with a con. I dressed hurriedly; my years of dreading the unexpected made surprise unwelcome.

The range was quiet as I walked to the duty office. Dusk was the nicest time of day in Millhaven. The harshness of the fluorescent lighting mellowed, no longer conflicting with daytime's natural glow, and the shadows of the night textured the sterile passageways of the prison, softening their sounds and cushioning their eeriness.

Plug was alone, leaned back in his tilting chair thoughtfully examining the ceiling, his pudgy hands interlocked at the back of his head. I shut the door behind me as he motioned me to the chair opposite his. I folded my arms, waiting; the minutes went by sluggishly, until Plug finally looked at me, sadly, bringing his right index finger to his lips, rubbing them, then slowly licked the dryness away with his tongue, first the upper lip, then the lower. His Adam's apple twitched as he prepared to speak. I blinked as though I hadn't noticed.

"I want you to help me, Julius."

Looking away from the directness of my responding glance, Plug reached for a half-empty pack of Marlboros on the table. He crumpled the foil and tapped the open pack on the palm of his hand, reawakening my resentment when I had last watched a pack of Marlboros being opened, in Aaron's cell. Plug's action ejected two cigarettes into his hand.

"You want one?... I forgot, you don't smoke."

I took one anyway, accepting a light from Plug across the desk. I took a few puffs without inhaling, using the time to think.

"What do you mean, Plug? What can I do?"

"I'll lose everything if you don't help me. I'm three months behind on my mortgage. Everything's gone wrong since my business went down the tubes."

"What business were you in?" I asked.

"A business, it doesn't matter. I could have sold it all and quit this job. I hung on until it was too late. That's why I work all this overtime. I made twenty-five thousand dollars last year in overtime, but I can't stay ahead."

I empathized with Plug even while calculating the cost of boozing nightly: I knew all about doing it to yourself.

"I don't have any money, Plug."

"Don't bullshit me. I don't expect you to tell me, but don't bullshit me."

"I'm not, Plug. Have you asked Aaron to help?"

"Don't mention that fucker's name. He's holding me out to ransom after all I've done for him. Did you know he's on his way to camp?"

"Yes, he said he was going to Bath soon."

"Yeah, well, back in the fall they were going to send him to the clinic at Warkworth. I got his warrant pulled and I've pulled every string in the book to get him into Bath. He'll probably get out in the summer."

"I don't understand. You mean he's a sex offender?"

"Sure he is. He must have given you the same story about the big frauds in the States. Nah, he raped some kid in Kansas. She was just under age, no violence. It was chickenshit. I read the transcript. They bang you big for statutory rape down there."

"Doesn't he have any money?"

"There's something there. His father left him a trust or something. I'm not sure if Aaron controls it."

"Well," I asked, "why doesn't he help you? He told me he was going to give you a mortga——."

"So the fucker told you that, too. Doesn't matter. The way he goes on, everybody's starting to figure it out. I've got to get him out of here. Lobsters, steaks, garlic toast — too much."

Plug angled forward, touching his short legs to the floor for the first time that evening. He put out his cigarette with his shoe and hunched over, his elbows between his knees, his hands clenched just above his ankles. He stared ahead through me, then sighed.

"The cocksucker gave me something, but not what he promised. Now he says he'll give me the rest when he gets to Bath. Cocksucker."

"I'm sure he'll come through."

"I need money right now. My wife's driving me crazy. I never go home. She's getting calls all day from the bank. They want to repossess the house. My kid needs money for university next year."

"I don't know what I can do. I'd love to help you, Plug. You've been good to me. If you explain the situation, maybe I can give you some negotiating advice to help you deal with your creditors."

"I need fuckin' money, *now!*" Plug slammed his fist on the desk, once. "Look, you don't have to give it to me. Lend it to me. I'll give you a mortgage on my house. I'll pay it back."

"I can't, Plug. I don't need any more hassle and I don't have the money."

After pausing momentarily, Plug continued, softly now. "I've already put in a good word for you about Bath." A menacing offer.

"I don't want to go to Bath. It's too far for my daughter and my psychiatrist to visit."

"I thought it was funny that you didn't want to go to the Creek."

"I never said that."

"Never mind, you know where I got the information. You're better off in the Creek. It's nicer there, like a park. They're turning Bath into a program camp. Soon it'll be all sex offenders."

I shook my head. "I get it. Aaron doesn't want to go to Bath, does he? He has no choice. What a bastard."

"Don't worry, it'll be easier for me to get you into the Creek.

You don't need programs. Trust me."

"Plug, if you want to help me, I'd really appreciate it. God knows I can use all the help I can get. But I can't pay you anything."

"OK, OK, I understand. It's risky for me too, you know. I've only got a couple of years till I get pensioned off." Now Plug was pleading.

"It's not worth it."

"I don't want you to misunderstand. I'll do whatever I can for you. But it's hard to guarantee you won't go to Joyceville or the Bay, if you know what I mean."

"I know, Plug. The worst I can expect is what I thought was going to happen anyway. I always expected to go to a medium. But thanks. Let me know if I can help you out any other way. I'll be around. I'm not going on a holiday soon," I quipped lamely.

For the next few minutes, Plug apologized. He reviewed his many years with CSC, how things had changed, how he had changed, and the circumstances that had intensified his drinking, wrecked his marriage, and led to his relationship with Aaron and the conversation with me. "You know," he concluded, "I've never taken anything from a con. This was Aaron's idea, not mine." I had no doubt about the last part.

The nurse arrived at the barrier for pill parade, interrupting our uneasiness.

I stayed awake most of the night. Plug had played his hand and failed. So had Aaron. My refusal to enrol in their intrigues made me an outsider. I could jeopardize them both. How would they deal with it? Wedded to money as the tender of their being, would they believe I wasn't in funds?

At the extreme, they could arrange to have me silenced in fact or by threat, or have me transferred to a medium security prison immediately. None of those alternatives was likely: for the time being, I had no reason to hurt either of them; nor could they harm me without involving other inmates, to whose unstable temperaments Aaron and Plug would be in lasting debt. It was also unlikely that they would consult frankly, Plug having divulged Aaron's offence and Aaron having unveiled Plug's injudiciousness; each now had reason to mistrust the other.

Their best bet was to keep me happy. If I made it to camp, they could both claim to have helped me. I would be grateful, not vindictive, and they would be safe. If Plug wanted me in camp, he would lean to Beaver Creek; that would keep me comfortably distant from Aaron. When in danger, divide: Plug would live by that credo, as I had in his shoes.

Time to act. Tomorrow afternoon, when Plug came back to work.

I stood at the open doorway to the duty office, leaning on the threshold casually as Plug reviewed the day shift's reports.

"Plug, about last night. I —" An expectant glint in his eye.

"About last night," I started again, "I appreciate the opportunity and all you've done for me. I'm sorry I couldn't do anything to help you. Even if I had the money, it's not right for me any more."

My words drew his eyes away from mine, into the vacuum where our hearts sink. He was as gracious as he could be without looking at me.

"It's all right. Don't worry about it. We'll get you out to camp soon."

His state of mind was tailor-made for my pitch. "Like I said, Plug, I'd appreciate anything you could do to help. I've been thinking about it and I really prefer Beaver Creek. It's so close to Toronto, it would make my time a lot easier."

"I think you're right. I'll push for it."

"Thanks, Plug. You know, I'm grateful for everything Aaron's done and I like him, but I don't think it would be good for me to be around him."

"That's just what I was thinking."

"Thanks a lot. I've got to get to work."

"You lazy cunt. You haven't done an honest day's work yet. Get out of here." We both laughed. Things were returning to normal.

At lunchtime the next day, Aaron signalled me to his newly disorganized room.

"I'm leaving for Bath tomorrow morning," he announced.

One last feast to clean out Aaron's supplies. Lots of laughs, even a big hug when he left the next morning. Promises to stay in touch. "Power lunch" were Aaron's last words to me.

As Plug and I watched Aaron push his belongings towards the Dome in a grey A & D cart, a caress of relief unlocked my neck, shoulders, back, and upper arms.

"That was fast," I said.

"Had to be," Plug said, with a penetrating look at me. "For everybody's sake."

I was still enjoying my release from Aaron's overbearing presence when the call to see my CO came over the loudspeaker after dinner.

"Just be straight with her, and everything'll be all right," Plug advised on my way into Sharon's office.

Sharon's frame filled all of her chair, the glasses halfway down her nose bestowing a matronly appearance at odds with her inappropriately short black dress and ornamental leggings. My thick file lay beside the keyboard. I felt like a schoolboy come to the principal's office.

The classification process consists of document collection, which Bob Bigelow had expedited, an interview, a Penitentiary Placement Report and recommendation from the CO, all followed by the decision of the Regional Transfer Board of CSC and the approval of the receiving warden.

Sharon, having completed an outline of my personal history and my crimes, started our session with the remark that I was a "different kettle of fish, quite an experience for me."

"You mean that I'm a first-time nonviolent offender."

"Not just that. The length of your sentence for a property offence. Your accomplishments, your education, your background."

"Yes," I joked, "those are the things that got me the nine years."

Sharon giggled; with the ice broken, we got along famously. She was an intelligent, no-nonsense type, whose warmth surfaced with honest interaction. The interview centred on my life, its motivations, and the events that landed me in jail.

I had resolved to be logical and straightforward; emotion would only complicate matters. As I talked, I found, as I would find for many months each time I repeated my chronology, that I could not restrain my feelings. My masks disappeared in wandering thoughts, in inchoate and run-on sentences, and in abstract, tangential meanderings that had little relevance to our topic.

As we talked, Sharon typed onto a standardized template of the Penitentiary Placement Report that appeared on her computer screen, clearly visible to me.

"Now," she said two hours later, when we had exhausted my life and more, "where do you want to go?"

"To camp."

"I don't think that's unreasonable. Where's that letter from the Crown?"

Her question put to rest any lingering doubts I had about my plea bargain.

"Is this it?" she asked, pulling out a sheaf of papers I had never seen before. "Take a look."

What Sharon handed me was a five-page parole report signed

by RCMP Sergeant Ray Porter, who had taken the unusual step of filing the document a year and a half before I was eligible for parole. Not only were Porter's opinions consistent with the letter he had signed pursuant to the plea bargain, but he had gone out of his way to be fair.

> *Melnitzer was cooperative and straightforward in all his dealings with the RCMP as were his defence counsel. He readily supplied details and admitted to the offences he had committed. As well, he indicated he wanted to have the matter dealt with in a quick and efficient manner by the Court. He displayed a realistic attitude in that he was well aware he would likely receive a lengthy sentence on conviction ... all matters were expediently dealt with by the Court. Melnitzer's cooperation during the investigation, while not essential, saved the Force, the Crown and the Court considerable time, effort and expense.*

As I read Porter's report, Sharon found Hutchison's letter. I glanced at her, pleased with myself.

"Any particular camp?" she asked.

"Beaver Creek or Bath, but I much prefer Beaver Creek. It's closer for my daughter and my psychiatrist."

"That's what I'll recommend."

In my suppressed elation, I could not help but think that Plug had talked to Sharon in some detail, but I was uncertain: Sharon had a reputation for independence both with Bob Bigelow and with the inmates.

"When will this go to the Transfer Board?" I asked.

"I'll have it ready for your signature first thing tomorrow and submit it right away. They'll make a decision Tuesday and you should know by Wednesday."

"What are the chances the Transfer Board will accept your recommendation?"

"Hard to say. Usually what the CO says, goes. It's very unusual to send someone to camp on a nine-year sentence — but then, you're an unusual inmate."

Remembering my mistakes when we were first introduced, I accepted Sharon's equivocation good-naturedly. "I'd like to take that as a compliment" — I smiled — "but I'm not sure."

Sharon beamed back. "I'll do my best. I go to bat for things I believe in."

I believed her. "Thanks. Thanks for listening too."

Despite the favourable report and Sharon's support, my powerlessness didn't escape me: Sharon could have singled out my firing from V & C, which she did not mention, as evidence of my need for "a period of gradual adjustment in a medium setting"; or she could have opined that "the length of the offender's sentence requires a period of incarceration in a medium security institution in accordance with normal CSC policies." In either case, getting to camp would have been a long, uphill battle, likely fought from Joyceville while I processed my appeal.

Time after time, I witnessed inmates prejudiced by overreactions to trifling incidents, by personality conflicts with their case managers, by unjustified inferences from unproven facts, and by bureaucrats covering their ass or passing the buck. With the help of Bob Bigelow, a little preparation, and perhaps a dose of Plug's desperation, I would luck out — if the Transfer Board saw it Sharon's way.

Friday afternoon, after Sharon handed me her completed report for signature, I anticipated a relaxed weekend awaiting the final decision. Despite the slow general turnover at Millhaven, the luck of the draw had emptied many cells on our range. At least half the occupants were new arrivals, but the range's makeup had changed: Plug had replaced many of his "old cons" with greying, white-collar, first-offender types, some of them accomplished businessmen.

The remaining old cons, however, had noticed my distance from Aaron before he left and silently approved; I had also unwittingly earned the respect of my range mates the previous Saturday by taking over the dishwashing job in Joe's absence. Plug was off until Monday, out of town, unlikely to drop in. After the riots in J Unit and the anxieties of the past few weeks, the range seemed unusually still. Things were as good as they could have been.

My relaxed weekend was not to be: the impending sense of doom that infects those who carry buried secrets stays with them long after the secrets disappear, likely because the sense of doom preceded the secrets. Although I had nothing to fear, I couldn't believe that my up-and-up approach would pay off in a transfer to Beaver Creek. Sleep was impossible. Into the morning hours I castigated myself for not buying insurance with Plug and Aaron — and alternately soothed myself with my newfound scruples. There would be no peace at Millhaven. I needed out quickly.

Unchained

I know well what I am fleeing from
but not what I am in search of.
MICHEL DE MONTAIGNE

The good news came on Tuesday afternoon. "When are you going to ship me out, Sharon?"

"The list for Beaver Creek's cleared up," Sharon said, "but it's not up to me. There's a load going Monday. You won't be on that, but I'd say no longer than a month. I'll speak to Plug. Sometimes he can do something about the list."

No doubt Plug could do something about the list, but I didn't want to hear about it. He could still make trouble for me by holding up my transfer; that was unlikely unless his desperation escalated, or unless he expected me to show my gratitude now that I had witnessed his influence.

When I saw him on Friday morning, Plug's good humour had returned. "Everything worked out, huh? We'll get your ugly puss out of here soon."

"Thanks, Plug. Thanks for everything."

"Thank Sharon."

"I did, more than once. I appreciate your talking to her."

"I told you I'd do what I could."

I was grateful there was no more mention of what else Plug

could do for me. "You did."

"By the way, you cocksucker, have you been writing up appeals for guys?"

My range mates, whatever their opinions of me, were not above seeking free legal advice when it suited them. My lawyers, ex-cons, and guards at the EMDC and at Millhaven had cautioned against becoming a "jailhouse lawyer": aside from endless, no-win demands from the cons, CSC would mark me as a troublemaker. For the most part, I heeded the warnings for the first five weeks of my imprisonment. In the last week, however, I had drafted five transfer appeals on a borrowed typewriter. Someone in Administration, perhaps the unit manager, had concluded that the style could only be mine.

"Yeah, I felt those cons were getting a raw deal. Did I do something wrong?"

"No, you dumb fuck. You did something right for a change. They can't wait to ship you out of here. Do a few more and they'll take you out by chopper."

"Great. Thanks a lot, Plug, I've got to change and get to work."

I was a few minutes late arriving at the servery for my lunchtime duties. Sharon was at the kitchen's open service door.

"I couldn't find him," she was shouting to someone inside, over the commotion. "Tell him he's going to Beaver Creek Monday morning."

"Are you talking about me, Sharon?" I hollered as I rushed towards her.

"You're the man. They took somebody off the load to put you on. I'm off until Monday afternoon and I wanted to tell you before I left."

I walked to the duty office to tell Plug. He wasn't there. Jerrold, a recent inductee to CSC, was standing guard. "You're out of here," he said, pointing to the newly issued transfer list for Monday that hung on the wall near the door. The third name on the list was crossed out; mine was pencilled in — in Plug's handwriting.

Leaving is serious business in prison. Sometimes it is a return to the rigours or horrors of higher security, accepted with a show of defiant scorn. Those departures, directly from segregation, leave no chance for discussion or goodbyes.

Most often, leaving is a step to greater freedom or to freedom itself. That is why departures are, for the most part, ignored by the cons remaining behind; nothing, I found, made us more aware of our helplessness, of the singularity of our existence. Cons may pass their days with varying degrees of diversion in the modern prison, but we all lived to get out, to a reinstatement of choice; saying goodbye reminded us of a world to which we had no access save at the whim of others. Out there, we may choose not to join those who leave us; oh, we make excuses — our jobs, our children, our previous decisions, our responsibilities — but what we really mean is that we have chosen to have no choice and deep down, we know that decision can be changed. Not so in prison.

The loneliest men I saw in jail wandered aimlessly down the ranges looking for company on the night before their release. Their packing was long since done, a ritual safeguarding the irreversibility of their imminent freedom, an uncoupling buffer between them, their mates, and their surroundings. Prison is nothing to reminisce about — not with those staying behind — for the future has no meaning to prisoners who are not sure when their own will begin, as next Christmas has no significance to the dying. The mutual, chronic complaints that are prison's social adhesions are suddenly a foreign language to the departing, suspending the syntax of jailhouse repartee.

Most of the time, the apprehensions of those leaving prison are unexpressed, bringing, as they do, only covetous responses: "What are you worried about, man? You're getting out." What else could we say? A more equivocal response, impliedly acknowledging the possibility that freedom was not absolute, would shade and denigrate our reason for going on, adding to the meaninglessness of our day-to-day lives.

Some inmates dreaded an unfamiliar world that was uncomfortable even when it was familiar. Keith, a fifty-one-year-old who had spent nineteen of the last thirty-two years in jail, was unsure about leaving. Exuding the breath of a dried-out Bowery wino through the empty spaces between his teeth, he explained his feelings one month before his release:

> I got no friends, no family. If they put too many stipulations on my statutory, I'll stay. I'm comfortable here, institutionalized. I got a roof over my head and three meals a day. I laugh at the guys who complain about the joint nowadays. They don't know how good they got it.

Keith didn't come back. He didn't stay out, either. Less than a month later, he hanged himself. Suicides by the liberated don't count in CSC statistics.

Tony, a black man in his late twenties, was released at the end of a three-year term for theft, culminating a string of sixty-six convictions for nonviolent property offences over the ten years of his age of majority. Tony was an authentic street kid, but with superior intelligence — self-taught, well spoken, and polite, doing his time in the weight pit or with his nose in a book or newspaper. His hunger for knowledge led him to seek my company, pumping me for information about a myriad of subjects at every opportunity.

As his release date approached, Tony grew restless. He spent two difficult weeks convincing CSC to pay his fare to Vancouver, where, he argued, he could get a fresh start, avoiding the haunts of the transient, antisocial crowd in Toronto who passed for kin.

His plans for the West Coast were acts of desperation, contrived to divert his sense of hopelessness.

"What am I going to do? I don't want to spend my life in here. I've got no one out there, Julius, no one. Do you know anyone who'll give me a job? I'll do anything."

There was nothing I could do to stop his life from slipping away. Criminals aren't well situated to provide character references.

Tony left jail in a blizzard with $80 in his pocket, alone, refusing the warden's offer to house him until the weather broke. Hitchhiking was impossible in the storm. He stole a car and drove to Burlington, spending the night with another inmate's girlfriend. After robbing a jewellery store the next day, he led police on a high-speed chase that ended in severe injuries to himself. Tony didn't hang himself, but I thought he was trying.

Now it was my turn to leave.

My unique passage through Millhaven was the stuff of prison folklore, prison anger, and prison tragedy. My range mates' envy was evident: "All that time in the duty office paid off, eh?"; "Did you get Aaron to send written orders from Bath?"; "Smell any booze when you were kissing Plug's ass?" But not even an awareness that my hasty departure marked me as effectively as one of Spike's black eyes dampened my enthusiasm.

Citing a newly minted tradition that transferees must work as dishwashers on their day off, Bryce cancelled my day off on the weekend. I didn't mind the extra work, which kept me busy, nor the dishwasher's job, which distanced me from my co-workers and from the hundreds of inmates coming through the servery line three times a day. Jason came by to congratulate me, and Neil, one of the guards I had helped out with an insurance case, gave me a much-needed, affectionate pat on the back. Kevin was his apathetic self, and we spent a good deal of the weekend continuing our chess series as if nothing had happened. Otherwise, prison ritual merited only "When are you going?" and "Take it easy" as the measures of goodbye and good luck, though I had been in closer quarters with my range mates for almost two months than I had been with anyone apart from my immediate family.

I monopolized the telephone much of Saturday and Sunday, sharing the good news with my friends and family. Even Deena mustered a little warmth, a sense of relief I cloyingly interpreted as caring.

Sunday night, just before count, Plug summoned me to the duty office. "I'm glad everything's working out for you. You'll like it at Beaver Creek." He seemed relieved.

"So am I. What can I say? Thanks again."

"Here's my home phone number. I know a lot of people in the system — if you ever need any help."

I took the scrap of paper from Plug, intending to throw it out.

"That's nice of you. I'll keep it in mind."

"Good luck, you fat fuck."

"You too, Plug."

Prison-wise cons had warned me that sleep was futile the night before a transfer. For me, though, the move to Beaver Creek was the end of a long journey; the shape of new beginnings had not yet intruded. I slept deeply, merged in hope with the scorpion under my pillow.

Peter stood over my bed as I opened my eyes, his serious face locked in a questioning but benign gaze.

"I've been here almost a year. You're the only con I've ever had to wake to go to camp. Better get moving. Bus leaves the joint at eight."

Peter handed me a list of check-out procedures, asking that I sign and return it to him when I was finished. I got up, took a quick no-soap alternating hot and cold shower to rouse me, shaved, and dressed. I stripped the bed, remembering the scorpion under my pillow at the last moment, and stuck it in my mouth for what I hoped was the last time; finally, I packed my own meagre belongings in a box I had scrounged from Rock at canteen the previous evening. I dusted the cell, swept the floor, and mopped up. In all, it took forty-five minutes to move my life.

Bryce was the only one in the kitchen as I prepared a simple breakfast. I ate silently, still drinking my coffee when Peter ducked his head through the serving window. Bryce clung to my hand momentarily, as if he was sending part of his next twenty-five years away to a better place with me.

"There's no hellos or goodbyes here, Julius. Take it easy, buddy."

I had nothing to complain about as I sat on my bed one last time, organizing my belongings for ease of carriage. I was on my way to Beaver Creek, the country club of prisons; I had survived Spike, Toronto East, V & C, Aaron, and Plug; I was outlasting loneliness and redefining catastrophe; I had made better, more liberated decisions than I ever had in the knotted mesh I knew as normal; I had cheered like a kid for my favourite sports teams, kept myself busy and fit, and carved the outlines of my own rectitude. Why was I worried? Why did things going right trouble me? This time I deserved them, didn't I?

Plug's telephone number had turned up when I emptied the pockets of my surplus clothing that morning. I pitched the note in the open toilet. And hesitated. Unable to stop myself, I read the fading ink and recorded the information. I was still hedging my bets. No wonder I was worried.

"One step at a time," I told myself. "You've got to catch up on a lifetime."

In the meantime, I needed insurance.

At A & D, I sensed a renewed freedom: Bruce was nowhere to be seen; the A & D cleaner was the only inmate in the room, and he went casually about his work, joking with us about the glories of our destination; the officer on duty was equally informal, benevolently returning our stored property.

There was plenty of room to sit in the bullpen where we awaited our transport. The severity of my introduction to Millhaven seemed a distant whisper, as though our status as "minimum" had revived our humanity.

Only a few minutes passed before our escorts arrived. Without restraints, we walked alongside two guards to a paddy-wagon.

At 8:45 A.M. on Monday, March 30, 1992, I was on my way from maximum to minimum. *Right on schedule.*

Minimum

I never saw a man who looked
With such a wistful eye
Upon that little tent of blue
That prisoners call the sky.
OSCAR WILDE

The ferry to minimum was among the most uncomfortable and confining four hours of my incarceration, comparable only to the waits in the East and Millhaven A & D, and exacerbated by my impatience that went beyond the hard seating and the monastic surroundings. The sole view outside was through a plastic panel that separated the guards in the front seat from the prisoners, but that called for a ninety-degree jerk of the neck, which brought on nausea in minutes, more quickly at my attempts to read the ever-present paperback in my pocket. Even the Grey Goose had windows and regular bus seats. Was this mobile hole CSC's way of reminding us of our place?

We ate our box lunches in a McDonald's parking lot. I craved the coffee the guards brought back to the van; two months earlier, I wouldn't have given in to the insipid, watery concoction served at fast-food outlets.

At 1 P.M., our van turned off Highway 11 between Bracebridge and Gravenhurst onto an unpaved road, indistinguishable in its serenity from others I recalled from more memorable visits to the area. We passed the par-three golf course that has no connection with CSC, but has for years contributed to the exaggerated, media-inspired myths about the country club amenities at the Creek. Two minutes and another kilometre later, the flatlands of Muskoka airport with its array of single-engine planes appeared to our left, followed shortly by the entrance to Beaver Creek.

No sally port, no watchtowers, no fences, no uniformed guards, just an open barrier and a sign announcing Beaver Creek Institution, succeeded by the Corrections Service Canada designation in a discreet font. Our migratory jail turned right onto the camp's paved road, ending our journey beside the main building, a chalet-type structure the size of a small country hotel.

Spring slush overshadowed Beaver Creek's natural beauty on this cloudy day. The torn-up asphalt road that wound its circular way through the site suggested a logging camp in the muddy throes of construction. As I stepped out of the van, I could see a tennis court, a miniature-golf course, and a baseball diamond. The curious who approached to check out the new arrivals wore the breezy garb of vacationers, making it difficult to distinguish the inmates from the staff.

Perry, my first acquaintance at Millhaven, greeted me. "How ya doing?" He grinned in his bearish way. "Plug finally got you here, eh?"

Perry's friendliness surprised me. In the two weeks we spent together on the work range before Perry left Millhaven, our association had cooled. Perry had little use for Aaron, whom he regarded as an arrogant windbag. At every opportunity, Perry had reminded me of his role in my various liberations to the work range. I reacted with cordial and correct appreciation, but the time I spent with Aaron spoke clearly about where I believed my bread was buttered.

Despite Perry's business background, he and I had little in common. The feeble attempts I made at interaction were thwarted by his self-made man's distrustful, misplaced sense of inferiority to the educated. Perhaps Perry's present warmth sprang from the renewed opportunity to be my patron.

"I'm fine, Perry. You look great." Perry, no taller than five foot six, weighed two hundred and sixty pounds when we first met.

"I've lost fifty pounds. Most of it here," he gushed.

"Good for you."

"Actually, the food here is great. They have a pastry chef, and six or seven desserts every day. You can eat as much as you want, but I just made up my mind. And I started working out."

"Yeah, that really helps. Do you like it here?"

"It's great. Nobody bothers you. I'll tell you more about it later, at dinner. You better catch up to those guys."

Inside the main building, enormous picture windows, extending to the full height of the twenty-five-foot ceiling, dominate Beaver Creek's indoor visiting area. A nine-by-six TV sports screen, most often tuned to CMT, hovers over the far end of the spacious room, used by the Creek's one hundred and twenty-five inmates, one-fifth Millhaven's population, but twice the size of the cloistered, windowless visiting area Down Under.

In the duty office, which was separated from V & C by a glassed-in counter, a mustachioed man in his early forties who spoke with a Maritimer's inflection was briefing the new arrivals. He looked up as I walked in.

"Hi, I'm Conrad. I'm the Inmate Committee chairman. I'll be showing you guys around."

"I'm Julius."

"I know. Melnitzer. We heard you were coming."

A dissatisfied pause before Conrad went on. "I was just telling these fellows that you guys would be bunked in the six-pak for a few days."

I let the others ask the questions. Up to two weeks in the six-pak; two to three months double-bunked in the trailer; another three months single-bunked; finally, a permanent home in Accommodations.

"And you can't sign up for Accommodations until you're in a single in the trailer."

The voice behind me came from Leo, the slim, dark man who was sitting behind the standard office desk taking in Conrad's instructions. The hair on his lip failed to hide Leo's youthfulness, and his unnecessarily stern manner gave away his inexperience.

"Around here, we expect you to take responsibility for yourselves. Same as on the street. You find out what the rules are, you follow them. If you can't do that, you're not ready for the street."

Leo pointed to a pile of orange booklets in front of him. "Read these. It's all in there. No excuses if you screw up. If you have any problems, ask any of the staff — or Conrad."

"I'll be back in a while, Leo. I've got to see the warden," Conrad said. "If you guys can just hang around here for a while —"

"Not in the office," Leo interrupted, in a voice that delineated the order of command. "I've got to get some information from them. They can wait their turn in V & C; when they're finished, they can go back out there until you get back."

To pass the time, I read the innocuous letter-sized memorandums on the bulletin board that set out the rules for visitors. Visiting hours were six to ten on Wednesday evenings and nine to seven on weekends and holidays. Visitors drove past the open barrier, parked their cars, and announced themselves at the duty office, where they turned in their car keys if the officers remembered to ask for them. Apart from a cursory check of their bags, often limited to a verbal inquiry, the procedures were indistinguishable from those at a security-conscious resort. Rumour had it that road-weary travellers occasionally mistook the Creek for the campground they had missed down the road, arriving at the duty office to seek accommodation; from time to time, misguided tourists could be seen driving through the camp unhindered, trying to figure out what the place was. One story had a prisoner escaping from the Creek by calling a cab.

Inmates and their guests were free to stroll up the drive to the camp entrance and back again by the administration building, past the parking lots to the visitors' yard, which ran almost the length of a football field beyond the end of the main building in a grove of grass and tall Canadian pine and maple; the yard's amenities included picnic tables, barbecues, and a children's play area complete with slides and swings. Guests brought food in as they saw fit, cooking it indoors in the microwave or outdoors at the barbecues; junk-food addicts could choose from three well-stocked vending machines in the vestibule on the far side of the duty office, where two pay telephones were conveniently available. Visitors sometimes dissolved in tears of joy at the emancipation of their loved ones to this clean, informal, and mostly friendly holding station.

I browsed through the rule book I had taken from Leo's desk: cons could carry $30 cash, to be used at the pay phones or the vending machines; possession of greater amounts or of bills larger than $5 were grounds for expulsion. All the inmates were obliged to work, go to school, or participate in rehabilitative programs; the institution offered AA, NA, Coping Skills, and Cognitive Skills programs, as well as sessions with the part-time institutional psychologist, Dr. Mike Quirt. After supper, the cons were on their own until bedtime at eleven on weekdays, one in the morning on weekends, but could leave their rooms anytime to use the vending machines in the main building, the washrooms, the showers, or the microwaves in the housing units.

As Leo motioned me to the office, I anticipated warnings to put me in my place, pointed references to my stash to emphasize my incorrigibility, and reminders that I was a criminal like the others. But he stuck to a few questions confirming my particulars and my medication, though his wariness lingered. I resigned myself: there was little I could do to temper the intimidating effects of my name, my profession, and my crime. *Funny, now that the world's tucked me away, there's no place to hide.*

Leo identified my case management officer, Chandler (technically my CMO, commonly shortened to CO), and my LU, or living unit officer, Phil, the guard who was to be my day-to-day liaison.

Conrad returned just as Leo handed me a key to the six-pak — no more electronic cell doors — bluntly telling me it would cost $10 to replace a lost key.

"Inflation at CSC is terrible," I cracked. "I can cut a key for about one dollar on the street."

"What's a few zeros to a guy like you?" Leo said. "Conrad, do you feel sorry for this guy?"

"No way," Conrad relished, "and now that you're at Club Fed, think of it as a little holiday to get up enough strength to carry all that cash around."

In maximum, no inmate would have dared to join a guard in mocking an inmate's crime. There was a different Code here. I hoped that I could learn it with less heartache than the old one.

We left by the back door of the duty office, through the vestibule to the rear exit of the building. Facing us was a miniature-golf course, its green patches soggy after months in the northern snow. Through a window in the large building beyond the course, I could see a pool table and a vending machine

"What's in there?" I asked Conrad.

"That's the gym. The canteen, pool tables, music room, hobbycraft are in there, too," Conrad replied, leading us along the path to our quarters.

"And this is where you eat. The food's good," he added as we passed double wood doors with glass inserts that were the front entrance to the freestanding cafeteria and kitchen. Almost the entire side wall of the dining room was glass; napkin dispensers, salt and pepper shakers, and sugar jars were set on thirty round tables that took up most of the space in the airy room, each table encircled by four chairs. At the front of the cafeteria was a large, spacious kitchen separated from the eating area by a serving counter; on the far side stood a salad, condiment, and cutlery bar.

Ahead of us was an appealing two-storey wood structure, tinted red, its sloping roofs, rural architecture, and modular window arrangement all environmentally compatible with the surrounding cottage country.

"That's Accommodations," Conrad answered before anyone asked. "We're going to the trailer."

The trailer, four attached, unattractive, yellowish-white mobile homes configured much like a mini-Millhaven, contrasted unfavourably with neighbouring Accommodations, reminding me of the dichotomy between the work range and the rest of A Unit.

Inside the trailer, which housed two-thirds of Beaver Creek's population, a short hallway led to a dingy L-shaped vestibule with low ceilings, dirty walls, four aging wall telephones, decrepit armchairs, and linoleum scuffed beyond redemption. A once-white fridge stood in the vestibule's corner, its exterior competing with its stained, greasy interior whose odours wafted to our group when a brave inmate, dressed in a colourful headband, Benetton shorts, and a Pit Bull Gym sweatshirt, opened the door to retrieve a jug of milk.

The six-pak just off the common area, on the other side of the trailer's three ranges, was a welcome relief. The room was clean, amply ventilated by two windows that looked out on the woods, with a rural ambience that soothed. The uncrowded room had ample space for three bunk beds, six gym lockers, and three small desks. The standard door and the absence of bars, a toilet, or a sink distinguished the six-pak from a cell.

My roommates rushed off to check out the camp and find friends from previous bits. I stayed behind, making up a top bunk with the bedding that lay folded on each mattress. The day's emotions had drained me, and I tried to sleep, unsuccessfully. Restless, I wasn't ready to call my family, unwilling to let a festering despondency spoil their elation over my transfer.

The incipient hostility from Leo and Conrad and the shabbiness of the trailer were insufficient cause for my depths: Spike, Toronto East, Millhaven A & D, and my firing from V & C were all much ruder shocks; on the work range, I had become acclimatized to the harsh reactions of other convicts and the needling of staff. Still, sensations of hopelessness tingled over my body like a frozen Popsicle on a warm tongue, leaving me dazed and disoriented, on the verge of tears.

Slowly, it dawned on me that this was as good as it gets. At the EMDC, at Toronto East, at Millhaven, and on the work range, hope for something better loomed: but Beaver Creek was the end of the line. My day parole eligibility date, sixteen and a half months away, was almost as far off as it was when I was sentenced. All I had set out to do on that Saturday night in Montreal was done; all I had left to do was time.

To curb my restlessness, I explored the trailer's three ranges. A third of the Creek's population was double-bunked in twenty rooms on one range; the second range, the "long range," had twenty-five single rooms along a dark hallway; in contrast, a surfeit of natural light permeated the spick and span brightness of the "short range," occupied by long-timers who had chosen to stay in the trailer: either they were comfortable where they were, or their friends or lovers lived in the trailer, or they had enemies in Accommodations.

In the trailer's U-shaped bathroom, however, the chipped mirrors above the washbasins reflected an unbroken squalor, from the wet, sloppy floors cluttered with clammy toilet paper and paper towels to the streaked walls to the overflowing garbage bins. Several days' grime had accumulated on the sinks and counters, the showers were mouldy, three of the curtains were ripped and yellowed, the fourth missing; one toilet had overflowed, reeking of excrement that spilled onto the floor.

Disgusted, I went outside. Apart from a few people on the path between the housing units and the main building, and a few loiterers in front of the library, Beaver Creek was quiet and empty. As I had on my first day on the work range, I glanced around warily, expecting to be told where to go and what to do. But I was free to do as I pleased and walked uphill along the camp road, counting each step as a choice.

Three or four men came in my direction. It was pleasantly novel to be in a prison where everyone was dressed in street clothes. Too self-conscious to socialize in my prison uniform, I veered off to the trailer.

The only clothes I had with me were the white dress shirt, dark suit, tie, and black leather shoes I had worn to court. Deena was on vacation in Hawaii and would not be visiting for a month; Melissa had no access to my clothing or personal effects, which Deena had taken from our condominium and stored in her father's basement in North Toronto scant weeks after my departure — soon after she removed my pictures from the walls and the wedding ring from her finger, and changed the access code on the answering machine.

A long line at the cafeteria added to my frustration. I was in a fog, wondering where to sit, when someone put an arm around me.

"Man, you're spaced. I've been waving and hollering since you got in line."

At Millhaven, I knew Mickey only in greens; now, dressed in a bright plaid shirt and fashionable jeans, his cheeks reddened with the flush of days in the clean air, I was hard put to recognize him. His welcoming smile, robust carriage, and transparent pleasure at seeing me restored my equilibrium.

Mickey introduced me to Stan and Irwin, the two cons seated at his table near the back of the room. I noticed how easily the small talk came; in twenty minutes, I learned more about my dinner companions than I had learned in six weeks about many of my work range neighbours.

Mickey and I barely spoke to each other while eating, intimates unable to tailor their conversation to company. After dinner, we started around the walking track that surrounded the camp on three sides; its soft snow was packed from frequent use and comfortably navigable. A flat expanse of deeper snow, broken up by the footprints of inmate syrup collectors carving a trail among the maple trees, lay between us and Accommodations to our left. The path curved behind Accommodations and towards the small shack that housed the tapping operation. Periodically, yellow-tipped wooden boundary poles dotted our way.

"Beats the fence at Millhaven," I said vacuously, enjoying the unreality of a twilight walk in the woods of a prison. "Do you like it here?"

"Yeah, it's very slack. It's also small — everybody knows what you're doing. It's hard to keep to yourself."

I asked Mickey where he worked.

"I better tell you about that. Everybody knew you were coming, including the guy who's the head of the Work Board, Ted."

"What do you mean, everybody knew I was coming?"

"That's the way it is around here. You're a celebrity. Everybody's going to hit on you. Some people are envious that you spent only a couple of months in Millhaven on a long bit."

"Fuck," I muttered to myself.

"So," Mickey said, turning his head to me at my under-the-breath whisper, "you know what it's like. People talk in jail."

"What are they saying?"

"The usual stuff. You're a rat, you have friends with political clout, you paid somebody off. That sort of shit."

"Fuck, I'm not going to get away from this, am I?"

"Just keep a low profile. It'll die down when the next big shot comes here."

"Well, what about this Ted guy? What's his beef?"

"He was asking about you this afternoon."

"Like what?"

"Like what kind of shape you were in. Whether you could work on the bush gang. He said he was going to put you in your place. That you were an inmate like anybody else."

"I don't get it. What's his problem? Why has he got it in for me?"

"I went in front of the Work Board," Mickey explained, "but somebody warned me about him. The best thing to do is to agree with everything he wants. That's how I got my way."

"Like what?"

"I got assigned to the school. I work there as a tutor half-time in the afternoons. That's the place for you."

"How am I going to swing that with Teddy the Terrible after me?" I asked.

"Just play along with him. Try to get half-days in the school and do the rest of the time wherever he wants you. After a few weeks, it's easy to switch."

We walked past the trailer, then up the rise behind Beaver Creek's famous swimming pool, in reality an old reservoir destined for demolition; we picked our way along the outskirts of the baseball diamond and the single tennis court, trying to avoid the muddy pools that had accumulated as the melting snow trickled from the woods to the low-lying outfield.

"Anything I can do to smooth the way?" I asked.

"Tomorrow, I'll take you to the school and introduce you to the teachers, Janna and Eddie. Your chances are better if they go to bat for you at the Work Board."

"Who else is on the Work Board?"

"The guys who run the different departments. Works, the carpentry shop, the steward from the kitchen, the microfilm guy. Microfilm's not a bad place to work. Only place with air conditioning in the joint."

As we completed our circle of the camp, returning to the trailer by the paved road, Mickey explained Beaver Creek's pass system to me.

"After thirty days, you're eligible for group ETAs. Better put in for them right away. They can take two months to process."

ETAs were "escorted temporary absences," but I'd never heard of group ETAs.

"They also call them institutional passes. It just means you go out in a group. In the winter, they rent the hockey rink in town, they take guys to church and AA meetings, movies once a month, shopping passes. And the camp has sports teams that play in the community leagues. Let's have some tea."

Mickey's room was at least twice the size of the cells at Millhaven. Single beds bounded either side of the room; between the beds, a cluttered metal desk faced a large window, which looked out on the forest behind the trailer. On the sill, bottles of juice, jars of milk, fruit, and other perishables took advantage of Canadian temperatures. At the foot of each bed, a green, seven-foot-high metal locker commanded the corner, with additional storage space on two tiers of open metal shelving on the side walls. Despite the chewed-up linoleum floor and the fluorescent lighting, the shopworn room was cosy.

Thirty minutes later I filled out the pass forms near the telephones in the main building's vestibule, dropping the completed documents in the Inmate Requests box opposite the library.

The library was inviting, though small, and I walked in. Its wide armchairs, low lighting, and magazines strewn casually over the reading tables gave off no hint of prison. The book selection was a disappointing, disorganized collection of paperbacks, but the magazine rack was current, featuring everything from *Time* to *Sports Illustrated* to *National Geographic,* as well as an assortment of specialty literature, like *Omni* and *Byte.* Sections of the *Globe and Mail, Toronto Star, Toronto Sun,* and *Gravenhurst Banner* lay about the room.

I leafed through the newspapers, unable to read, my sense of well-being disturbing my concentration. Browsing in the joint was pleasantly animating in its dispersion, though tiring for its novelty. I dozed.

The scent of *eau de cologne* from the delicate hand that shook me awake made me think I was at home.

"Worn you out already, have we?" The pixie face in the pageboy haircut giggled.

I blinked to an uncertain awareness, momentarily lost in that zone of decision where we sort dreams and reality.

"This is Earth, Beaver Creek Station. I'm Sue." Another giggle. "It's close to eleven. Time to get back to the trailer."

"Sorry."

"No problem. Lots of time."

Unwilling to let go of my pleasant daze, I floated to the six-pak. My roommates were asleep, and I undressed in the dark, thankful I had made up my bed earlier. I left my shirt on and tucked myself in, leaving Sue's reassuring fragrance to lull me back to a cosmos unconcerned with the cleavage of fact and fiction.

Getting organized

Man, you are free to define yourself.

DR. ALBERT ELLIS

CSC has named its school system "Acheron College"; "Acheron" translates as "River in Hell" — a rare smidgen of humour in the CSC bureaucracy, or else a veiled acknowledgement of the verities of the correctional system.

After breakfast the next morning, Mickey showed me through the school's computer room dominated by fifteen PCs and a half dozen printers; several students were at work on the computers.

"Listen, I want to talk to you about Ted," Mickey said as we headed for the school office at the back of the building.

"What's going on?"

"He's still asking about you."

"Maybe I should go and talk to him first. Make him feel important so he doesn't have to show off to the Work Board."

"Might be worth a shot."

Mickey knocked on the solid door to the school office; a pleasantly overweight, very pretty, freckle-faced short-haired blonde woman in her late thirties or early forties opened the door.

"Hi, Mickey." She extended her hand to me. "You must be Julius. I'm Janna."

I took to her openness. "Pleased to meet you."

"Eddie's in, so we can talk to you together. Come on in."

Eddie, average-looking in every way but for the hint of an alert deficiency, sat at a desk in the tiny office, inputting data. He didn't turn around until Janna tapped him on the shoulder.

"You're the lawyer," he said.

"Yes, hoping to be a teacher."

"Well, tutoring is a voluntary position. You can only get in the school by being a student."

Mickey helped out with this unexpected development. "Julius wants to learn computers, but, if he gets in the school, he'll tutor on a voluntary basis."

"Do you have teaching experience?" Eddie asked.

"I've taught all over the place: high school, community college, police college, university. I don't have any training, but a lot of experience."

"You should come to our Laubach Literacy program tonight and get some training," Janna said. "It's a little different teaching at the elementary levels here."

"Oh, yeah, I forgot to tell you about that," Mickey offered. "I go every Tuesday night from seven to ten. The coffee and doughnuts are great."

"Sure. I'd like to keep busy."

"With all your education," Janna said, "it will be hard to get you into the school. They won't want you to take up a place."

"Can't they use good teachers? I don't imagine there's that many of them in here."

"Actually, we have plenty of good tutors," Eddie said dismissively, reminding me to watch myself.

"Oh, well, I'll be happy to come here when there's a spot open," I replied subserviently — and effectively, judging by Eddie's sudden change of heart.

"We'll try to get you in half-days. Ted will probably go for that."

"Great," I replied. "I'll give it a shot at the Work Board."

Outside, Mickey chastised me. "You can't come on that strong around here."

"What do you mean?"

"You're intimidating enough without telling them you've taught everywhere. They won't want you around."

"I don't understand, Mickey," I pleaded, dreading the tension of Millhaven all over again. "Don't they want qualified people?"

"Not more qualified than them. You don't have to be a genius to work here. You don't have to do a good job. There's no challenges in this environment and they don't like cons who go looking for challenges. You're an inmate, you do what you're told."

"OK, OK, what do you want to do now?"

"Let's go eat," Mickey suggested.

Stan, our table mate, was on his way out of the cafeteria as we arrived. "Out looking for a job? What job did you do at your last joint?" Stan asked.

"I worked in the kitchen at Millhaven Reception."

"They sent you right here from Down Under, did they? Must be a short-timer."

"No," I bragged, "I'm doing nine. I was just in Millhaven for six weeks."

"Oh, yeah?" Stan asked, showing no emotion. "Lucky. See you later."

Alone at our table, Mickey's hushed mood hung over our dinner. "It's all over camp by now," he said, out of the blue.

"What are you talking about?"

"What did you tell Stan all that shit for?"

"I just told him the truth. He asked."

"Julius, you don't understand. This place might not look like a prison, but the politics are worse than Millhaven. There's only one hundred guys here and everybody's into everybody else's business."

"So?"

"So some of these guys have waited for years to get to camp. They'll hate you for beating the system."

I picked at the rest of my meal in silence. Obviously, I didn't understand myself or the way I came across well enough to avoid the pitfalls of what was turning out to be just another prison.

Mickey reported to his afternoon job as the camp electrician; I went to the duty office, anxious to firm up Hans's plans to visit me.

"Melnitzer," blared a voice behind me.

Turning back, I faced a husky, grey-bearded man, wearing a baseball cap, jeans, work boots, and a red lumberjack coat.

"You're Melnitzer, the lawyer, aren't you?"

"Yes, I am," I replied stiffly.

"I'm Ted. You're at my Work Board tomorrow, aren't you?"

"Yes."

"Well, I need a guy to go around and pick up the recycling boxes. It may not be the kind of thing you're used to, but around here, you have to do what comes up."

"Sure, I'm here to work. Whatever I can do to help."

"The job doesn't take that long," Ted continued, "so I also want you to help the guys in the maple syrup operation for the next few weeks. Empty the buckets whenever they're full, depends on the weather. They'll call you when they need you. Could be any time of day."

"No problem. Whatever you say." But I didn't relish the idea of inmate bosses.

"Think you're strong enough to haul those buckets through the snow? You're pretty big, but I don't suppose you've done much physical labour. Spent most of your life behind a desk?"

"I work out regularly and I'll do my best.... I was thinking, though, that, in between, I could tutor in the school, and I wouldn't mind learning a little computers."

"You're pretty educated. Everybody wants to go to school to avoid working. They don't do anything down there."

"Just when I'm not doing my other jobs. Mostly, I'd tutor. I think Eddie and Janna think I could help."

"We'll try to put you down for half-days. I'll think about it."

"Whatever you decide. I don't want to cause any trouble."

"I think we can work it out."

The collect phones in the trailer were disconnected until suppertime, but the pay telephones in the vestibule worked like any other pay telephones, amenable to credit card calls and accessible all day. The staff made futile attempts to restrict the use of these phones. Oddly, that little triumph of us over them symbolized the difference between maximum and minimum: a reluctance to charge inmates over minor breaches (taking a walk just beyond the boundaries of the camp) naturally allowed for abuses, much as society, in the consensus of tolerance between the governing and the governed that acknowledges their indivisibility, selectively enforces its myriad rules of conduct (driving slightly over the speed limit). This symbiotic coalition recognizes that hierarchy is a function of human interaction, not its touchstone; at Beaver Creek, it helped reintegrate prisoners to society — paradoxically, by keeping them ahead of the rules.

Strohm was the correctional supervisor, or CS, on duty that morning — a tweedy, mustachioed man in his mid-thirties, casual in manner, who, with a pipe in his mouth, would have blended effortlessly into New England campuses. He and Sol, the other CS, were the camp's security chiefs.

"I don't think there will be a problem seeing Dr. Arndt privately," Strohm said. "I'll let you know in about a week, after I clear it with the deputy warden."

Strohm seemed sincere, out of place in his apparent understanding that promises to inmates meant something. "How are you doing around here?" he asked, solicitously.

"Fine. It's quite a change from Millhaven."

"I bet. Did you have any trouble at Millhaven?"

Fortunately, I was reborn about six weeks earlier. "No, why would I? I keep to myself."

"Guys with money sometimes have trouble in prison. People muscling them, that sort of thing."

"I don't have any money."

"That's your business. If the cons think you do, it can be a lot of trouble."

"Not for me."

"Good. I'm glad to hear that. You shouldn't have any trouble here, but, if you do, come see me and I'll take care of it."

I turned to go. "Where's A & D?"

"Right now they're using the nonsmoking visiting room, around the corner, you'll see the double doors out by the phones. Since they had that fire over at stores, A & D's a mess."

Several months earlier, three inmates had looted the canteen's entire store of cigarettes, burning down the stores building to cover their tracks. They were caught within three hours. Initially, the swift capture was attributed to the camp's extensive network of PC informers. Further investigation revealed, however, that the Three Musketeers had brought capture upon themselves: the pyromaniac who set the fire was still at the scene admiring his handiwork when the guards arrived; Genius Number Two, in an act of unprecedented civil conscience, alerted the volunteer fire department *before* the alarm went off; Genius Number Three, an entrepreneurial prodigy, was selling stolen cigarettes to the spectators drawn to the blaze. So much for the quality of criminal at Beaver Creek.

At 3:30, the mail line formed at the duty office's back window. The inmates' eagerness and the emotions on their faces as they received their letters or the news that they had none spoke volumes about their hermitage, their dependence, and their feelings about being in prison — any prison, even Club Fed. Mail call was a reminder that no matter how good it got, it was never good enough. But at least some of us had reason to line up; almost half the camp had no such reason: they couldn't read, couldn't write, or had no friends or relatives; they managed, for the most part, by forgetting the world that had forgotten them.

From here on, until I left jail, my correspondence sustained me. I had been writing steadily, religiously pumping out at least one handwritten letter a day since my sentencing. I wrote once a week to Melissa, Deena, and my mother, and responded promptly to my steadily growing incoming mail. Melissa wrote steadfastly, as did many friends, old and new, from all over the world. Writing was becoming my instrument of growth, of self-realization, of external discovery, and eventually, of self-love.

By the time I fell asleep that night, Beaver Creek had taken shape: I could imagine the parameters of my existence for the rest of my sentence, picture the places of work, of play, and of rest, and configure my days and nights. The concrete visualization of my activities relaxed me, because I could not conceive of living without doing. Doing was not — had never been — my expression of being: doing *was* being, through the process we call routine, or habit. Creatures of habit, as I was, are refugees from the present: routines become the substance of life, the pillars of safety that keep us from the exploration and risk our self-doubt denies us. When we venture to the fringes of vulnerability, routine is our tag-team partner, always there, always eager to take its place at centre stage, always allowing us to recede to our shelter beyond the ring of real life.

Club Fed

Life has turned into television for me.
I'm watching but I can't figure it out ...
JEAN CUMMING

The Work Board met after lunch on Wednesday. With a half-dozen others, I waited at one end of the cafeteria while the board deliberated at the other end, behind rectangular tables arranged for the occasion. Facing the board stood a single wooden chair, underscoring the servility of the "subject inmate" and prompting the effect of galley slaves in the chair's occupants.

Although inmates were otherwise called alphabetically, I went last: Ted, clearly in charge, had saved his conquest for dessert. The show came off as conspired: half-days in the school, half-days in forestry, doing the recycling rounds. Throughout, Eddie didn't open his mouth, as though we had never met, leaving me mindful that his alert deficiency was cross-wired with a short-circuited backbone and a streak of insincerity.

I left the Work Board looking for Mickey, anxious to tell him the good news. Janna hailed me in the computer room.

"Did you hear your name on the PA?"

I hadn't. "How long ago?"

"Ten, maybe fifteen minutes. They want you at the duty office."

Two months in jail hadn't freed me from expecting the bottom to drop out, but the news was good: I was moving to the double-bunked range, a few doors from Mickey.

My room was identical to Mickey's, twin beds, twin everything, double the space of the cell at Millhaven. I carried the first of two loads in and made up the bed, happy to see that my roommate had a colour television; the Creek, unlike Millhaven, did not supply TVs for the inmates' rooms. I made a mental note to ask Deena to bring in one of the eight we owned.

The ample space in the room and the large bulletin board allowed me to surround myself with remembrances that were contraband in the bucket and at Millhaven: one picture of Deena and three framed pictures and at least a dozen snapshots of Melissa; my "World's Greatest Dad" coffee mug; my "Superdad" sweatshirt; packets of fruit-flavoured herbal tea Melissa had lovingly sought out in the health food stores; and an accumulation of greeting cards from my daughter, including my favourite: *Love Does Not Dominate, It Cultivates.* It's tough, I thought, patting the scorpion in my pocket, when your daughter is more mature than her father.

Sherman, my roommate, announced himself at 10:30 P.M., through the daze of my half-nap. Scrawny and hirsute he was, with a moustache and sideburns contrived to hide the baby face that reduced his twenty-eight years to teen status.

"Fuckin', what's up, stud? I'm your new partner." He stuck out a bony hand.

"I'm Julius."

"Where'd you come from? Fuckin' Wallyworld? I heard some cons came from there."

"Our bus stopped at Warkworth and picked up two guys. I came from Millhaven Reception."

"Fuckin' A. I just got back from there myself."

"Back?"

"You bet. The Man sees me outside a bar in Gravenhurst and

charges me. Good thing I had the brains to ask for a urine test when they put me in the hole. Bobby had no trouble beating the charge."

"Bob Bigelow is your lawyer?"

"Fuckin' yeah. He does good for me."

"He's my lawyer too."

"Fuckin' A, stud, fuckin' A, that fuckin' Bobby, he's a mean legal machine."

Three "fucks" in a single breath were living proof that caricatures are not inventions; otherwise, Sherman seemed harmless enough. Now in the eighth year of a ten-year bit for a date rape committed when he was eighteen, Sherman had come to Beaver Creek on a "residency," a form of statutory release where the inmate returns to a minimum security facility nightly.

The precise rules of residency were unclear, a constant source of jurisdictional friction between Sherman's parole officer and the camp staff, who resented Sherman's special status and general exemption from their supervision and rules. Sherman's institutional history as a drug user and trafficker gave Beaver Creek security the excuse they needed to harass him. Whether the harassment was justified or merely the venting of despotic frustration was unclear to me. On the one hand, Sherman swore that his relationship of six months with the welfare-dependent alcoholic mother of four young offspring of four different fathers had opened his eyes to life's fuller possibilities: Terry bore his child and, Sherman said, he would risk nothing that jeopardized his residency. On the other hand, Sherman obsessively set booby traps to ascertain whether our room had been searched, was often found in the company of the camp's most notorious drug users, and forayed regularly to the woods behind the trailer between the infrequent nighttime counts.

I drafted Sherman's grievances, advised him on dealing with his parole officer, the guards, and his wife's problems with her ex-husbands, ex-boyfriends, and ex-occasional lovers; I played father confessor on his bad days and lent him money, cigarettes, and canteen when he was short. In return, Sherman let me use his TV and brought pizza, Chinese food, and odds and ends that I needed from the street. When he was there, which wasn't often, he was the perfect roommate. I might as well have been single-bunked again.

With four days to myself before starting work, I slept late, spent the afternoons in the almost empty computer room writing letters, checked out the gym after dinner, played Scrabble with Mickey, and watched TV on Gravenhurst Cable's thirty-three channels. Deena was still in Hawaii, and I relaxed, as though by going away, my wife couldn't get further distant; Melissa was busy writing exams.

Having no visitors to share my relief made for a sad first weekend at the Creek; the blaring PA seemed to call everyone but me to V & C. I comforted myself with Beaver Creek's proximity to Toronto, looking forward to the promise it brought of regular guests. In the meantime, I participated in the pool and athletic competitions that, with card tournaments, were regular weekend highlights at the Creek.

Mickey and I got to know each other better. Sacrificing unmanly tears for the choked-off words he tried to bury with a fixed gaze at the complexities of our Scrabble board, he talked of his common-law wife of three years, Pat, and the hardships she had endured by sticking with him.

Mickey wanted wealth, quickly, and his capitalist politics put him over the right horizon of the political spectrum, apart from a narrow streak of civil libertarianism based on his hatred of the police, who had beaten him badly on his arrest. Mickey showed me pictures: I cringed, recalling the brutality of the Barrie police from my days as a criminal lawyer. Ill at ease with the anger Mickey's plight aroused in me and my helplessness, I changed the subject.

"I guess what bothers me most about being in jail so far is

missing Melissa's graduation," I complained.

"Put in for a UTA," said the always pragmatic Mickey.

"I can't. I'm not eligible for unescorted passes until my day parole date."

"When's your day parole?"

"August 1993."

"Maybe she'll flunk," Mickey quipped.

"Not funny." Since my arrest, I had fretted about its impact on Melissa's schooling.

"Why don't you apply for a CE to Melissa's graduation?"

"A CE?" I asked.

"Citizen's Escort. A volunteer from the community takes you instead of a screw. CSC likes it because it saves on overtime."

"How am I going to find a citizen escort? I don't know anybody around here."

"There's a list. The guys who go on them regularly can give you the names of the good ones. If you're worried about it, ask for a staff ETA or a CE."

"Mickey," I argued, "I'm only four months into a nine-year sentence."

"They can only say no."

I filled out the application that night: "My daughter is the most important thing in my life," it started. That was true. No conscious imperative. No manipulation. No mask.

Hans's Easter Friday visit perpetuated my awe at his unnumbed compassion through thirty years of practice. A hug, which I needed badly, came easily to the Freudian bear of a man, accompanied by a warm smile and sparkling brown eyes.

We talked for two hours in the classroom downstairs. "Julius," Hans said when it was time to leave, in the Old World accent that complemented his big heart, "you know I do a lot of forensic work and I know jails and the system. Usually, 'correctional system' is a misnomer; it really is a penal system. In your case, 'correctional' might be appropriate. You've come a long way."

Visitors occupied me most of Easter weekend, my second at the Creek. Melissa, Joan, and Jules, an old friend and one of my victims, dropped in at different times. In a quiet moment, as we walked back and forth along the roadway in front of the administration building, I told him about the changes I felt.

"I'm glad for that, Julius," he reflected. "It always bothered me that someone with your intelligence didn't use it more kindly."

"What do you mean?"

"It's just the way you talk," Jules fumbled, as if he had said too much already. "You put people down."

"We've kidded around as long as I can remember."

"Yeah, but it's not a fair fight."

"I don't mean anything by it," I said.

"That's not the point. You do it. Not just to me. I've got a pretty thick skin, you know."

Jules lowered his eyes. "This is hard for me, Julius," he went on, in a hushed voice almost lost in the spring breeze. "I know you didn't mean to lose my money, either. I still have the cheque with the return. But you didn't have any right to take the chance. Don't get me wrong. I'll always be your friend. It's just that you were as reckless with the money as you are with your mouth."

"I'm sorry." I was, but ended the conversation to assuage the pain — his, as well as mine.

Deena had visited twice at Millhaven, oases in an otherwise deteriorating situation. After her first visit at Millhaven, she reacted badly to my over-the-phone pressure for another visit soon, insisting on time for herself. I cut back my phone calls and letters, in the hope that giving Deena her own space would strengthen what remained of our relationship — and by way of cushioning the blow if it didn't. That seemed sensible when no postcard came from Hawaii; Deena hadn't written since we parted. But her vacation had mellowed her, and for a few weeks we talked as friends. Her busy schedule, however, split her between her legal practice and her budding acting career, made the timing of her first visit to Beaver Creek uncertain.

Weekdays at Beaver Creek were almost as relaxed as the weekends. Like most federal penitentiaries, Beaver Creek has an unemployment problem: a "job" is really a "position," not "work"; few of the camps jobs were full-time in any real sense — a lousy model, I thought, for inmates returning to the street after a prolonged absence.

Having properly asserted himself, Ted became my protector, taking every opportunity to coach me on the ins and outs of getting along in camp and keeping me up to date on the gossip about me. His own unhurried pace made him oblivious to my undemanding workload: he spent his days in the camp bus reading the newspaper, while his charges, the bush gang, worked in the community and countryside cleaning highways, clearing trees and trails, cutting grass in city parks, and at other volunteer activities. For a few weeks, I reported to Ted at eight in the morning at the Forestry office, until he made it clear that he had no use for formalities.

My tour of the recycling boxes in the camp took no more than twenty minutes a day, at a time of my choosing; soon, I learned that pickups were necessary only twice or three times weekly. As for my duties in the maple syrup operation, two weeks went by before I responded to a surreptitious request from Andrew, the inmate in charge of the tapping crew. But the call wasn't to work: Andrew wished to discuss his legal problems in seclusion. From then on, the call-ins were infrequent, rewards for my free advice. When I did help with the sap collection, the work was as enjoyable as it was strenuous: sap runs only in warm, sunny weather, bringing welcome relief from the school's muskiness.

After completing my recycling duties, which took no more than twenty minutes, I reported to school, staying there most of the day. "Reported" was another Beaver Creek misnomer, for Eddie, an administrative disaster, rarely took attendance except in hindsight as payday approached. Most students and tutors wandered in and out of the computer room at will, with Janna doing her best to give meaning to the term "education" by doing as much teaching as she could while trying to keep Eddie organized. In the months I was at Beaver Creek, Eddie taught only one class, a two-week course in basic computer hardware, which lasted for five working days before he lost interest — four and a half days after his half dozen students, who lost interest in the first half hour on the first day; Eddie, it seemed, had his set tuned to the wrong channel even when it was on. Absent any meaningful structure but Janna's valiant efforts, many inmates assigned to the school whiled away the hours playing pirated computer games.

Unusual bursts of activity transpired at month's end, when CSC reports came due and long-awaited completion certificates were finally handed out to oft-snickering students: Eddie was known to award grades based on his quotas without reference to the curriculum.

My own teaching load was minimal, never more than one or two private literacy and high school math lessons daily and a bit of marking for Janna. As word of my background got around, the inmates who were taking university correspondence courses showed themselves, and soon I was helping them with psychology, economics, and business studies.

The literacy tutoring was rewarding and frustrating in turn: Janna's persistence paid off in some remarkable successes, but more typically, students showed up eagerly only for their first few lessons;

as the work became more trying, the dropout rate accelerated.

All this left me with free time on my hands, and, true to form, I developed a routine, starting the day by writing letters on the school computer. My correspondence, for the most part a review of my life and my losses, was so draining that I could write for no more than an hour or two before quitting, emotionally spent, taking up the rest of the morning with consulting work.

In the months between arrest and sentence, I had, trading on my reputation as a marketer, started a small business consulting practice, motivated by financial need, by a desperate urge to feel useful, and by the opportunity afforded by a few friends who recognized my abilities and my desire to be busy. Several of my clients sent work to the Creek for me: the camp accepted courier deliveries and faxes, and the money I earned was a welcome bonus for Melissa, who nonetheless spent much of it looking after my needs.

In the afternoons, I concentrated on computers. Within two months, I developed an excellent working knowledge of numerous applications and was well on my way to proficiency in several programming languages. That was enough to make me a useful resource in the computer room, and, informally, I took over elementary problem-solving tasks, freeing up Janna and Eddie. The arrangement left me with a great deal of flexibility in the organization of my day, interrupted only by periodic, short inquiries from the students.

Near the end of April, when Janna asked me to draft a literacy grant application to Ontario's Ministry of Education, Eddie agreed to put an outdated computer in the library: our silent understanding was that the computer was for the use of all inmates, but its availability would not be advertised. Inevitably, some inmates, ever alert to nuances of favouritism, realized that I controlled access to the library computer. That was a no-no: inmates didn't supervise other inmates.

The multi-acre camp and relaxed atmosphere made it easier to escape the resentment than at Millhaven, so I ignored it. I shouldn't have.

Thoughts of Spring

You are free and that is why you are lost.
FRANZ KAFKA

Within a fragile membrane, my good spirits persisted through April. Emotional and physical subsistence were no longer in issue, as they had been Down Under, where bare existence and emptiness were spiritual partners; at the Creek, existence shed its barrenness, gorging on the reawakening of initiative, learning, diversity, and spontaneity, allowing day dreams and pretence. Although emptiness and its ingredients, isolation and estrangement, were never far away, quick to assert themselves and to displace the overlays of diversion that kept them at bay, my thinking grew more expansive, positive, and hopeful.

On a Thursday evening three and a half weeks after my arrival at the Creek, I found myself happily engrossed in my activities and routine, despite a discouraging game of Scrabble against an inmate with grade-school education who had memorized every word in the Scrabble dictionary during his nine consecutive years in the penitentiary. Mickey had again declined an invitation to play, intent on solving the most recent programming puzzle on his laptop, but had invited me back to his room for our now habitual ten o'clock tea break.

Three or four cons stood by the open door to Mickey's room;

from within came sounds of a scuffle and the agitated voices of Mickey and Stan. Stan was six foot four and well conditioned, outweighing Mickey's five-foot-seven frame by at least forty pounds. Mickey was surviving, keeping his head low, his arms in front of him, fighting off Stan's jabs by charging him with the whole of his compact, solid body. Apart from a reddening around Mickey's right eye, neither seemed hurt, and both were tiring.

"What's going on?" I asked Coco, the psychopathic, handsome bisexual Québécois who was nearing the end of his thirteen-year term for several violent rapes — including a stint in the SHU following his sexual assault on a helpless seventeen-year-old in Quebec's Archambault prison.

"It's a beef, buddy."

"Stop the fight, Coco." I was worried that, as the combatants tired, Stan would use his size to advantage.

"It's their beef, man, nobody's business, eh?"

"I know, but some rat must have gone to the coppers. I saw Tim heading over here in a hurry." I had indeed seen the guard on his hourly rounds as I returned to the trailer, but he didn't seem in any particular hurry.

Coco could relate to that; he stepped between the fighters, his bodybuilder's physique and fearful reputation instantly quelling them.

"You guys finish it later. The cops are coming."

"I'll be out on the walking track in fifteen minutes. You be there," shouted Stan, shaking a clenched fist at Mickey.

"Fuck you," Mickey howled. "I'm not risking my parole over an asshole like you."

"You're a fucking goof," Stan said as he turned to his own door across the corridor, adding "Fucking rat" as he slammed it shut.

Tim came around the corner a few moments later. Someone had definitely tipped him off: he stayed around the trailer for a full twenty minutes.

I sat quietly with Mickey on his bed, acutely aware of the thin walls. When Tim left, Coco and his pal Bernard returned.

"What you gonna' do, Mickey?" asked Coco.

"Nothing. He's not worth it."

"The guy, he call you goof," Bernard chimed in, in his thick French accent. "Your life, it not gonna be wort two cents. You got to take him out."

"*C'est ça, mon ami,*" Coco agreed, his French an unconscious concession to Mickey's fluent bilingualism.

Two sets of eyes gleamed at us from the dark hallway, expectantly piercing with bloodthirsty pleasure.

"What's the point?" I asked. "Stan's twice his size and he doesn't give a shit about his parole. Mickey's out of here in a few months."

"You can never say who going to win a fight," said Coco. He stepped into the room, leaned over, and patted my tummy. "The blade, she go in easy. Big guy, little guy, it don't matter."

"He's right," Mickey burst out. "I'm tired of putting up with that piece of shit."

"Right, Mickey. And what's Pat going to say when they deny your parole?"

That calmed Mickey down. He started to say something, but couldn't finish.

"Let's go for a walk," I said.

"Maybe you right," Bernard conceded grudgingly. "This ain't no jail. Rats. Diddlers. Motherfuckers. Anywhere else, you fight or you die."

We walked circles around the camp road. My own thin layer of detachment burst as I contemplated the brawl's senselessness and the coldbloodedness of the spectators.

Mickey and Stan had started out as friends, but Stan was a bit of a deadbeat. After Stan borrowed things once too often without returning them, Mickey, no fool, ran out of supplies when Stan needed them. Angry at the withdrawal of his mark, Stan accused Mickey of stealing cigarettes from his room, resulting in the fisticuffs. *Tell them no, and see what happens. Then tell them no again.*

I wanted to talk to Mickey, talk him down, maybe put my arm around him, but I too was locked up, lost in my own helplessness, disgrace, and loneliness, with nothing to look forward to and no one to put their arms around me. Yes, this was Beaver Creek, the Fantasy Island of prisons, an illusion, a "delete" button, a memory eraser. Only partially effective. Still a jail.

May came. The sun alternated with the rain, modelling my emotions. I was comfortable and relaxed, but hollow. Late spring brought baseball and tennis to the Creek, sports the doctors warned me not to play after serious knee injuries left me bedridden for two months in 1988. But I missed the camaraderie and competition.

"I'd just as soon spend a few months in the hospital as in jail," I thought. What better time to give this a try?

So I played first base on the camp baseball team, seniors division, a designation that influenced my intermittent thoughts about my future. I took up tennis again, playing regularly with a debonair lifer named Philippe Clement, soon to become a *cause célèbre* of the Keep Predators in Jail Forever movement when he escaped from Beaver Creek in September 1992 and sexually assaulted a Gravenhurst woman, almost killing her; I also renewed my interest in basketball through biweekly pickup games with a group of mostly black inmates and their white co-leader Nick, the only other ex-lawyer in camp.

From an administrative point of view, things were also working out. Both my group ETAs and a CE to Melissa's graduation were approved, as was a three-day private family visit in early July in the pretty cottage facing the main building. The group ETAs meant I could join the baseball team for away games in Gravenhurst, with their attendant perks at McDonald's, Dairy Queen, or Tim Horton's, catch a movie on Monday evenings, go fishing or play golf if the appropriate groups could be organized, and look after my needs on regular shopping excursions.

Chandler was enthusiastic about my chances for early day parole, confiding the deputy warden's view that "Melnitzer is exactly the kind of guy we have to get out of here as fast as possible." I was heartened by Chandler's competence, his long working hours, and his genuineness, and only slightly bewildered at his habit of talking to his favourite tree, Fred, daily. There was much to commend Melissa's prediction: "This is the beginning, Dad, not the end."

Stupidly, I made no secret of my good fortune, expressing my exultation over my pass to Melissa's graduation to all who would listen, cheerfully insensitive to the note of triumph I conveyed and to the bitterness behind the congratulatory "Right on, man." I had no conception of the grief my pleasure would bring.

My personal life was more immediately disquieting. Beaver Creek's easy pace and holiday atmosphere gave me too much time to think, even on my busy days. In April, I expended much of that energy considering my future, but in May, my professional losses hit me. For the first time since my arrest, I missed my career and its trappings.

Since I abandoned criminal law, I hadn't cared much for the practice. That made it easy to rationalize my disbarment at first by connecting it to the disappearance of long hours, clients' expectations, and the rest of the rat race. Then I came to recognize that I defined myself as a father and a lawyer. The father part continued: my relationship with Melissa was tribute to the only melding of honesty, success, and happiness in my life. The rest of my self-esteem with its imperfect accomplishments depended on the lawyer part. On the one hand, the status facilitated the workings of my various masks; but to the extent that life was real, my genuine legal triumphs and academic proficiency defined it. I missed the satisfaction of exercising my abilities to their fullest. Disbarment was a loss of the way I looked at myself, and a visit to the camp by a group of judges, many of whom I recognized, underscored the rout. A new identity was a turnaround still incomprehensible to me. I dealt with the vacuum in fear that, on and off, begot its progeny, depression.

In early May, on her second visit to the Creek, Melissa told me of her plans for a six-month trip to Greece and Israel. I encouraged her to go with all my heart: she had thrown her energy into propping up her dad for the better part of a year, without missing a beat at school; it was time to look after herself. Inside, I was apprehensive and forlorn. The kid was my mainstay, my rock: whom would I call when things got tough? I was some way from discovering, in the words of my friend Joan, that we must pass through the greater darknesses on our own.

Deena was an unlikely alternative. After the brief respite following her return from Hawaii, the ups and downs between us reappeared, her anger resurfacing whenever I thought things were getting better. Deena was genuinely relieved at my removal from the dangers of Millhaven, but she resented the Creek's opulence and leisure. Her own life was hectic, and the emotional devastation I had caused shattering, but she seemed equally distraught at the sudden burdens of everyday responsibility. In many ways, her life was more difficult than mine: choice can be a greater ordeal than its absence.

Deena followed Melissa to the Creek, more than a month after I got there. We were still close enough to hold hands at our table at the back of the visiting room, but Deena's discomfiture at the surroundings and the people told me that she would never bear the shame of being an ex-con's wife, adultery or no adultery.

She left two hours before V & C closed. We kissed goodbye in the parking lot. I was glad to hold her. Touching gave me hope as it blinded me.

A few days later, Deena told me, brightly, that she had the lead in a summer stock at the Griffin Playhouse in Barrie, a forty-five-minute drive from Beaver Creek; she talked of combining weekend visits to me with overnight stays at her sister's cottage near Gravenhurst. At the time, I was too needy to connect her warmth to the euphoria of her new acting job.

Afterwards, Deena's busy schedule made her difficult to reach. Within days of my incarceration, Deena had warned me of her embarrassment at my phone calls to her office; I depended on haphazard evening and weekend calls to reach her. When we connected, I passed off her renewed distance and outbursts to the pressures of her busy life.

On Wednesday, May 27, my concerns about my marriage once again took up most of my weekly half-hour telephone appointment with Hans.

"Well, she's coming to visit next weekend," I said cheerily.

"Yes, I know," answered Hans.

I was sure I hadn't told him. "How do you know?"

A flash of painful awareness struck me before Hans could answer. "Did you speak to her?"

"She called me. She told me she was coming to visit you."

My sinking feeling was worse than when the RCMP called me in Montreal. "Why? That's not like her."

"I think it's best that you speak to her first."

"Hans, tell me what's going on."

"I promised her I would keep our conversation in confidence until after her visit."

"Hans, don't play games. Who's your patient? Me or her? Tell me what she said."

"Call me after you see her Saturday."

"Don't give me the shit," I shouted. "I'm your patient and I want to know. I'll tell her I wrestled it out of you."

Hans paused, forever. "She wants out."

My world came to an end.

"What do you mean, Hans? She told me she wanted some freedom. You know she said that I abandoned her by going to jail and that we might need to separate before we could get together again."

"She was talking permanently, Julius. She wants to end the marriage."

"The relationship or the marriage?"

"My impression was that it was over."

"You'd think she'd have the guts to tell me herself."

"She wanted to. That's why she asked me not to tell you. She thought you might be in bad shape after her visit and wanted me to know."

"Fucking sweet of her. I'm going to call her. Are you sure she was talking about a permanent end?" By now I was crying openly, for all in Beaver Creek's vestibule to see. Nor could I keep my voice down.

"Why don't you let it go for a day?" Hans suggested.

"No, Hans, I want to hear what's going on from her."

"If you must. Call me at home tonight, please."

"If I'm still around."

I hung up, without a partner for the first time in my adult life. *I'm free.*

Part Four

REJECTION

*I believe in the reality of the accidents we
subconsciously perpetrate on ourselves, and so
how easy it was for this loss to be not loss but
a form of repudiation, an offshoot of self-loathing
(depression's premier badge) by which I was
persuaded that I could not be worthy ...*

WILLIAM STYRON

Acquisitions

The car, the furniture, the wife, the children
— everything has to be disposable. Because, you
see, the main thing is — shopping.

ARTHUR MILLER

I came as the conqueror and sat high on the judge's bench above the four contestants in the University of Western Ontario's Faculty of Law Moot Court Competition. It was March 1981 and in hindsight, I remember only Deena's — Jewish, nice name — fervent blue eyes set in her pale freckled face and brown hair, looking directly back at me, no matter how tough the questioning. The moot court over, I changed masks, offering to assist the mooters to prepare for the provincial competitions before real judges at Osgoode Hall in Toronto.

Deena took up my offer. Her youthfulness, her intelligence, her vulnerability, and the eyes of everyone on her as she walked into my office captivated me. The Beauty Myth incarnate. If this went anywhere, it would be a romance, not friendship. Deena was young, beautiful, tender, and insecure enough to worship me: the perfect wife, as daughter, as conquest, as possession. With fantasy as the aspiration of my shallow reality, a real relationship had no chance. I wanted in to the game; with Deena at my side, I could come out and play.

Two months later, near the end of April 1981, Cathy and I separated. There was no reason to leave Cathy, other than that my new mask seemed a better fit for the times: it was easier to move on, run away from myself.

Deena moved into my London condo in August 1981; we married in July 1986. From the outset, I tried to stay beyond Deena's reach, fearful that I could not meet her expectations. I could not tell Deena, who loved me for my strengths, about my weaknesses; I couldn't tell her that it wasn't my strengths, but the strength of my weaknesses that I wanted her to love. We were both looking outward, afraid to reach in, unaware that our love was properly tested only against our qualms about its frailest links. I sold myself to Deena: I saw the shelf she favoured, and put myself on special; she bought the groceries, oblivious to the artificial sweetener — and inevitably, its aftertaste.

Deena's attitude to money and wealth was motivated by insecurity, a feeling that all could be lost anytime, a nagging compulsion that debt, bankruptcy, disgrace, and the loss of her home and roots were just around the corner. We are all insecure in our comforts when we feel unworthy of them. In the scheme of life, the progression is banal: the larger the estate, the greater the need for insurance. When my arrest tore Deena's world apart, luxury had long since overlapped necessity and become a way of life for both of us.

When I met Deena, my finances were not unreasonable. I was earning between $100,000 and $125,000, with $200,000 of net worth. I had the usual burdens of a large mortgage and the uncertainties of a divorce, but my abilities assured a bright future and incremental wealth.

In my desire to move beyond criminal law and build a larger law firm, I was unwilling, ever again, to put up with the growth pains I had experienced in my first six years of practice in London.

While I loved the law itself, I hated the business end of the practice, the fight for clients, and the petty politicking of London's provincial mentality. I didn't want the hassle, but I wanted prestige and recognition; I was still dedicated to hard work and high standards, but I was no longer satisfied that these qualities alone would take me where I wanted to go as fast as I wanted to get there.

Anything important to me frightened me. Deena frightened me. What would it take to keep her? And what would it take to keep her after that? Leaving criminal law and starting to build a big firm frightened me. What would it take to succeed? And then, how would people know I was successful? And what was the point if they didn't know? Recognition from others is not static. It comes and goes, fed only by repeated stimulus; it disappears rapidly with any chink in the armour; it takes little to turn recognition to notoriety, "Wow" to "I told you so."

Successful corporate legal practices often originate in the firm's patrician ancestry, or the entrepreneurial, not the legal skills of its new blood. I decided to become not only Cohen, Melnitzer's litigator, but its promoter and deal maker. At first, I was far less successful at this than I was at trial work; I had no heart for business as an end on its own and no standing as a businessman.

In 1980, friends in Toronto — lawyers turned entrepreneurs — offered me shares and a directorship in Vanguard Trust, a private, closely held financial company. I agreed, convinced that my involvement would help bring corporate clients to Cohen, Melnitzer. When my attempts to put together an investment group failed, I approached CIBC for an investment loan, luckily at a time when London financial institutions were competing recklessly for business. I had a fair degree of clout with the bank, who, in the year since the firm had moved its account from the Toronto-Dominion Bank, was impressed with my legal reputation and administrative skills. CIBC readily advanced $100,000 on the strength of my signature, the Vanguard shares, and accurate financial statements.

The myth of the wealthy financier began, and I enjoyed it, realizing its potential. I followed with other legitimate and successful investments, tending towards long-term deals with conservative, honest partners who had strong managerial skills. In real business, as in law, I gravitated to the proper and the decent, filling my inner and outer vacuums. But no amount of intelligent investing could generate enough cash to meet my exorbitance.

It would not have done to let anyone, let alone Deena, know that Cathy's demands in our divorce proceedings, based also on her lack of appreciation of my affairs, were creating financial pressure. My practice was skyrocketing, fuelled by a string of unconventional courtroom successes and continual media coverage of the provincial government's three-year-long Commission of Inquiry into Residential Rental Tenancies following the Crown Trust–Greymac apartment mortgage scandal, a proceeding at which I was front and centre; but at the same time, the recession of the early eighties decimated Harris's commercial clientele, and our young litigation partners, Fletcher Dawson and Paul Vogel, were still riding my coattails. Yet my share of profits remained constant despite my ever-increasing billings.

Why, when it no longer made sense, did I continue with inequitable partnership arrangements? I guess I could never admit I needed anything, but that wasn't the reason at first; then, I believed a deal was a deal. When our partnership began, Harris and I agreed to a fifty-fifty profit split, unwilling to sacrifice the long term to bickering over billings and drawings. I wish I could go further and say that I accepted the arrangement with equanimity, but I didn't. I let my resentment simmer, punishing my partners with humiliating outbursts privately or publicly when the pressure got to me.

Once, I asked my father what he thought about the financial arrangement between Harris and myself.

"Do you trust Harris?" was his only question.

"Yes," I replied unhesitatingly.

"Then don't screw around with money. Money's not worth the aggravation. Honest partners are hard to find."

Initially, my father's advice made sense. As the years went by, it benefited me in an unforeseen way. Harris's honest ways were his blinders: a heart and mind that could not fathom dishonesty would not suspect it. That was true of all those closest to me: Cathy, Harris, Fletcher, Paul, my secretary Helen, and Iva, the firm's administrator, the people around me when I started out, whose authenticity protected my credibility.

The future brought other reasons to leave the partnership arrangement in place. While the split remained equal, my contribution regularly exceeded my remuneration. My partners, on the other hand, earned far more than they would without me and, like most people, lived to the limit of their means. That translated into virtually absolute power for me in the conduct of the firm's affairs. Power that was useful: as a cloak, no questions asked.

No legal partnership in the world could generate the income I needed. When my partners' cash flow demands did not abate and my desire to expand outstripped our cash flow, I stopped drawing from the firm: disappointment on my partners' part would have been failure on mine. In the mid-eighties, my capital account reached $800,000, and I started living off personal bank loans. As my thinking grew more dishevelled, I went beyond minimizing my draw to supporting the firm's cash flow by secretly paying clients' receivables or drafting phoney accounts, never sending them to the clients but paying them myself. Over eleven years, I injected $6 million into the firm's coffers; my partners knew nothing of this, except that they were getting what they imagined to be their fair share.

Let me be clear: neither my partners nor Deena were in any way responsible for my self-imposed indulgences. Their ambitions were not within missile distance of my imagination. Without exception, my partners were average in their tastes, honest and decent without question. But, like Deena, they were human, and they could not resist joining the party, particularly when I was willing to carry the load. Somehow, I always pulled it off: legally, I really did have the knack; financially, I had set myself on a suicidal course, my ego unable to accept the unrealistic nature of my aspirations, my hunger for recognition driving my greed for money.

As I reflected how easy it had been to obtain the loan for the Vanguard shares, my morality crumbled with my awe of financial institutions. Each bank branch, I surmised, was just a glorified retail store; each manager, credit chief, and regional vice-president just another operator with a bottom line on which his career depended.

The Vanguard shares were a profitable investment, except that I didn't tell the bank when I sold them a couple of years later. Instead, I convinced CIBC to lend me money for a fictional purchase of new shares; as security, I typed up a phoney certificate for hundreds of thousands of new shares, traded in the fraudulent document for the original, legitimate security, and promptly turned the original over to the buyer in the real transaction. That was the beginning of a roll: CIBC, impressed by Vanguard's performance, lent me money again and again over the next few years for what I led them to believe were progressive buy-outs of Vanguard and Melfan Investments, the company my father had set up as an estate freeze. I forged the Melfan security as I had the Vanguard shares.

As the loans grew, Melfan became the mainstay of my frauds. I eventually altered Melfan's balance sheet to show $15 million of term deposits and marketable securities, some thirty times the company's real worth, tantalizing my bankers with promises of Melfan's business. Around a tale of intrigue based on my father's alleged obsession with privacy, I warned my bankers not to discuss my affairs with anyone, including my accountants; I would not even divulge the location of Melfan's deposits or securities. Once the banks, in their anxiety for Melfan's cash down the line, accepted my story and the phoney shares without as much as a phone call to Melfan's accountants, whose office was virtually across the street, I knew I was safe. I was right. None of the banks made a single enquiry about Melfan until *after* my arrest.

When the police arrested me, they were hard put to believe that anyone other than a chartered accountant could have formulated the phoney financial statements. I had been cross-examining accountants for years and understood financial statements thoroughly; the work was tedious, I told the police, but quite manageable intellectually.

With the high interest rates of the early and mid-1980s and the increasing demands for cash as Cohen, Melnitzer expanded to my impatient visions of glory, the CIBC loans were not enough; I aggravated the situation by investing in anything remotely reasonable, both to promote legal business and to enhance my wealthy image. The National Bank and the Royal advanced millions with little more scrutiny than CIBC. But I needed a source of funds from outside banking circles.

Nothing makes banks happier than cash flow, revolving loans, money coming in and out, loans paid up and down fluctuating within ever-increasing increments, all creating the illusion that cash is available to pay the interest that represents much of banks' profits. Turnover, as it is for most businesses, is the banks' sustenance.

When money is moving, banks rarely question its source, which explains why money laundering was so easy and effective for organized crime for many years. With tougher regulation, things may have changed for the Mafia, but not for Canada's financial power-brokers. In Canada, we need only look to the collapse of the Reichmann empire, the fall of the Royal Trust financial icon, and the incomprehensible corporate intertwinings of the Bronfmans to appreciate that financial institutions' business practices are sloppy, clubby, reeking of conflict of interest, and sealed with buzzwords rather than caution. The élitist incestuousness of those practices makes fraud easy — which is not to suggest that the business practices of our corporate structure are dishonest, or akin to fraud, nor that fraud is justifiable. It merely reveals that the legitimate practices we condone are flawed, to the prejudice of those not in the club. My professional reputation, my burgeoning practice, and my impressive and influential clientele gave me the credentials to become a member of that trusted élite, those who did not need checking.

It was quite the vicious circle: the more money the banks lent me, the greater their belief in the image their cash propagated, and the less likely they were to look behind it. Only the trust of friendship, however, would complete the circle of deceit.

I met Allan Richman, a London developer and property manager with investments concentrated in apartment buildings, in the mid-1970s, at meetings of the London Property Management Association. Both arrogant egotists, we were unlikely candidates for friendship. Allan overlooked our mutual gratings when, ever the pragmatic business person, he decided to confront rent controls head-on by maximizing his rents through the regulatory process. He put his personal misgivings aside to take advantage of my expertise.

As we prepared Allan's cases for hearing in spirited one-on-ones, the tension between us gave way to respect and friendship. We were both dysphoric by nature and viscerally lonely, with a similar approach to life. In the spring and summer of 1979, we trekked and rafted in the Grand Canyon, the first of many shared business and personal trips over the next twelve years.

As our friendship flowered, so did our business dealings. Allan's extensive network and shrewdness, coupled with my own contacts in the real estate industry, exhaustive knowledge of rent controls, and negotiating skills, led to the creation of Grand Canyon Properties, our investment vehicle that grew into a venture with assets of several million dollars in Canada and the United States.

Allan and I were both restless: I, never satisfied; he, bored with a property management business that ran itself. He wanted to experience the excitement of creating, planning, and developing: expand beyond buying and selling properties, see the world, deal in international markets. Guided by the images of myself that I crafted for him, he sought that stimulation through me.

As victory after legal victory piled up, Allan, like my wife, my partners, my bankers, and my other friends, began to believe in my infallibility — and making them rich conveniently nourished the perception. In Allan's case, I baited the hook of legal invincibility with the trappings of financial genius, initially earning his gratitude by lending him money when his own cash flow choked in a sedentary real estate market; then, I purported to invest small sums of his money in nonexistent schemes that earned enormous returns in short order.

In a pool hall, observers would say Allan was sandbagged, lulled into a false sense of security by my contrived posturing and his own greed. Impressed by the rate of return on his initial loans to me, he kept lending me more money at rates ranging from prime plus three to thirty percent, believing he was sharing in complex, private investment schemes that would be jeopardized if I divulged his participation. In one year, I paid more than $3 million in interest to Allan and the banks, but the money kept moving around, generating more and more capital with nothing but the force of its activity.

As I discovered how to get money out of people, my success at it blinded me. Over time, I fell out of touch with reality, content that the merry-go-round would whirl forever: the banks would earn their interest, Allan would make his profit, and I would do whatever I needed to achieve whatever I wanted. There was no question of proportion; since money meant nothing, it didn't matter how or where I spent it, so long as its use had the right effect: if investing money and giving people fictitious returns made them likely to advance more money to me and institutionalize my Midas touch, so be it; if supporting the law firm secretly with my own money meant it could be the largest firm faster, so be it; if paying clients' accounts to keep my partners happy until I could try the cases only I believed in kept my hold on the firm tight, so be it; if buying my girlfriend a condo and a BMW after we split up eased my guilt, so be it; if making legitimate investments in companies with impeccable principals helped me get away with everything else, so be it.

I went from a Duster to a Mercedes; from a small apartment to a beautiful home in London, a Rosedale house and Yorkville condo in Toronto, and a ski chalet in chic Deer Valley, Utah; from jeans to $20,000 in clothes at a single sitting at Versace; from rebel to the Patrons' Council of the National Ballet of Canada; from criminal lawyer to developers' lobbyist; from drunkenness defences to national news; from camping trips to $2,200-a-night hotel rooms in Marrakesh; from teak furniture to Chagalls, Mirós, and Neimans; from no holidays to hundreds of thousands of double-bonus first-class airline mileage points; from strumming folk songs to seats behind the conductor at the Vienna State Opera. Each time the banks and Allan advanced funds to a new level, my financial bulimia intensified. Nobody noticed the connection.

As for Deena, my masks kept me out of her reach. They, and her special vulnerability to them, answer the question, "How could she not have known?" Deena's weaknesses were not powerful enough to make her break the law. Mine were. Deena wanted security and freedom at a price, not any price; I wanted everything, at any price.

In the end, there was only one game left: was there anything money couldn't buy? And why wasn't it making me happy? Is it significant that we express the accumulation of wealth, our treasured power to acquire, by adding zeros to our net worth?

Getting caught

Why had I taken risks that very competent men had declined?
And the quick answer, of course, is — to pull off the impossible.
ARTHUR MILLER

In April 1991, less than four months before my arrest, a picture of my barefoot self, in full courtroom regalia, on the water's edge of the Grand Bend beach appeared on the cover of the *London Free Press* Saturday supplement. Eight months later, the same newspaper published a twelve-page pullout dedicated to my plunge from grace.

I had indeed reached the pinnacle before the fall. At the zenith, I basked in thoughts of the bluebloods in their plush chairs at the Hunt Club and the London Club, fulminating at my victorious smile beaming at them from their daily newspaper, arching their eyebrows with ever so slight a furrowed brow, speculating over the imminent invasion of their sanctum by remnants of the Twelve Tribes, the lawyers among them wondering what the profession had come to. At the bottom, I fought a tendency to misplaced self-righteousness over sensationalistic journalism by remembering that I had had no such qualms the previous April.

It is, of course, a distortion to describe anything in my life as a "pinnacle." The April cover story was simply the polish on the mask. Since December 1990, when my friends, whom I guaranteed a hundred percent return, advanced millions of dollars for a nonexistent real estate venture I called the Singapore Deal, I had been searching for a way out. Previously, apart from Allan Richman, whose own greed made him a target about whom I could rationalize, I had scrupulously avoided financial dealings with friends or clients. When the desperation of potential discovery drove me to betray them, my ability to compartmentalize also ended. For the first time, I lost sleep; I couldn't socialize without a keen awareness of their trust in me; I could no longer accept their thanks for my generosity and pour it into my ego without a bitter pang of conscience reminiscent of aspirin without water, chewed over and over in a desperate attempt to swallow; nor could I repay them without resort to the banks, whose demands for repayment precipitated my treachery on my friends. Allan could not help either, his credit limit taxed by the recession and the $8 million he had put out to me.

In the early 1990s, banks were preoccupied with liquidity: loan paydowns, cash security, bonds, or publicly traded stock in blue-chip corporations. I had overlooked the vulnerability of my imagined empire to the vicissitudes of the larger economy. When pillars much more solid than mine faltered in a prolonged recession, all security held by lenders came under scrutiny. Mine, based as it was on trust and fiction, was particularly susceptible; trust alone, the commodity of fraud, was no longer acceptable security.

Never one to remain passive, I continued my ostentatious personal spending in the face of the financial pressure. Offence was the best defence, I had always believed: it allowed the attacker to control the momentum. Who would believe that a man on a multi-million-dollar spending spree was in serious financial trouble? That part of the plan worked fine.

As the pressure mounted, however, dysfunction set in. Work, always comforting, became an annoyance, holidays a waste of precious time. I became detached, prone to excessive outbursts which, for public consumption, I attributed to the demands of a busier-than-ever two-city law practice and to the high-profile, politically delicate, thankless job of guiding the Fair Rental Policy Organization through the hazards of an NDP government committed to increasingly restrictive rent controls.

The idea of manufacturing my own stock market certificates had occurred to me from time to time, but I discarded the thought as offensive to the secrecy I relied on. Unlike private company shares, which were routinely typed on standard forms in private offices, stock exchange certificates, which are numbered, registered, water-marked, printed on paper of limited availability, and handled by institutional transfer agents, were impossible for me to duplicate without professional help; I was unfamiliar with bank practices relating to their verification; finally, my usual warnings to my lenders about the need for confidentiality made no sense in the context of public stock, because a routine inquiry about a publicly traded certificate would bring an impersonal response from an administrative functionary that did not encroach on my privacy.

Eventually, I had no choice but to change the ground rules. In the spring of 1991, I called my trusted friend Sam Hassan at his home in London; Sam was comptroller of Sterling Marking Products, a graphics and printing company of impeccable reputation. I told him of my involvement in a case in which it was alleged that my banker client should have known that the shares presented to him as security were fraudulent. In my client's defence, I told Sam, I wanted to prove that even my opponent's expert witness could not recognize a good forgery. Would Sterling attempt to make duplicates of originals that I obtained from a broker?

Over the years, I had given Sam, the company, and Sterling's owner, Bob Schramm, often unconventional but impeccable and original legal and business advice. They had no reason to doubt me: my tendency towards effective "stunts" in cross-examination were well known, and the off-the-wall idea I was proposing was perfectly plausible coming from me; in the circumstances, my request for absolute secrecy, the cornerstone of my frauds, was understandable. Sam's, Bob's, and Sterling's propriety and ethics had been relentlessly consistent in my ten-year association with them; I relied on that purity of spirit to trample their trust.

Having no choice but to expose myself to the greater risks, there was no sense in it unless I upped the stakes. My current cash squeeze had alerted me, painfully, to the snowballing that would eventually catch up to me. The only way out was to change directions: if the banks wanted solid-gold security, I would give them what they wanted, but in return, I wanted a lot more money than the banks had ever advanced before — enough to get out of the mess I was in.

On the back of a cigarette pack, I methodically worked out a plan. I needed $10 million to pay out Allan; $7 million to double the investments of my friends in the Singapore deal; I owed CIBC $8 million, the Royal $3 million, and the National $2 million: $30 million overall, plus various personal financial concerns totalling $5 million; interest at ten percent for three years on $35 million of bank loans amounted to $10 million. Fifty million dollars would be just about right.

In time, the $50 million would have to be repaid. To do that, I would have to make money — lots of money. That would take an additional $50 million of investment capital; I would devote myself to the growth of that fund as singlemindedly as I had to excelling at law. That meant leaving the law practice, which, understandably, had lost its allure amid the pressures. At heart, though, I realized that my change of direction was no change at all: it was a money-laundering scheme, no less illegal than its predecessors.

After satisfying myself that routine checks of stock certificates' validity were not the norm, I presented my proposal to the banks, insisting, once again, on absolute secrecy and discretion. All the banks jumped at the opportunity to lend millions to the perfect recession borrower, flush with blue-chip liquid security: CIBC was delighted at the simplicity of the transaction after years of convoluted lending arrangements and put up $20 million; the Royal jumped at the opportunity to cut into CIBC's stranglehold on my account with a loan of $8 million; the National Bank increased my credit line from $2 million to $15 million; and the Toronto-Dominion threw $21 million at its newest catch.

None of the banks knew of my dealings with their competitors. They had no idea that their overall commitment of $64 million was based on copies of the same forgeries; nor were they aware of the existence of another $1 billion of certificates for circulation if and when necessary. The $100,000 cost of Sterling's painstaking, innocent participation in my scheme was about to yield the biggest return of all.

There was much to do in the first week of August, sandwiched between the trip that Deena and I had just taken to the Middle East and the two-week holiday to Japan that Melissa and I planned for the middle of August (not, as the post-fall wags would have it, a "getaway" trip to Singapore). On Sunday of the upcoming long weekend, our family would attend the ceremonial unveiling of my father's tombstone in Montreal. In the meantime, there was three weeks' legal work to catch up on, an Ernst & Young forensic seminar to co-chair, conferences with the four banks to complete the financings, a board meeting, and, most importantly, arrangements to be made for repayment to Allan and the Singapore investors.

I met with CIBC, the Royal, and the National and finalized $43 million of loans; the remainder was coming from the Toronto-Dominion Bank the following Tuesday. I wrote postdated cheques for August 30 to the Singapore investors, doubling their investment with a $3-million profit in nine months. There was nothing sinister in the postdating: I habitually left bank advances in place for a while — to let my lenders know that I didn't really need their money; August 30 also coincided nicely with my return from Japan and with the interest due dates on the Singapore notes. Allan and I arranged to meet Monday night, on my return from Montreal, to do our final accounting and pay him out.

I dozed on the Friday evening shuttle to Montreal and slept well into the morning on Saturday, still catching up on months of fitful sleep. My late morning awakening took its toll on Saturday night, but I didn't mind, as I lay open-eyed beside a sleeping Deena in the bedroom of our Four Seasons suite, hugging her, savouring the success of my scheme.

About the same time, the police were meeting my partners at our London office. My account manager and his supervisor at the National Bank, cautious because I had never mentioned the existence of my stock market holdings on previous financial statements, ran a routine check on my certificates. Their cursory search exposed me.

It was inevitable. Although the National Bank duly received credit for my detection, the Royal, in a sudden fit of prudence, had sent their shares for verification one day after the National did. One way or another, the fall was inescapable.

I gave Deena the bad news on the way back from Montreal to London.

"It's all right," she said, fighting the shock. "We'll figure out a way to survive."

"You don't understand, Deena. I'm going to jail. For a long time."

"Will we lose the house?"

"Probably. Everything, Deena, everything."

The next two months were a nightmare of every horror I had imagined, more or less as I had imagined them. Unrealistic as I was about going on forever, I had no delusions about the consequences if I was caught.

Cohen, Melnitzer expelled — not suspended — me immediately, demonstrating how quickly human nature overrides principle when our own ass is on the line. My partners' pragmatism in refusing to delay was understandable, but, as a lawyer, I wondered how Fletcher Dawson, who made the announcement and was vice-president of the Ontario Criminal Lawyers Association, could keep a straight face the next time he raised the defence lawyer's battle cry of "innocent until proven guilty" to a dubious judge or jury. In any event, I never crossed the firm's threshold again.

Front-page national media coverage had the press knocking on our door and lying in wait with video cameras at my numerous civil and criminal court appearances; all our bank accounts were frozen and assets seized; our Rosedale home was broken into and its furniture repossessed without notice by our decorators, Gluckstein Design, within forty-eight hours of my arrest, using the key with which Deena had trusted them; our creditors demanded that we vacate both Toronto properties and return both leased cars; CIBC unsuccessfully tried to seize Deena's Acura and Melissa's car. Worst of all were the hurried overnight moves from Rosedale to Yorkville to protect Deena's interest in the condo and the surreptitious removal of our furnishings from our London home to shield them from the trustee in bankruptcy.

Allan Richman, devastated, had two brief conversations with me designed to ascertain my assets and intentions. For the most part, my remaining friends disappeared, but were replaced, surprisingly, by people I had forgotten, who, for one reason or another, remembered me.

As for Harris, I saw him once, in Mike Epstein's office a few days after I was arrested. Sentimentally, I called him a few times from jail; he was friendly, which was probably more than I deserved.

He lost no money, but, apart from my family, may have been my most tragic victim. There was no way he could have known what was coming: living in different worlds when we met, we had grown less intimate as our lives converged.

As November 1991 arrived, one hundred days had elapsed since my arrest. In the tumult, Deena and I were working together well, she at the legal job she had managed to get, and I, doing whatever I could to help out and preparing myself for jail. Notwithstanding our inexperience with reality, our core resourcefulness and worldliness surfaced.

For three months after my arrest, I saw Hans twice weekly. He sent me to relaxation classes, also twice weekly, to help with my fear of confinement, to learn to be alone with myself, and to learn that doing nothing, relaxing, is not necessarily empty.

Through August, September, and October, with Melissa's fervent support and the encouragement of a small circle of friends, I tried to fight a growing depression by staying as active as I could. Still, I sank constantly into unprovoked tears, long periods of withdrawal, memory lapses, disorientation, fits of possessiveness so acute I could not bear to have Deena leave the room without asking where she was going; with all this came a despair provoked by a growing appreciation of the enormity of my crimes, the façade that passed for my life, the pain of my victims and their families, and the proportionate certainty that a fifteen-year sentence was inevitable. Unwilling to face my psychological problems, I compounded my depression by clinging to the unrealistic needs for control that caused it, and resisted Hans's suggestion that I resort to medication.

By the end of October, negotiations with the Crown and the police began. As a sentence in the range of the eight years I was hoping for became realistic, my spirits improved, allowing me to focus on an opportunity to make some badly needed money in a small consulting business. My self-respect rebounded with the chance to contribute financially, and the need to function made the bouts of tearfulness and withdrawal less palatable; I agreed to a daily regimen of Prozac. The drug took two weeks to work; simultaneously, the consulting opportunity became a reality, guaranteeing steady employment until the New Year, and my lawyers reached a final agreement with the Crown: I would plead guilty before Christmas and give up my freedom to a nine-year sentence two months later.

Saying goodbye

... growth is betrayal. There is no other route. There
is no arriving somewhere without leaving somewhere.

JOHN UPDIKE

On Wednesday, I called Melissa, telling her that Deena was leaving me. She promised to visit that evening. But the prospect of seeing Melissa didn't settle me down. I called Deena, who refused to tell me more than Hans had told me, insisting we needed to talk in person. Not only was I going to lose my wife, I would lose her by the Chinese water torture method.

By now I was crying uncontrollably, furious and helpless, a spectacle for the rumour-mongers at the Creek. I called Melissa again, analysing my conversation with Deena to death, seeking shreds of hope in phrasing, intonations, and hypotheticals. Then I called Hans and had much the same conversation.

Mickey came over before dinner. "You OK? Perry's telling everybody your wife's leaving you."

"How does he know anything?" I asked angrily.

"Said he heard you on the phone."

"I'll kill him. I don't give a fuck. There's nothing to get out for anyway. What else did he say?"

Mickey grew hesitant at my rage. "That's about it."

"Don't play fucking games with me," I screamed, grabbing the front of Mickey's sweater with both hands. "What did he say? Tell me."

"Take it easy, Julius," Mickey urged. "Let's take a walk where no one can hear us."

That made sense.

"Perry doesn't like you," Mickey told me, as we started around the walking track.

"I know. So what did he say?"

"He said he was glad an arrogant son of a bitch like you was getting what you deserved. He was really happy your wife was leaving you."

"I'll kill him," I threatened, turning towards the trailer.

"Let it be, think about it," Mickey warned. "Don't do anything in the trailer. The rats will be to the coppers in no time at all. You're not exactly popular, you know."

"Fuck 'em," I replied. But Mickey's words were sobering, and I calmed down.

Melissa arrived that evening as visiting hours began. A short, cool spring had not quite allowed the Muskoka countryside to flower and bloom, though the days were lengthening and the sun was only beginning to sink on the horizon, mellowingly diffusive in a clear sky. We walked arm in arm along the road for three hours, connected as never before, interspersing my tears with open, unmasked discussions full of hope.

As 9 P.M. drew near, we returned to gather Melissa's belongings from V & C. She patted my arm reassuringly.

"You'll be all right, Dad."

"What do you mean?" I asked.

"I don't know. You just seem OK. I expected you to be a lot worse."

"Right, I've been crying for three hours," I replied. "But it's funny, you know — and don't get me wrong, I'm really sad. And I'm scared — but I don't miss Deena. It's just being alone."

Melissa's warmth lingered as she drove off in her bright red convertible, but the soothing interlude was short-lived. Just off to my left, Mickey was saying goodbye to Pat. We took another walk, part of the ritual unwinding prison visits necessitate.

"How was your visit?" I asked.

"Tough. Pat's having a hard time. She's two months behind in her rent. That friend of mine who was supposed to lend us some money hasn't come through yet. How about you?"

"Good. I feel a lot better. Melissa's great."

"Yeah. I was watching you guys. You're lucky you've got her. Have you talked to Deena yet?" Mickey asked.

The fury sublimated by Melissa's visit welled up in me. "Yeah. The bitch won't tell me what's up."

"That could be a good sign."

I turned my wrath on Mickey. "Get real. Are you trying to tell me that she's keeping the good news from me? Prison scrambled your eggs, or what?"

"Easy, Julius," said Mickey as we neared the trailer. "You don't want the whole camp to hear you."

"And why not?" Cupping my hands to my mouth, I began shouting in the direction of the trailer. "That cunt Perry's been getting his jollies all day shooting off his mouth. I know what'll make me feel better. I'm going to kill him."

"For Christ's sake," Mickey warned, "they'll ship you back to the Haven just for saying that. Take it easy."

"Fuck it. I'm going to clean his clock."

I stormed ahead of Mickey. Perry's room was dark. Enraged, I kicked the door. Nothing happened. I leaned back against the opposite wall for leverage and kicked it again. It flexed, but didn't open, and I hurled my shoulder at it in frustration, only to tumble into the room, belying my disguise as Van Damme.

Perry, a heavy sleeper, flicked the table lamp on as I rose. James, his roommate since Mickey had got his own room, sat bolt upright on his bed.

"What's going on?" James demanded.

I ignored him and turned to Perry, shaking my finger two inches from his nose, my upper frame bent over his face. Mindful of James at my rear, I glanced back; he sat quietly on the bed, his best prison face on.

"I'll fucking kill you. If you don't keep your nose out of my fucking business, I'll kill you. I'm not even going to ask. If I even hear from somebody about my wife or my daughter or anything about me, I'm going to assume you told them."

Perry cowered, trying to look nonchalant as he did so. "What are you talk—?"

"Look, you toad," I yelled as my finger came closer to his face. "Stay away from me. If you're close enough to touch, I'll smack you. If you're even close enough to hear what I'm saying, I'll kill you — the same night. If you don't come out to the woods with me, I'll drag you. You better not even be in the fucking building when I'm on the phone."

Perry shook his head, seemingly at a loss. The motion reminded me of the guard — the one who couldn't pronounce my name — who had hailed me from the bullpen at Millhaven A & D. Months of restraint came undone; my fingers withdrew to a fist as I put my knee on the bed and pulled my right hand back; spit flew from my mouth.

"I'll fucking kill you. I don't give a damn what they do to me. I'll be happy for the rest of my life. I'll cherish the photographs of your body in bits. And I'm just not talking about my wife. If I hear one more word about the pass to my daughter's graduation, I'll assume it came from you."

As I brought my knee forward to his stomach, the thought of Melissa brought me to my senses, and I hesitated, losing my balance as I raised my leg.

"Sorry, I was just leaving," I said sarcastically, standing up. Perry rolled away. I went to the door and turned around, pointing my finger again.

"Do me a favour, go rat out to the coppers, because it'll give me a chance to do what I really want to do to you."

I tried to slam the door shut behind me, for effect, but it swung open, its frame bent from my opening salvo. Mickey was down the hall at the door to his cell. "I just caught the end of that. I didn't know what you were going to do, so I stayed outside watching for the coppers. It's almost eleven. They'll be around for count. Did you hurt him?"

"I just scared him a bit. Let's talk about it tomorrow."

I felt better. I had blown off steam, no more constructively than in the past, but I had blown off steam. I smiled to myself: I was getting good at this prisoner business.

I spent most of Thursday on the phone to Hans and Melissa. To Melissa, I worried, conjectured, and cried, always letting her bolts of warmth through; to Hans, I complained, rationalized, demanded explanations and advice, and obliquely threatened suicide, aware throughout of the cry for attention it represented. At the peak of my frenzy, Hans doubled my Prozac intake to forty milligrams.

Thursday night was sleepless, but, by Friday at noon, I had calmed down, though I remained agitated enough to stay awake that night, thinking clearly for the first time in days.

Deena arrived at 11:30 on Saturday morning. We kissed hello, exchanging genuine hugs. Mindful of Beaver Creek's elephant ears, we talked outdoors.

A hazy drizzle came and went, weather suited to the partings of Harlequin romances; drifting, thick clouds promised no sunlight, nor did they warn of deluge, as if the sky needed time to brood before committing itself.

"So what's doing?" I asked.

"Essentially," Deena said, speaking slowly and softly, "what Hans told you was correct."

"Permanently?"

"Yes."

"Do you want a divorce?" I asked. I was still standing on the landing at the top of the stairs, just outside the door to V & C. Deena leaned against the railing, her eyes tearing.

"We can worry about that later."

"Don't you think we should talk about it? We've both got eleven years in it. I think it's worth it. I know I haven't been calling you much before Hans told me about this," I added.

"It's got nothing to do with your not calling me. I promise. It wouldn't have made any difference."

Deena went on. "You'll never let me lead my own life. You're too controlling. I want to do things the way I want to do them. The last few months, I've done quite well on my own."

"Are you telling me I can't change? Maybe you should look at yourself. Who refused to go for counselling after I was arrested?" Our loud argument was catching the staff's attention through an open window.

"Let's not fight," Deena pleaded. "Yes, I can see the changes in you, but I don't believe you'll ever stop manipulating and controlling enough to let me be the kind of person I want to be. And I don't trust you."

"I won't be down and out forever."

"I know that. I'm sure that in five years, you'll be making more money than all your lawyer friends."

"Don't you think," I asked, "there are things worth talking about?"

Deena was now weeping openly. "How could you treat me like you did if you valued me? You don't appreciate me, you never appreciated me. I don't even know if you cared about me."

"I didn't show it." I caught Deena's eye. "I know, I know, that's a lot more than an understatement. But it doesn't make sense to throw eleven years away without talking about it."

"My heart's not in it. I'd just be going through the motions."

I was about to protest, when one of my early conversations with Hans about Deena came back to me.

Ask.

She won't like it.

That's her problem.

What if she says no?

That's your problem.

Then and there, I grew up, accepting Deena's decision as hers to make.

"OK, Deena, let's just call it. No sense in fighting."

She had come prepared to stay all day, to talk, to say goodbye. "Julius, I said I wouldn't abandon you in jail and I won't. I'll visit and help you out as much as I can, if you want me to."

"No, thanks," I answered abruptly. "Pity's not necessary. I'll be fine."

"If you change your mind, I'll be —"

"Come on," I said, "let's get your stuff."

Deena was crying again. We went back inside for Deena's belongings, then walked silently to Deena's car.

"Goodbye, Deena. Good luck," I said, standing at the back of the Acura as she unlocked the door.

"How about a hug?" Deena asked.

"No sense going through the motions," I said, turning away, resigned, not cold.

I walked a few feet and looked back. The car wasn't running. Deena was in the driver's seat, her hands in her lap, sobbing so deeply I could see her heaving. At that moment, we were closer to love in parting than we had ever been before, refusing to let fear destroy us by keeping us together.

I retreated from the half-step I had taken back towards the car. Deena had grown enough to leave me; four months on her own had convinced her to take a chance on herself. I didn't like it and I liked the way she went about it even less. Maybe she was just changing outfits, or masks; I might never find out, but then it wasn't my business any longer.

From the top of the stairs, I watched Deena back the car out and drive away, as lonely in her flight as I was in my prison.

Graduation

Ye shall know the truth, and the truth shall make you free.
VICTORIA COLLEGE MOTTO

On Sunday night, two days before my pass to Melissa's graduation, Deena phoned. The conversation dissolved into an angry shouting match as Deena defended her financial decisions with accusations about the "millions you have stashed away." With her warning "not to try to get into the apartment unless I'm there," the finality of her decision came home. I deflected that reality, determined not to let my troubles intrude on Melissa's celebration.

On Tuesday morning, June 9, I presented myself at the duty office waiting for Richard, an ex-lawyer and ex-con who was a volunteer citizen escort at the Creek. My designer suit and tie brought a stir from the inmates who habitually gathered in V & C for morning coffee. Yet I was insufficiently sensitive to the impact of my "easy" transition on inmates who had spent years in prison, only to be refused passes even to family funerals — an impact aggravated by a brief, innocent, and unexpected visit from Judge David Cole, incidental to his finalization of a judges' tour of the camp.

It all went over my head as I signed the paperwork while Richard gathered up the sealed bundle of information he was to turn over to the police at the first signs of escape. On the two-hour ride to Toronto, I chatted easily with Richard and his wife, Anna, pausing only to gaze at the passing greenery in a detached way, unaffected by any newfound sense of freedom, more mindful of the weather, a warm, beautiful day made to order for graduation.

The private chapel ceremony for outstanding students was in progress when we arrived. I strained, catching a peek of Melissa up front, glowing in deserved serenity in the low light of the hall; and of Cathy, seated in the middle rows, leaning slightly forward, beaming without smiling, the pride of a single parent evident in her determination to take in every detail, every sound coming from the mouths of the academic deans dressed in their bright robes on the raised dais. I saw Mark, Melissa's boyfriend, exuberantly crouched near her, manoeuvring for the best possible camera angle.

Only then, standing at the back of the packed sanctuary, rich and colourful in deep-toned carpets, handcarved woodwork, and ornate stained-glass windows, and lost in the formality of a ceremony warmed by tradition, did I understand how wrong it would have been to miss this moment. My jet-set life had had no place for ceremony or ritual but those of my own contrivance. Now I knew why: I had attended many such occasions, my own and others', but I had never truly been there before.

I yearned for the feeling that Melissa must have had right then. *Her* moment, *her* happiness in the success of the goals *she* had chosen, the liberty to be herself and end up where she wanted. The sadness disappeared quickly in the joy of the occasion.

On the two-hour drive home, I was quiet and very much alone, unwilling to let conversation interrupt the day's reminders that life was worth living.

"The TV station called," Sue, the duty officer, said excitedly as I walked in the door of the main building, ten minutes early.

"What TV station?" I asked.

"Toronto, Global, the London station. Wait a minute, Julius." She handed some notes to me, messages from the media.

"They've been calling all day," Sue volunteered.

"Did you talk to them? What did they want?"

"They wanted to know about your pass."

"What did you tell them?"

"Nothing. We have very strict instructions not to tell anybody anything, we don't even acknowledge that you're here. There's a sign up on the board, over there." Chandler, my CO, had posted the sign after I expressed my concern about media interest back in April.

"How the fuck did the media find out?" I asked.

"Nothing's secret around here," Paul, my LU, said as he walked out of the back office. "Julius, there are no secrets in this camp. Inmates are calling the papers all the time. There's a lot of jealousy about your pass."

"Inmates, my ass," I growled. "The fucking staff here are worse than any criminal I've met. Just about all of you guys have been poking your nose into my pass ever since the word got out."

"It wasn't staff who called the media, Julius."

"Well, who was it? What's with the games?"

"Think about it. Who was around this morning when you were signing out?" Paul asked, in the affected, fatherly way that fed his ego.

"I don't remember! Who was it?" I shouted.

"I can't tell you," Paul said.

"Then fuck you and your games."

I stormed along the path to the trailer, puzzling over Paul's intimations, lowering my eyes as I passed a group of inmates outside the dining hall.

"You're really a heat score," came a voice from the group. Jody, standing among the inmates, was a tall, chunky, bleached blonde in her late thirties, gruff in manner, the female version of a boot camp drill sergeant; she had come to Beaver Creek after several years as a guard in Joyceville Penitentiary. Jody had taken a dislike to me, treating my elementary questions about camp procedure with disdain and greeting my visitors with a stringent orderliness that let them know they were tainted. Jody was infamous for her attitude, quick to pull out the charge sheet at minor provocations.

I played dumb. "Heat score? What's that?"

"Heat," Jody went on, "as in hot. All the media's coming down on this place. Guys like you make it tough for everybody."

"Fuck you, Jody. You've got no business talking to me like that. I'm not your goddamn dog."

"Watch your tongue, or I'll charge you. You'll go right back to the Haven."

"Go right ahead." As I glared at Jody, I kept an eye on the curious, but silent, inmates around her.

"All these guys gonna back you, a copper, or me?" I said to Jody, nodding at the inmates and turning to Red, a veteran of the system. "Eh, Red, what do you say? How about I make a note of all of you guys' names — so you can back me up when she charges me." I pulled my address book and pen from the breast pocket of my suit jacket.

"Here, let me write down what she said. 'Heat score' is what she called me, in front of a bunch of cons." I made a deliberate show of tucking my book and pen back into my pocket.

"Don't fuckin' single me out," Red sputtered. "I'll do what I want, not what some waterhead lawyer tells me."

I leaned forward towards him. "Good to know we're all solid cons here." I laughed as I walked away, as hatefully as I could.

Beaver Creek's staff made regular references to my stash, my wealth, and my connections, often in the presence of other inmates. Some of the remarks were good-natured, others were tinged with the envy I had come to expect. When word of my application for a pass got around, many of the staff laughed at me, discouraging my chances, and reminding me, again in front of other inmates, that "being a wheel on the outside won't get you special privileges here." When my pass was approved, their smirks became the hostile embarrassment of the bested.

Still other staff took me into their confidence, seeking me out for legal and investment advice and even asking me to come down to the duty office on the midnight shift to discuss real estate opportunities. This type of special interest made life harder for me among my peers, but, stuck in my desire to please, I lacked the wisdom to avoid it.

Back-stabbing was as rampant among the staff, divided philosophically into hard-liners and doves, as among the inmates. The hard-liners operated by the book, convinced of the incorrigibility of all inmates, forever lamenting the country club atmosphere they attributed to modern-day prisons. The doves talked to the inmates, let them wander through the woods beyond the camp boundaries, looked the other way at harmless contraband, shared the odd drink with a trustworthy inmate when out on passes, and ignored the smell or sight of a joint on an inmate — if he wasn't a trafficker or troublemaker. Both groups had bones to pick with the warden, the deputy wardens, the correctional supervisors, and the administration generally.

Often, it seemed that the staff spent more time bickering among themselves than tending to security. The opposing factions made no bones about their mutual dislike and made no effort to hide the friction from inmates: "Why the fuck did he do that?"; "Is *he* your LU? Watch out for him"; "That idiot never does anything right. I've got to do all his work for him"; "Did she say no? You know what she's like. Wait till I'm on the morning shift and I'll let you do it."

Conniving cons played on the divisions to confound security and make life as comfortable for themselves as possible, leaving the camp drug- and alcohol-ridden, disorganized, and ineffective in its rehabilitative objectives.

By morning, the camp buzzed with gossip: Global TV and the London media had broadcast the news of my pass, with appropriately indignant commentary; federal and provincial politicians were reportedly poised to raise the matter in the House of Commons and the provincial legislature. Before I completed the short walk from the trailer to the main building, I was stopped at least five times by smug inmates anxious to remind me of my renewed notoriety. For four months now, I had been privy to the pain of prisoners, but only now, as I became the system's pariah, did I understand the extent of their bitterness.

Staff did nothing to help me; some of them took as much joy as the inmates in reminding me of the adverse effects of the publicity on the performance of their duties and on other inmates' chances for passes. Their comments hinted at the origin of their rancour: "Maybe the media wouldn't have noticed if you hadn't worn the fancy suit."

On Friday, Eddie gave me a computer for the single room I had moved into earlier in the week, right next to Mickey's room. In return, I agreed to write computer manuals for CSC "under Eddie's direction" and to share credit for the publications with him. Word quickly spread that "Melnitzer's got a free computer from the school."

I sought refuge at the computer, intensifying my study of computer science and stepping up the correspondence that had become my cathartic mainstay. By now, I was writing two or three lengthy letters a day and receiving the same amount of return mail. Writing always brought peace; I turned to my correspondence as regularly as I took my Prozac.

Over the next week, things slowly returned to normal, though not a day went by without a reminder of my pass. Even when the clamour died down, I felt as I had at Millhaven: an outsider, remote, different, still wanting to play the game and still willing to buy my way in.

I had spoken to Beaver Creek's warden, Les Judson, only once, in late April, when I attended a meeting of the Citizens' Advisory Committee. As its name indicates, CAC is made up of local citizens, Inmate Committee members, and penitentiary staff who serve as liaison between the institution and the community. At BCI, which is how we referred to the camp, the committee met every month; inmate observers from the population were welcomed and encouraged to participate.

When experienced cons told me that CAC meetings were a good place to make contact with citizen escorts, I attended, seating myself along the wall near the warden's end of the table. Les Judson was a slim, handsome, neatly groomed man of about forty. The immediate warmth in his eyes and the smile that didn't fit preconceived images of custodians was consistent with his reputation for straightforwardness and fairness among many inmates.

As I sat down, my natural discomfort with any authority that wasn't mine came out in a straight-ahead stare and a loud silence.

"I'm Les Judson," the warden said. "Why don't you come and sit at the table with us? There's plenty of room."

I didn't introduce myself, either out of a misplaced attempt at control, or because I forgot that I was no longer wearing clothes with my name tag on them, or because I was unsure how to respond to the unexpected kindness. I should have accepted the warden's gracious gesture.

"No, thank you, I'm fine here."

As the meeting went on, I regretted my knee-jerk reaction. "Excuse me, warden," I asked during the coffee break, "would it be all right if I stepped into the next office and looked out the window? I'm expecting my daughter and don't want to be late for her visit."

"Go ahead," he said — coldly.

I sighed as I looked out to the parking lot: the battle lines were drawn.

Now, almost two months later, dutifully compliant with his summons, I was on the warden's territory, sitting in the small waiting area in Administration. Fifteen minutes of waiting let me build a head of steam. I amused myself by reading the paper that I took from the receptionist's desk without asking; by deliberately stretching my legs over the narrow passageway to the front door, I caused staff who went by to hesitate ever so slightly before I grudgingly granted them passage.

A short, sallow man in his mid-thirties approached me. I pretended not to see him.

"Mr. Melnitzer?" he asked politely, though I sensed his disapproval of my insolent sprawl.

"Yes?" I answered, a tad too quickly for a man distracted from his newspaper.

"I'm Dave. I don't think we've met. I'm the head CO." *Big fucking deal. And I'm Ambrose, the Amazing Armadillo.*

"The warden wants to see you," Dave went on. "Down this way, please."

I followed Dave to a large office. There the warden and Marie-Andrée Drouin, the deputy warden, belle of Beaver Creek and rising CSC star, awaited me. "Tough but fair" was the word on Marie-Andrée, but she seemed slightly nervous.

"Mr. Melnitzer, I hear you've got an arrogant attitude that's causing a problem," the warden said.

"Can I sit down?" I asked.

"Go ahead." I sat down, drew my left ankle over my right knee, leaned back, and stared at the warden. We glared at each other for almost a minute. I waited until his eyes left mine.

"Is that remark about arrogance a statement or a question?" I asked.

"I'm just telling you what I've heard," the warden replied.

"Who told you that?"

"It doesn't matter. We don't give out names around here."

"That really helps solve the problem," I said. "Well, then, why don't you tell me what've you heard?"

"What I've heard," he answered, "is that you've been bragging about your pass, telling people about your connections that got you the pass. Some people heard you say that you weren't worried about the media because you could buy them."

"That's a pile of shit," I replied. "Even if I got the pass through connections, which you know I didn't, would I be stupid enough to brag about it, for Christ sake? Maybe you should check things out a little better."

My emotion returned the warden's authority to him. "I don't want to have to ship you out of here for your protection."

"Don't threaten me," I said, my voice rising. "Where are you going to ship me? I'm no security risk. What are you going to tell the media? You let a security risk out to Toronto four months into his sentence? Let's get real here."

"I didn't say you were a security risk. We'd ship you to another camp, same security level, for your own protection."

"Right. And we'd go right from camp to court. You could call your precious informants as witnesses, in their rat skins. Then you'd have to ship out half of the Creek's population."

"I'm just telling you to keep a low profile. We try to avoid trouble here."

"I'll tell you what I think." I offered, "I asked for a pass. I didn't think I'd get it. I didn't press. I just asked. The Unit Board approved it. The deputy warden signed it. Now the media shit has hit the fan and you got political heat from Ottawa."

"Not very likely." It was the warden's turn to be agitated. "We did everything by the book. Isn't that right, Dave?"

"We got a call from national headquarters," Dave replied. "I checked the file and told them everything was by the book."

"I wasn't born yesterday." I laughed. "You guys think that just because I'm a convict, I'm stupid. Well, they took everything away, but my brain's still here."

"I'm just telling you to keep a low profile," the warden repeated.

"You mean don't bother applying for any more passes." On the day after Melissa's graduation, I had filed for a pass to see Hans.

"Not at all," the warden replied, too hastily to be convincing.

"Look, I've been in the system for four months. People can't change the minute somebody snaps their finger and says, 'Now you're in jail, be somebody else.' There's no orientation course for this sort of thing, you know. I'm doing my best. Why don't you help me by getting your staff off my back?"

"Just do your best to keep a low profile. Have a nice day." Dismissed.

I left without a word, irritated but unshaken, convinced I had won the battle — but I had missed the point again.

For someone devoted to image making, I had considerable difficulty comprehending the role of perception in prison. My meeting with the warden was an opportunity to learn, but my ego chose form over substance. True, the warden was not skilled at diplomacy and was oblivious to personal dynamics; he had made a valid point imperfectly because his insecurities paralleled mine, turning what should have been a discussion into an argument.

His simple message was: being who you are, you're in a difficult spot in prison, whether you like it or not; so why don't you just cool it, stay in your room, mind your own business, keep your mouth shut, and eat a little crow? Had I digested the advice, I would have found it unappetizing, but nutritious.

War and peace

Changing masks is easier than changing faces.
EDWARD DE BONO

The isolation I felt in the aftermath of Melissa's graduation left me with a much keener feeling of imprisonment than my inability to leave the camp at will. Although jailhouse friendships are limited by an assumption of impermanence, I was deprived even of the "us against the world" camaraderie that is prison's way of imitating community. I could talk to Mickey and Nick, but our mutual psychotherapy was consoling, not mending.

Despite my overt rebelliousness in the warden's presence, I made a deliberate and successful effort to tone down. I kept my opinions to myself, cut down on the sarcastic barbs I had passed off as jocularity, stayed away from the high-visibility area of the duty office, and limited the easy contact with the guards that was my way of asserting dignity but raised the ire of my fellow cons. I spent afternoons as well as evenings in my cell, confining my social contact to Mickey and to my weekly outings with the camp's baseball team, including away games in Gravenhurst on group passes.

By the beginning of July, the grapevine had new fish to fry. When Angie, the drag queen, arrived in camp, both my pass and my presence became old news. As my peers afforded me a grudging acceptance, I turned to my relationship with Melissa, convinced that there, I could find a starting point, if not the answer, to my perplexed search for love.

I loved Melissa, as expressed by my commitment to her over twenty-two years; by the same token, I had loved none of the women in my life, none of the people in my life, and few, if any, of the things in my life. How could that be? I had never *felt* uncaring; throughout my life, I had a strong *desire* to give and to care. My next step, I decided, would be to learn how to act on that desire, and then act on it by reaching out to the people and the things I cared about.

Inevitably, my examination of my relationships with others led me to questions about the place of people in this world — questions of faith. Hans, convinced that mental health and forgiveness of my father went hand in hand, had urged that I reintroduce myself to my past.

"Go to a synagogue," he said, a few months before my internment.

"I've tried, Hans. I can't sit still there. I don't feel anything."

"You do feel something. That's why you can't sit still. Go to an empty synagogue. Sit there alone."

It was the only one of Hans's suggestions that I had ignored.

At Beaver Creek, I remembered Hans's advice. Although I was intensely schooled in religious orthodoxy, I was inexperienced in matters of faith. I wrote to Beaver Creek's part-time Jewish chaplain, Rabbi Barry Schneider from Toronto. He visited in early June, just after Deena left me, and regularly through the summer. Although my views of faith remained inconclusive, the rabbi, with the aid of literature he provided, helped me put religion and my Jewishness in a therapeutic context; as Hans had predicted, the peek at my roots brought me face to face with my father. In late June, during the Jewish festival of Shavuot, I lit the traditional

memorial candles for my father, the first time I had done so since
his death.

As family assumed a new perspective, my relationship with my
mother deepened. Her support, as I awaited incarceration and
endured it, had been unconditional, awakening me to her love. It
was time to explore that bond, and she and I did so on her monthly
visits and during our twice-weekly phone calls and regular correspondence. With our historic programming as a retardant to change,
our journey was winding, but forward.

Theory and practice didn't merge quite as effortlessly in my feelings about Deena, though I removed all her physical traces, including my wedding ring, on shifting my belongings to a single cell ten
days after she left me. I fell asleep and awoke with Deena as my
first and last thoughts every day, but in between, I was much more
ambivalent. I teetered between a sense of loss and a sense of freedom, sometimes revelling in the lack of responsibility, sometimes
thinking that it had been forever since I spoke to Deena and that I
missed her more and more as time went on. In denial, I fantasized,
regretting that I might never get the opportunity to savour our com-
patibility when we were both healthier and more mature. Joan, a
regular visitor, opined that I was "more sad than depressed."

With our anniversary coming up on July 13, I wanted to get
in touch with Deena. Hans didn't deter me, but recommended that
I put my thoughts in writing.

"There's no need to talk to her. You're both too angry."

I agreed. After many drafts, I typed up the final version of a
letter to Deena on July 10, but never mailed it. That decision
unearthed a healthy progression from my fixation with the past, a
move on to the future through the present. Patience, I learned, was
not always passive, and activity not always positive.

As my evolutionary pace quickened, I found myself looking to

Hans for advice more and more. With the immediate crisis of Deena's departure behind me, Hans and I returned to our regular pattern of weekly phone calls and monthly or bimonthly visits, but more frequent, personal contact was necessary to sustain progress. Hans could only make the trip to Beaver Creek occasionally, and I sought other ways to see him.

When I first visited with Judge David Cole after my arrest, he mentioned "parole by exception": laws that permitted unescorted passes in exceptional cases, limited to serious personal or family illness. David told me that, some years previously, he had used these provisions to obtain passes for a client whose mental health was deteriorating because the required psychiatric intervention was unavailable in jail.

Naturally, I jumped at the prospect of unescorted passes before my eligibility date in August 1993. Bob Bigelow warned me that the chances were very slim, suggesting that only a prognosis of imminent disaster would meet the legal requirements; he felt, however, that it was "worth a shot."

I applied for parole by exception soon after my transfer to Beaver Creek. The hearing was scheduled for August; pending the hearing, I applied for escorted passes to see Hans.

Paul, my living unit officer, a prototype of bureaucratic indolence, didn't process my application for over a month, despite repeated promises in the interim both to me and to Chandler.

In mid-July, Strohm summoned me. "I've been looking at your pass application," he said, in his business-like way.

"What's the problem?"

"I ran it by the warden this morning, informally. No way."

"Am I a security risk?" I asked.

"I can't answer that."

"You mean the warden doesn't want any more heat."

I was determined not to be pushed around; if the warden

insisted on bypassing my rights, I would fight him. I was encouraged by support for my parole-by-exception application from my case management team, composed of Chandler, Paul, and Dr. Quirt; even the Toronto police department supported the application, citing the benefits of psychiatric help. The only objectors were the parole officer in Toronto who prepared the community assessment and Dave Davey, who took the unusual step of dissenting from the opinions of his staff.

Spurred on by my unresolved emotions over the separation from Deena, I started my "paper war." In the last week of July, I filed a careful, technical grievance against the warden's refusal of my escorted passes to see Hans; next, I took on Davey, blasting him in a second grievance that was a scathing rebuttal of his dissent from the case management team's report. What I didn't admit to myself was that my crusade wasn't restricted to the attainment of my goals: irate at the power the warden exercised over me, I wanted to best him.

But the fallout from graduation had taught me a bit about prison politics, and I kept my activities to myself. A move to Accommodations earlier in July had eased my quest for anonymity.

Accommodations, which housed forty-two inmates, was divided into three upper and three lower ranges: the lower ranges were close to the tiled, private showers with heated floors and to the common rooms; the upper ranges, where I lived, were more isolated, located off narrow, winding, dark passageways, and featuring attractive, fifteen-foot-high sloping wood ceilings in rooms half as large again as standard CSC cells.

Accommodations' inhabitants tended to be loners, discreet in their indiscretions, inclined to time in their rooms and inbred social circles. As long-term residents of the camp, they cut an influential swath with the staff and were privy to official and unofficial privileges inaccessible to new arrivals. The trailer's population was younger, noisier, much more gregarious, and more inclined to bravado and drug-induced trouble.

Drawing on five months of practical joint experience, I put a screwdriver through the existing holes in the worn, stained mattress left behind by the previous occupant of my room in Accommodations, enlarging the holes sufficiently to meet SIS's damage requirement for the mattress's exchange; for two bales (prison slang for pouches) of tobacco, an inmate who worked in the paint shop redid my room in cheerful baby blue on the afternoon of my move, and I spent the evening stripping and waxing the floor. I decorated the desk, the bulletin board, and the shelves with the Mac-Tac Melissa had brought to the camp for me; as a finishing touch, I strategically set a large, stuffed "Maude" representing my beloved bitch on my pillow and carefully positioned my mementoes of Melissa, including graduation snapshots, all over the walls, shelves, and bulletin board.

This was my twelfth residence in less than five months in prison, an average of twelve days between moves; it was also my fourth room in ninety days at Beaver Creek, and, I hoped, my last. A prisoner's permanence. From here I would go home.

The camp's patricians were the group that formed around Nick, the other ex-lawyer in the camp, who was serving a twelve-year sentence for cocaine trafficking. In December 1991, the Parole Board turned down his application for day parole, but Nick won a rehearing scheduled for the following September.

Nick's group was made up of three blacks, two of whom, Nelson and Rolph, were lifers; the third, Clint, was serving a fifteen-year sentence for an armed robbery resulting in the paralysis of the shooting victim. The entire group lived in proximity on the upper floor in the Accommodations building, avoiding the mainstream politicking, backbiting, bickering, and petty envy that characterized most of the camp.

In late April, I had a brief run-in with Nelson over the use of the pay telephone. Nick took it upon himself to smooth things over, offering fatherly advice on Beaver Creek etiquette as it applied to high-profile lawyers. From then on, Nick and I maintained a friendship that flourished with my move to Accommodations. He introduced me to the group's biweekly basketball games, and I slid effortlessly into their smooth routine.

Vitalized, I looked forward to my three-day family visit with Melissa, scheduled to begin on the morning of Tuesday, July 28, just ten days before her departure abroad. Inmates are entitled to bimonthly three-day trailer visits with close family, common-law spouses, and even with girlfriends. Beaver Creek's small population made these visits possible every six weeks.

The two-storey private family visit (PFV) cottage facing the main building was configured to shut out prison. The main bedroom on the top floor overlooked a large back yard surrounded by the Muskoka woods and an attractive eight-foot-high solid pine fence. Nature was also the focal point of the ground floor, consisting of a kitchen and a combined living and dining area which led, through sliding glass patio doors, to the back porch, complete with lawn chairs and a barbecue; only a picnic table and a sandbox interrupted the yard's greenery.

Our visit was undisturbed: security rules called for a twice-a-day personal check on the cottage, but my only contact with staff was a single phone call from Paul, asking if Nick could borrow my baseball glove. I could have been halfway around the world by the time I was expected back at the duty office at 10:30 on Friday morning.

Melissa and I stayed in for two days, talking, reading, watching TV, and listening to music on the tape deck supplied by the Inmate Committee. Our conversations were emotional torrents, but I reserved my tears for moments of silence, when Melissa didn't know I was watching her, thankful that the one thing I was left with was the one that mattered.

Deena wasn't far away either, her absence a respectful testament to finality. Here, safely sequestered with Melissa, my ego suppressed its affront over the trophy that got away, and I mourned, temporarily displacing my anger. The mourning engaged me in its authenticity, dissolving my masks, allowing me a glimpse of the joy that is in all honest feelings: even the saddest moments pulse with the energy of life.

Melissa departed early Friday morning, promising to return for a final goodbye on the following Wednesday. Drained by the intensity of our time together, a common reaction to trailer visits, I napped until lunch. Eddie, his attention in its customary hold setting, either didn't notice my absence from school or didn't care.

I decided not to go to the dining room, choosing to spend the afternoon working on the manuals I had promised Eddie. Still unable to face prison after my brief respite, I had myself counted at mail call and skipped dinner. At 5:30, I was absorbed in the computer when Mickey walked in without knocking.

"Have you been to the duty office?" Mickey asked.

"Just for mail call. Why?"

"There's a parole list for August with your name on it."

"How long's that list been up?" I demanded.

"It doesn't matter, Julius. It's all over camp."

"What's all over camp?"

"Everything. You've made a deal. You're getting out. Your daughter's going to Israel to get things ready for you."

"They're going to take that fucking list off right now."

I hurried to the duty office, imagining the inquiring, blaming glances of everyone I passed. I knocked on the back door, noting the parole list as I did so. Sue, who seemed to be on duty whenever something was happening to me, greeted me with a smile.

"They've got no right to put my name up on that list," I announced unceremoniously. "If they don't take it down, I'll get a goddamn injunction right away."

"What are you talking about?" Sue asked, obviously intimidated. Youthful and not yet indoctrinated in the knee-jerk authoritarian responses of more hardened CSC personnel, Sue spoke to me as an equal.

"That parole list on the window. It's already all over the goddamn camp. I don't need the grief. I want you to take it down."

"That's the way we've always done it as long as I've been here," Sue explained innocently.

"I don't give a fuck. That doesn't make it right. First of all, it's a breach of my privacy. The cocksucking inmates here don't have any right to know what's going on with me. And the other thing is, they have to give me proper notice of my hearing. That means an envelope to me, not a sign in a public place."

"I'll take it down for now," Sue said, "and give Strohm a memo. He can decide what to do Monday morning — Tuesday morning, it's a long weekend."

"Thanks." I softened. "I really appreciate it."

Back in my room, I wrote a memo to Strohm urging him to keep my name off the list. Still agitated, I followed it with two sarcastic responses to the Toronto parole officer who had objected to my parole-by-exception application.

The remonstrances did not address my basic problems. My life was operating at extremes. On a practical level, things were going well: the Work Board transferred me to the school full-time, relieving me of an uncomfortable position as a computer clerk in SIS, which I had taken on in early July in preference to the garbage pickup job. Some of the staff had taken advantage of my skills to help them with personal problems and their workload on an ad hoc basis, rewarding me with an occasional stretch of the rules that went beyond the general laxity of Creek security.

There is a strong argument that I had it made; things could have been very relaxed and pleasant, but for my tendency to push everything to the limit. Despite Melissa's absence and the loss of Deena, I was cheered by the loyalty of three of my staunchest legal clients, all of whom applied, during the month of August, to visit me. My personal friends communicated regularly and I was still earning money from the consulting work couriered between Beaver Creek and Toronto. Hans had stood by me, there whenever I needed help.

Maybe it was all too rosy. Maybe I didn't feel punished enough. Slowly but surely, my life pattern was re-emerging, mutating to the new environment, repainting the masks without removing them. Nowhere was this more evident than in my association with my first real circle of friends in prison, Nick's group.

As I had been in London, I was the newcomer; as in London, my brains, energy, talent, and gregariousness took me to the inner circle; as in London and Toronto, my friends respected me, sought my advice, and looked to me for leadership. Predictably, I felt dependent on their opinions, certain my unworthiness would be discovered and I would be unmasked.

Soon, I found myself searching out the approval of those who had accepted me; life at the Creek became as serious as life on the street. I struggled at basketball and baseball, increasingly frustrated at my inability to keep up with men younger and fitter than I; I listened to others' problems, affecting a confidence that suggested I was above it all; I calmed them in their fears about the future by painting a rosy and exaggerated picture of my own possibilities; I railed with them against the system, raising argument to conviction, prematurely hawking victory in my battles with CSC.

In mid-August, I met with Dave in an attempt to settle my three grievances. Our meeting was polite and as satisfactory as could be expected when bargaining power is so grossly imbalanced. He agreed to strike my name off the parole schedule before it was reposted, but he would not withdraw his opposition to my application, adding that he had not intended an attack on my good faith or sincerity.

"If you succeed, it will open the floodgates. Everybody who can't get treatment in here will be looking for a pass."

Mollified by his assurance that the dissent wasn't personal, I withdrew my grievance. As for my escorted passes to see Dr. Arndt, they had become academic with the imminence of the parole hearing and were no longer worth pursuing.

We parted on good terms, I thought. I went right over to Accommodations and bragged to Nick and Mickey. That evening, the parole list went back up, with my name removed: my "victory" raised my stature.

It was all a show. I wasn't happy with the compromises I had made, as I had never been content with the results of the cases I settled. Compromise had always been defeat for me, slowing down the pace of conquest; no matter how good my intellectual and professional judgement, anything short of clear, public victory tore me apart inside.

What I had feared most was happening. I wasn't changing: I was retrenching. I had lost much of my desire for privileges that could draw attention, resentment, and perhaps, more media coverage. But obsession bested reason again, and I continued fighting — the fighting still more important than the fight.

Rock bottom

I crawl into my loneliness
But cannot find a place to hide.
BERNICE LARSEN WEBB

Sparked by two spectacular escapes, tension mounted at Beaver Creek in August. The first escapee was a lifer with a previous escape record, who wasn't missed for almost six hours; the second was Angie, the pill-popping drag queen whose arrival in late June had turned the spotlight away from me; she roared away under cover of night in a CSC truck, using one of the keys that floated loosely around the camp. "Inmate Flees Beaver Creek in Pink Jumpsuit," screamed one local headline. Lax security of this kind was the norm in Beaver Creek. Apart from the lack of attention on my family visit with Melissa, I had twice dozed through the dinner count; nobody bothered looking for me until 7 P.M.

Upset at news coverage that pointed to security lapses at the camp, the warden decided to take attendance on his own, and with Sol, the correctional supervisor, toured the camp to check things out. My tennis partner and I were the first suspects, coolly playing out our point while the warden and Sol waited on the sidelines. Only then did we meet at centre court, in the manner of Wimbledon. Sol, carrying a clipboard, looked uncomfortable.

"Mr. Melnitzer," the warden said, "and what are we doing?"

"Playing tennis, Mr. Judson." I kept a straight face.

"Why aren't you at work?"

"Janna told us the school would be closed this afternoon because somebody's been sabotaging the network."

"Did you check in?"

"Check in?"

"Yes, check in?" mimicked the warden, incredulous.

"I don't know what you mean." I didn't.

"I mean did you check in and have attendance taken?"

"There's nobody at the school to check in with. Janna said she wouldn't be there at one and Eddie's away today."

"Write that down, Sol. We'll confirm it."

"Can we get back to our game?" I asked.

"You're supposed to be in your room if you're not working," the warden replied.

"I didn't know. Nobody's ever objected before." Sol winced noticeably.

"Well, I don't want you playing tennis on my time."

That was too much for me. Puffed with the truth of my explanation about why I wasn't in school, I did a mental calculation that told me I was earning between seventy and eighty cents an hour. I reached in my pocket and pulled out a two-dollar bill.

"Here. This should cover the rest of the afternoon."

The warden wasn't amused. "You know the rule now. Don't let me catch you here again during working hours."

As he stomped away, my tennis partner and I went home, laughing our heads off.

A few days later, Bob Bigelow and I appeared before a Parole Board panel of two. I was relaxed going in, not expecting much.

Bob would have to convince the Parole Board that my mental health was deteriorating. Hans's report, the crux of my case, didn't go that far: I was "making progress" with my emotional problems, but the progress could be accelerated considerably with greater access to therapy. I took an inner satisfaction from my lack of desire to manipulate the evidence.

"I read your rebuttals to Mr. Davey and the parole officer, and I didn't see any evidence of thought impairment." That statement was the chairperson's, Max Stienburg's, first question.

"I don't have any problems intellectually or cognitively," I answered.

With that admission, Stienburg warmed to me. His questions were pointed but fair, addressing the relevant factual and legal issues.

"What would you do if you couldn't get to see Dr. Arndt?"

"I'd manage." Bob almost choked — it was true, but the kind of frankness lawyers don't like.

"That's an honest answer," said Stienburg, "not the histrionics I expected when this case started."

The board denied my application because my "mental health was not likely to suffer serious damage." The reasons carefully pointed out that the result of this "exceptional" application was not to be taken as a reflection of the societal risk involved in my release, nor of the probability of my reoffending.

I left the hearing content: the board had been fair and that was all I expected. The chairperson had taken Bob aside afterwards and confided that he was impressed with my candour. That meant more to me than success.

At Beaver Creek, inmates hang around the main building on parole board days, checking out the tos and fros at the administration building through the large windows in V & C. My deletion from the parole list had done its job temporarily, but now the secret was out.

My satisfaction at the conduct, if not the result, of the hearing disappeared on my way back to Accommodations. Accosted repeatedly by curious inmates, I replied with "No comment," "My lawyer told me not to say anything," and "I really don't want to talk about it." The new me had learned the value of silence, and the old me was glad to avoid admitting defeat. Since only Chandler and I, in the camp, knew the outcome, and Chandler was strictly professional about privacy, not even the staff could discover the result.

Unfortunately, my silence came across as insolence, causing as much trouble as my exuberance had previously: in cons' eyes, I was privileged, and if I didn't admit it, that didn't make it any less true. I would have been better off acknowledging the hearing's result, allowing the fallibility of defeat to reduce my imagined privileges to earthly proportions.

The staff were no less curious than the inmates. At least twice during the next week, I overheard guards discussing my case with cons. Lewis, an LU who was one of my favourites, confided that his "sources at the Parole Board" had confirmed my release in six months after paying back my creditors; my daughter was in Israel to retrieve the money. Inmates repeated the story often enough to make it clear that Lewis didn't keep his information to himself.

Elaine, an offenders' programs specialist, approached me in the dining room lineup. "Julius, I've never heard of parole by exception. You still have your lawyer's bag of tricks, don't you?" I could hear the grumbling above the din of a roomful of convicts.

I was back in a fishbowl. There is nothing worse for an attention seeker than attention he does not seek. I was becoming the outlet for the increasing tension in the camp, fed not only by a third escape but also by the passage of tough new prison and parole laws, which put everybody's release plans in jeopardy. In anticipation of the legislation, all recreational passes, including movie, sports, and shopping outings, were cancelled without explanation, causing a dangerous uncertainty in an uncertain, powerless population.

About the same time, I sought a half-day ETA to meet with Hans in Huntsville, some thirty miles from the camp. When the warden turned down the request out of hand, I rushed to the correctional supervisors' office, slamming the door behind me as hard as I could; I sat down nose to nose with Sol in the small office.

"You tell the fucking warden that he should try for an honest bone in his body," I shouted. "If the warden doesn't want to play straight, we'll try out some of your security practices on the local newspapers. Or the histories of some of the guys running around this place. I bet the umpires in Gravenhurst would be calling a lot less strikes on our guys if they knew whom they were aggravating."

Inmate tantrums were commonplace to Sol. "What's bugging you, Julius?"

"What's bugging me is a straight answer. I know fucking well why I can't get ETAs. Why don't you guys just admit it's politics and we'll go from there?"

Sol exhaled and bent over. He was a large man in his thirties, and the forward movement of his bulk intimated that I was about to pay for being a major prick. But I liked Sol. He had always treated me well.

"Look, Sol. I'm sorry. There's a better way to handle this, I know. It's got nothing to do with you. Things have just been building up."

"Didn't you just get parole?"

"I got shit." Weary of the tug-of-war, I told Sol about my hearing.

"You're kidding," he said.

"If you'd keep your goddamn staff out of my hair," I said, furious again, "I wouldn't blow up like this."

"Something you want to tell me?"

"No, I just think you'd have less trouble around here if you told your staff to mind their own business. Things have been crazy around here lately. What's going on?"

"There's a lot of pressure," Sol divulged.

"What kind of pressure?"

"Upstairs. The community."

"Looks to me like the warden's feeling it," I said triumphantly. "You didn't look too happy when he was on the rampage through the camp a few days ago."

"I'm not," Sol said. "Keep this to yourself. I asked for a transfer. Well, I filled out the documents. I'm not pushing it, but you know...."

"Why?"

"I still travel back and forth between here and Kingston weekends. It's not worth it if I have to put up with all the bullshit."

With Sol exposed, I took him into my confidence. "Me, I can't just leave. What should I do about the warden and my passes?"

"I'm not sure the warden knows how you feel. I'll try to set up a meeting between the two of you for tomorrow morning."

"I'd really appreciate that. Sorry again about the outburst."

My correspondence that day brought a curt note from Deena saying that she didn't want me to use our Bell credit card beyond September. The telephone was my lifeline in jail; the regular pay phones, not limited to collect calls, were among Beaver Creek's most liberating and humane features.

Deena's note energized the stress of my session with Sol. Powerlessness was one thing; helplessness was worse.

I called Hans, who promised to speak to Deena, avoiding a confrontation. She was gone for the weekend. Patience and helplessness are poor bedfellows, breeding distrust; I spent a sleepless night worrying about what Deena would do with my personal possessions, the household goods we had agreed to split, and the dogs.

My state of mind had not changed by next morning, when I arrived at the warden's office. Peripherally, I saw Chandler on the couch, beside Dave Davey, and Sol across the room from them.

"They told me you were a gentleman when I agreed to accept you here so early in your sentence," the warden said.

I didn't answer him.

"What's this I hear about you running into Sol's office, slamming doors and pounding desks and threatening me?" he continued.

"I wasn't threatening anybody. I just figured the public should know about the bullshit that passes for security around here."

"Would you mind explaining that to me?"

"I mean that I can't get passes for legitimate medical reasons. I'm no security risk. I can't even get reasons for your decision."

"I apologize for being late," said the warden, sarcastically.

"I could live with that if you just told me the truth. The last time I was in here, you denied that there was any pressure over the pass to my daughter's graduation. Why don't you just give me the straight goods? 'Julius, there's been three escapes, you were all over the media the last time and we can't let you go.' I'm telling you, I could live with that."

"My problem," the warden said, "is that I'm too fair. On my last job evaluation, the deputy commissioner complained that I gave inmates too much consideration. He used your pass as a specific example."

The warden opened the desk drawer on his right, pulling out a sheaf of paper.

"If you don't believe me, I have my evaluation right here. Would you like to read it?"

"No, thank you."

"Beaver Creek's a media draw for Toronto. There's no way you're going to Toronto."

Finally, the truth.

"What about my rights? The new Act, section 86, entitles me to reasonable access to mental health facilities."

"We could send you to RTC if you insist." RTC was the

Regional Treatment Centre, the maximum security psychiatric facility inside the walls of Kingston Penitentiary.

"Send me wherever you fucking well please and we'll let the Federal Court sort it out. I don't give a damn. What else can you do to me? You haven't got any basis to send me to RTC and you know it."

"That outburst in Sol's office sounded pretty serious."

The furtherance of the threat infuriated me. "You just go ahead and try to make me out as a head case. Yeah, I pounded the table and slammed the door, just the way you went running around the camp like a chicken with your head cut off when the pressure got to you. But I said my piece and I apologized to Sol."

"I hope so," said the warden, looking at Sol, who nodded vigorously, playing both sides of the fence.

"What about seeing Dr. Arndt in Huntsville?" I asked.

"You're not going to his cottage."

"You mean it doesn't look good."

"That's exactly what I mean."

"What about meeting somewhere else? All I want is the therapy, not the cottage."

"That sounds reasonable. If you can arrange neutral territory, I'll give you the pass."

"Great. I'll talk to Dr. Arndt and see if he can get access to an office or a hospital or something like that."

"I'll go further. If you can't find a place, I'll ask Dr. Heath to let you use his office." Dr. Heath was the camp doctor, whose private practice was in one of the nearby towns.

"I appreciate that. But I'd like to make it as easy as I can for Dr. Arndt, and Huntsville is closer. Let me ask him and I'll let you know."

"Anything else?"

"No, thank you."

I got up, not feeling dismissed as I had the last time and wanting to extend my hand to the warden. Uncertain that the gesture was appropriate, I thanked the warden again, and Sol. Chandler left with me, shaking his head as we exited the building.

"Did I do something wrong, Chandler?"

"No, I thought things came out all right in the end."

"So, what's the problem? I wasn't going to let him get away with any more bullshit."

"You certainly did that." Unmindful of the hidden warning in Chandler's remark, I gloated.

The meeting was good enough for me, but not good enough for my image. Back in my room, I bragged to my friends as long as they could tolerate it.

Everything was well in hand. I was a hero, the rebellious toast of my circle, and soon I would be out on a pass again. I just wished I could get Deena out of my mind.

On Monday, I ran the warden's proposal by Hans.

"It's not worth it, Julius, for one pass. I don't want you fighting the authorities all the time. I'll come to Beaver Creek."

"When?"

"Next Saturday. On my way to the cottage."

"Great. Have you spoken to Deena?"

"Yes, I left a message at the condo. She called me long distance."

"What did she say?"

"She was callous. She said the relationship was over."

"I can figure that out for myself," I said bitterly and despondently.

"She said you wouldn't speak to her. That you keep giving her messages through Melissa."

"I'm just following your advice, Hans. What did she say about the credit card?"

"She says she's broke."

"I've heard enough, Hans. I'm going to call her myself."

"If you must. But try to avoid a big blowup."

"We've already had a big blowup. I'll see you Saturday."

Deena wasn't in. I left a message.

Later that afternoon, I memoed the warden that I wouldn't need the pass to Huntsville: the gesture was but an outward flag of surrender.

On Tuesday, September 1, Deena returned my call. She accused me of "manipulating Hans," of "not having changed at all," and thought I would "manage fine without the credit card."

That evening, our group from Accommodations played basketball. The games had become incrementally intense as the same teams played each other repeatedly: arguments were frequent and a roughness had crept in. Still, the exercise was an alleviating constant, the bickering a release of my frustration. This night, I played fiercely, as if my being was at stake. No one was going to push me around any more. I'd had enough from the warden, from the staff, from the inmates, from Deena.

Nick and I argued over possession of a loose ball; Nick stood on the sideline, preparing to inbound. I was still nattering at him about who had touched the ball last, when, unable to find an open man, he tried to bounce the ball back out of bounds off my leg. It hit me in the groin.

Without warning, I attacked Nick, pushing and swinging wildly at him; Nick, facing a parole hearing in less than two weeks, did little but defend himself. Four men wrestled me to the ground. I flailed at them until they let me up. I went at Nick again, with only Clint trying to keep us apart.

"You rat. You goof," I taunted Nick. Clint moved away, and I stepped right into a punch between the eyes; the ring on Nick's finger cut a gash in my nose, which bled profusely. As Nick and I continued dancing around each other, an alert con grabbed the cleaner's mop, furiously mopping up the evidence.

Clint stepped between us again. After a few more insults, I returned to my room, disposed of my bloody clothes, and took a shower downstairs, leaving my room unlocked. In the bathroom mirror, I saw that the bruising from the cut was spreading, racoon-style, under both eyes. Back in my room, I opened my *armoire* to find a paper cup with at least six ounces of Scotch in it, placed there by an unknown friend with access to Beaver Creek's readily available stocks. I drank it in a gulp. Anxious to avoid company, I set off across the baseball diamond, resting on a boulder just beyond the boundary.

Eventually, the Scotch calmed me. I returned to Accommodations well before the guards started their evening walk. As I stopped by our range's fridge for a cold pop. Nick came by, apologetic, but I brushed off his attempts at conciliation.

I turned off the lights in my room, shielding my condition from the patrolling guards, and, exhausted, soon fell asleep.

In the morning, I covered up my shiners with the $200 designer sunglasses that I usually saved for visits. I waited for school to open, as I did most mornings, with a cup of coffee in V & C.

Sol arrived for work. I removed my glasses as I approached him.

"Wow," he said, "what happened to you?"

"I thought I'd better tell you about this before you heard any rumours. I caught an elbow playing basketball last night."

"Quite an elbow," Sol said.

"Just thought I'd tell you," I said, putting my sunglasses back on and returning to my table.

Nick sat there. We looked at each other. And I grinned.

"I shouldn't have hit you," Nick said.

"You were just defending yourself," I replied. "It had nothing to do with you. Things have been rough lately."

"With Deena?"

"With Deena, with the parole hearing, with the warden, with everything. I'm sorry, Nick."

"I thought things were all right."

"Forget it." As we shook hands, Nick surprised me with tears. Again, I had failed to appreciate how strongly my friends felt about me; again, all I had wanted had been there all along.

"It's 10:30, Eddie," I announced. "I'm going back to my room. I want to give Clint a computer lesson and work on those manuals."

"Security wants everybody to stay here, especially you," replied Eddie.

"What for?"

"I don't know. They just told me to keep you in sight."

"Fuck them. Clint's waiting up there for me."

Unable to think, I paced until Clint arrived. "What's going on out there?" I asked him.

"They don't believe it's an elbow. They think you were being muscled or something. Conrad and Nick are in there right now explaining things."

"Am I in trouble?"

"I don't know. They're treating it seriously."

I skipped lunch for a walk with my old solace Kevin, who had arrived at the Creek in June, promptly enrolling himself in an education program at the government's expense — as he had promised when I first met him on the Grey Goose.

"Are they going to ship me out, Kevin?"

"No way. They'll fine you maybe, or take away some privileges."

Taking what I wanted to hear as gospel, I got up the nerve to return to V & C. I went to Sol's office, unaware that Conrad had just left. Several months later, when I accessed my Internal Preventative Security (IPSO) file under the Privacy Act, I discovered Conrad's complaint that "something has to be done about Melnitzer, he's causing a lot of trouble in the camp": the inmate chairman, whose job was to intervene on my behalf, was trying to get rid of me.

"I had to report this to the deputy warden," Sol said. "The warden's away."

"So now what?" I asked.

"I don't know. I told her it was no big deal."

"Did you speak to Nick, Sol?"

"Yeah, he told me it was all over."

"So what did you have to report it to the deputy warden for?"

"Because you lost it in here a few weeks ago and then you had that outburst in the warden's office last Friday."

"Outburst?" I screamed. "Sol, I thought we resolved things. That's what you told the warden."

"It's out of my hands," said Sol.

"Like fuck it is. It's of your making. What happens now?"

"Hang around here. I'm pretty sure she'll want to see you soon."

At 2:30, the deputy warden called for me. As I approached her office in the administration building, I noticed a CSC van just outside the rear exit; the van's back door was open for loading.

"I don't believe the story about the elbow to the face" were the deputy warden's opening words.

"Let's not deal with the obvious," I said.

"Then I must tell you that we don't tolerate fighting in a minimum security institution. I've decided to send you to Warkworth."

"Without hearing a word from me?"

"That's why we're here now," answered Marie-Andrée.

"But you've already decided. I saw the van."

"I'm here to listen," she insisted.

"Then what are your reasons?" I demanded.

"Deteriorating behaviour, fighting, and threats to another inmate."

"Have you spoken with Nick?"

"We can't disclose the names of informants."

"Well, I want Nick here," I said. "I can't make my case without him."

"I'm sorry," said the deputy warden.

"Well, then, I'd like to call my lawyer."

"You can do that when you get to Warkworth."

"I guess you've made up your mind."

"Our information is that there was a prolonged fight, that you were the aggressor, and that you threatened to kill another inmate."

"Who are your informants?"

"That doesn't matter."

"What's this bullshit about 'deteriorating behaviour'?"

"The correctional supervisor tells me that you became hysterical in his office a few weeks ago and threatened the warden; also, my information is that you were very agitated in a meeting with the warden last Friday."

"Bullshit. The warden agreed to give me a pass at the end of the meeting. Ask Dave."

Marie-Andrée looked at the head CO quizzically. Davey shook his head. "It doesn't matter," she said.

"You mean what I have to say doesn't matter."

"I'm the one who approved your pass to your daughter's graduation because I thought it was the right thing to do. Since then, all we've been getting from you is a flood of paperwork."

Marie-Andrée caught my sneer. "Of course, the grievances you've filed have nothing to do with this. It's not a question of paper —"

"Then why did you bring them up?" I was rather enjoying my line of questioning.

"Mr. Melnitzer, you don't control the camp. We do."

"What's that got to do with transferring me? I'm no security risk."

"I don't agree with that. I believe that medium security for a while would help you adjust."

"Ten days ago, my CO told the Parole Board that I should be out on UTAs. What are you talking about?"

"Do you have anything else to say?"

"This isn't fair. This fight is the first infraction I have of any kind and it occurred during a sports match. You know damn well nobody gets transferred for a sports fight."

"I'm sorry."

"I'd like to call my lawyer."

"At Warkworth. Now, would you sign this, please?"

The document she put in front of me was a notification of reasons for my transfer, culminating with a consent form that amounted to a waiver of my right of appeal.

"I'm not signing this. I'm going to appeal."

"You are?" The deputy warden seemed genuinely surprised. I wondered, not for the first time, how many inmates unthinkingly renounced their rights. "I think it would be better if you accepted the decision. If you show progress and there are no further incidents, I'll consider taking you back."

"You wouldn't mind putting that in writing, would you?" I asked.

"We can't do that."

"Then fuck your form."

Marie-Andrée started to say something, pursed her lips, and started over. "If you step outside, the officers will escort you."

I left the office. The guard handcuffed me, but didn't search me, and loaded me in the van. The driver stopped the van at the main building, where the vultures gaped while he went inside for the paperwork.

Ten minutes later, we pulled away from the Creek. I was stripped barer than ever, without even the meagre belongings that had accompanied me to every other destination. All I had now, aside from the address book that I always pocketed, were the green shorts and white T-shirt on my back, my underwear, socks, and deck shoes — and, happily, the gift pouch from Melissa, which held my "SuperDad" key chain. That and the scorpion in my pocket reminded me of a verse I had read in the writings of George Iles, a 19th-century Canadian author:

Hope is faith holding out its hands in the dark.

Part Five

REMORSE

I would far rather feel remorse
than know how to define it.
THOMAS À KEMPIS

Medium

*Zen masters say that when we become
convinced that the human situation is hopeless,
we approach serenity, the ideal state of mind.*
TOM ROBBINS

Warkworth is set in eastern Ontario's Kawartha Lakes district, not
far from Peterborough, two hours east of Toronto and three hours
southeast of Beaver Creek. Chain link fences over twenty feet high,
topped with barbed wire, surround Canada's largest prison, a medium security institution. Raised, squarish, grey watchtowers sit just
beyond the fences, but the freestanding variety of buildings on the
spacious grounds, the greenery, and the neighbouring farmhouses
modify the prison's austerity; the barbed wire disappears in the
irregular, pastoral pattern of the undulating hills.

Unlike Millhaven, which speaks to a world of fences, Warkworth
seems separated by fences of necessity, like a factory or an army
base. The large parking lots on the northern and western perimeters
reinforce the impression that people work, but do not live, within.

Warkworth greeted me privately and quietly, for I arrived at
5 P.M., during the supper count. The A & D staff, quartered in
a mobile home, noticed me only long enough to hand me a plastic
bag of basics; at Reception's back door, Martin, a smiling, kindly
guard, guided me along a bright yellow corridor of thirty double-
bunked cells.

Cell number ten, opposite a small lounge area adjacent to the bubble, was cheerier than most, looking out on the countryside beyond the parking lot. Three card tables and two couches took most of the lounge, which also had two telephones; a television was perched atop an aging refrigerator located at the end of an L-shaped utility counter closest to my cell; on the counter sat a microwave, a toaster, and a coffee urn.

I recognized my cell partner, Dino, a red-haired, baby-faced, twenty-five-year-old first offender, in for a number of break and enters. Dino had lived across the hall from me on the long range in the trailer at Beaver Creek; we were comfortable enough with each other to shake hands warmly. My young friend had been evicted from camp in the summer for impetuously refusing to work after a disagreement with his boss. His impishness disguised a testy, childish streak that had involved him in scrape after scrape through his two and a half years in the penitentiary. While the incidents were minor by prison standards, in the manner of schoolyard fisticuffs, Dino's long list of institutional offences kept him in prison beyond his parole eligibility; he was awaiting statutory release next summer.

Dino was relaxed and respectful with me, restricting his squabbles to punks his own age; we talked easily about Warkworth's ins and outs until supper was announced.

The circuitous route from Reception to the dining room took us along an outdoor breezeway, past the Health Care Centre to Two Control, Warkworth's central security post and main intersection, encased in the same heavily smoked glass as the control towers at Millhaven. Beyond Two Control, a grassy, open area on our right afforded a view of the nonsmoking Eighty-Man Unit, or EMU, CSC's Holiday Inn: the two-storey grey concrete block structure, barely a year old, sported garishly yellow aluminum siding, giving the appearance of an oversized Lego construct.

So far, Warkworth was more reminiscent of Beaver Creek than

of Millhaven — like a camp with fences; on the walk from Reception to the dining room, I saw only three guards. Here, the herding endemic to Millhaven and the buckets gave way to loosely monitored individual movement. Greens were supposedly mandatory during working hours, but sweatsuits were in evidence much of the day. In the evenings and on weekends, Warkworth became a fashion emporium as inmates dressed to distance themselves from their drab days. In the living units, the bubble opened cell doors electronically at the push of a buzzer and inmates shut their own doors, except in Reception.

Tiny, one of my first acquaintances at Warkworth, had recently arrived there. His reaction was typical of inmates who had come from higher security institutions:

> Well, life here at Warkworth is sure different than in max. Ten times better, I would have to say. Coming from where I'd just come from, this place gave the impression of utopia.

The dining hall at the breezeway's end was flooded with natural light from the floor to the twenty-foot-high ceilings. But the noise from the open scullery was deafening, and the room as a whole was uninviting, all metal tables and cement floors.

Although I acknowledged a few inmates I had encountered elsewhere in the system, I ate with strangers. Vegetarian fare was available, but the food was awful, barely a chip wagon to Beaver Creek's cuisine; and dinner in my cell at Millhaven was preferable to eating among Warkworth's population of seven hundred. As I ate, I imagined the whispers about my racoon eyes, but my arrival was not trumpeted, and no one bothered me, a welcome change from the tea party atmosphere at the Creek.

I returned to Reception to discover three acquaintances from Millhaven: Peter, the unit clerk, had made it to Warkworth that same day; Mike, the barber, had been in Reception for about a month; and Spanky, one of A Unit's range cleaners, had been shipped to Warkworth in June to serve out the last four months of his sentence. All three had remained aloof from the tension around me at Millhaven; I welcomed their familiarity and friendliness as we reintroduced ourselves.

Just after six o'clock, rec-up was called. Warkworth's enormous yard boasted two weight pits, exercise bicycles, Stairmasters, a miniature-golf course, two tennis courts, a soccer field, two baseball diamonds, a small single-hoop basketball surface, a punching bag workout area, water fountains, an ice-cream stand, and a central recreation shack. Spectators sat on bleachers along the playing fields, and idlers gathered about hexagonal cedar tables built around the trunks of the yard's shade trees. A three-quarter-kilometre, two-lane walking and running track, heavily used, encircled the yard; in one corner, the inmates who had been lucky enough to win the annual draw for gardening plots grew their chosen assortment of vegetables and fruits.

The slow, uninterrupted walk in the fresh air cleared my head, but terror rushed in: Melissa was in Israel; Deena was out of the picture; neither Hans nor Bob Bigelow knew I had been transferred. The measure of my shock was my failure, to that moment, to contact anyone. I returned to Reception. The doors were locked.

I interrogated Spanky at the tennis courts, where I had seen him while walking.

"They lock the doors five minutes after rec's called," he said. "You can't get back in until changeover at eight o'clock. Then you can use the phone."

"What does that take?" I asked, remembering the bucket.

"I'll see what I can do," Spanky volunteered. "I'm the Range Rep."

Discouraged, I walked the track until eight. Spanky waited by the phone on my return to Reception.

"I've arranged forty minutes for you," he said proudly.

I phoned Hans at home. Without prompting, he offered to visit Saturday. Then I called Bob Bigelow. When he overcame his surprise, we discussed an appeal against my involuntary transfer: the humiliated part of me — humility was still a way off — wanted back to the Creek; the rest of me wanted no part of a return. In any case, I would be in Warkworth for a few months at least.

Twenty-five of my forty minutes were up. I called my mother, upsetting her greatly; she promised to make the long drive from Montreal on Sunday. Then I called Cathy, with whom Melissa stayed in touch by phone.

I was about to call Deena, on the pretext that my friends still called the condo, when a rough-looking inmate walked over.

"Hey, buddy. It's after nine. I've got the phone."

On my way over to my cell, Martin, the guard who had introduced me to Reception, waved me into the office.

"I have to do an intake interview. How are you doing?" Martin asked.

"Fine. Are you guys worried about me? Is that why you put me in cell ten, so you could keep an eye on me? Did someone from the Creek call here?"

"You don't look that great," Martin said coyly.

"Am I on a suicide watch?"

"We're keeping an eye on you. An inmate hung himself in here not so long ago. That's why the guys in the top bunk have to sleep with their heads towards the door."

Almost anyone who had been in the system for any length of time knew of an inmate who had killed himself. Kingston Penitentiary had nine suicides in one year; between January 1983 and March 1984, the thirty-two suicides in the correctional system quietly outnumbered the thirteen homicides. Media releases from CSC often obscure suicide's prevalence, using the term "violent deaths" to colour the tragedies.

"I am depressed, but I'm not going to hang myself."

"Have you ever attempted suicide?"

"No," I lied.

"Have you ever thought about it?"

"In passing. Nothing serious. Everybody does."

"Are you thinking about it now?"

"No." I felt depressed, but not hopeless.

Martin seemed satisfied. "I'd like to see a psychiatrist," I added. "I've been in touch with my own psychiatrist all the time in jail and I saw Dr. Quirt regularly at Beaver Creek. How do I arrange to get some help here?"

"Talk to your CO in the morning."

"Who's that?"

"I think it's Ward."

"Are you my LU?" I asked hopefully.

"No, Slinger is."

"Will he be on tomorrow?"

"In the afternoon."

We made small talk about the Creek for a few minutes, and, as lockup neared, I returned to my cell. Dino thoughtfully turned off his ghetto blaster.

For the next couple of hours, Dino filled me in on Reception's routine. Lockup all day, one fifteen-minute coffee break in the morning and one in the afternoon; one hour recreation after lunch in the small asphalt walled area outside Reception. After dinner, recreation in the yard or the gym. Most of the guards were all right, except for Slinger: some people got along with him, some didn't; Adolf, the copper in Eight Block, was the worst. The average stay in Reception was three months, then inmates went to the Blocks, the regular living units; things were much better there, even with six months of double-bunking, sometimes more.

I now had enough information to give Melissa some idea of the conditions. I handwrote a long letter to her, becoming distraught at my loss of computer access. *It's hard,* I wrote, *but I'm fine, and if I need you, I'll let you know. I promise.*

Plug's phone number stared up at me from the address book I was searching for Melissa's whereabouts in Israel. I had thought of Plug many times at Beaver Creek: a steady inflow of well-heeled white-collar types had invaded the Creek after I got there, many of them Plug's friends who had made it out of Millhaven in short order. The refugees from A Unit also bandied about stories of trailer visits in A Unit "going for a thousand bucks." I didn't know quite how much to believe, though there was a consistency in the stories I heard that raised them above rumour.

Plug, I guessed, could throw his weight around, even at Warkworth. Disgusted at myself for even thinking about it, I tore Plug's phone number from the address book and threw it in the open toilet, flushing it before I changed my mind.

Next evening, I called Deena, clinging to my pretences. "Deena, I'm not at Beaver Creek any more. I was in a fist fight and they kicked me out."

"I'm sorry." But her voice was cold. "Will you be going back?"

"Not for a while. I have to appeal this transfer."

"How long will that take?" Deena asked.

"Listen, I thought if anyone called, you could tell them where I am. I don't know who you've told that we've split."

Deena responded with an awkward silence. "Once I've got you on the phone, Deena, I thought I'd ask how you feel about us."

"I feel the same," Deena replied, without hesitation, "I don't trust —"

"OK. Just thought I'd ask. Take care."

"Julius, I'm still willing to come visit if you need me, or do whatever I can."

"No, thanks, it's too painful." I thought I sensed relief at the other end of the line.

As the protective mantle of shock wore off over the next few days, my depression worsened. I spent as much time as I could on the phone, but my outbursts of temper and pessimism distanced me from my friends. Irrationalism touched me, prompting two of them to call Warkworth to express their concern about my mental health. The same friends also called Hans; in an indignant snit, I denied the accuracy of their observations.

Ward, my CO, seemed hard-working and efficient, but regretted that "psychology was backed up"; he would try to get me in to see a psychologist "next week" and, as for my medication, I was listed for an appointment with the institution's very part-time psychiatrist on his next visit from Kingston, whenever that might be.

Professional commitments forced Hans to cancel his visit at the last moment; the disappointment was debilitating enough to keep me in my cell all day Saturday. My presence didn't calm Dino: a boxing match on Saturday night put him back in the hole, where he spent most of the month. The privacy brightened my mood, raising my sadness to a philosophical bent for my mother's visit the next morning. And her devotion further dammed my despair.

On Sunday, I received unexpected, concerned messages from my brother in San Francisco and my sister in Calgary, my first contact with them in more than a year. I was touched by and badly in need of their attention, finding a satisfying affinity in the weekly telephone conversations with my brother that followed. A new, smaller world was shaping up, one built around myself, my family, and a few close friends.

I finally saw a psychiatrist six days after my arrival, on Tuesday, September 8. Presumably I had been on a suicide watch in the interim, but if the guards had been watching me more closely than usual, it was beyond my powers of perception. Had I wanted to commit suicide, it would have been very easy with the articles I had in my cell; not only did I have the freedom and tools to kill myself, I could so at my leisure. Though Warkworth is hailed as a model treatment centre for offenders, only three staff psychologists care for the mental health and rehabilitation of a prison housing two hundred and seventy-five sex offenders, and one hundred and fifty lifers; of the remaining two hundred and seventy-five inmates, the majority were incarcerated for violent crimes and drug offences.

If Warkworth's visiting psychiatrist had my file, he hadn't read it. After admitting as much, he pointed to the forty cases on his desk and ruefully told me he had to get through them all in one morning. He politely listened to me for no more than ten minutes, quickly and definitively concluded I wasn't a danger to myself or others, advised me that Warkworth had no facilities to help me, and encouraged me to maintain my relationship with Dr. Arndt.

Two weeks later, a report arrived from Beaver Creek, prepared by Chandler, who had no mental health credentials, suggesting that I was suicidal, prone to violent conflict with others, and an escape risk. Chandler cited my fight with Nick, my first since I was a teen-ager, and information gathered from "unnamed inmates." Less than a month earlier, Chandler had told the Parole Board I was a model inmate who presented no risk to the public and should be released on UTAs.

The psychologist I saw at the end of September laughed out loud at Chandler's conclusions. Natasha gave me two valuable, fully professional hours, but made it clear that regular therapy was unavailable.

"One, you're not a priority. You're not going to go out and kill anyone. Two, we don't have time to treat anybody individually. We can't even keep up with assessments for the Parole Board. But if you're having a serious problem, let us know, and we'll try to see you." Her emphasis was on "try."

Hans and I spent most of our two hours together in mid-September discussing the pros and cons of returning to the Creek; finally, I admitted that I didn't want to return — except to prove something to Les Judson.

My anger continued to grind away at Deena and the warden each night and during daytime lulls. Through the haze, there was something about Warkworth I liked, an ease I had not felt elsewhere. Despite the *Toronto Star*'s publication of an exaggerated version of my fight with Nick, I didn't become a target of attention. The guards, unlike Plug at Millhaven and virtually the entire staff at Beaver Creek, treated me like everyone else; their responses to my special requests were exercises in discretion, decisions related to the circumstances; I got no sense of Millhaven's insidiousness or the endemic favouritism that plagued Beaver Creek; I even learned to trust a few of the staff. The evenhandedness freed me of extracurricular concerns about audience reaction, translating into a degree of anonymity that left me with a measure of dignity in my misery.

"Melnitzer to Control, please." There was something uncommon about the announcement; it wasn't until I slipped on my bathrobe and made my way to the office that I pinpointed the anomaly: in eight months in prison I had never heard the word "please" over the intercom; in fact, I had never heard the word "please" from a guard — except Plug when he was up to something. A new face was in Control, finishing another message on the PA — "please" again — before he turned to me, looking at the name tag on my bathrobe.

"They want you in the hospital," he said.

"Oh, yeah, they told me I'd have to get a physical. Would it be all right if I took a shower first? I just woke up."

"That sounds reasonable to me," he replied.

I stared at him, dumbfounded. "Are you all right?" he asked, noting my perplexity.

"Actually, yes." I laughed. "I've been in three prisons and two buckets and it's the first time I've ever heard the word 'reasonable.' Makes me feel almost human.... I'm Julius."

The guard reddened. "I'm Dwayne, Julius. I don't know any other way. It keeps me out of trouble."

"Well, I appreciate it," I said, remembering my habitual cringe when V & C staff called me to the bubble in the presence of my visitors: "Melnitzer, to the office," as in "Rover, get over here." I tried to measure the insidious hatred building up inside people treated like indentured servants before their wives, children, and friends; surely, there wasn't a regulation against "Mr. Inmate, come to the office please." More than once, I thought of taking it up with the V & C staff at Warkworth, but I backed off, for I was learning my place.

When I returned from the hospital after lunch, another new face, Adolf from Eight Block, had replaced Dwayne. Adolf was proud of his nickname, earned through years of reciprocal loathing between himself and virtually every prisoner he encountered.

At precisely one o'clock, as the stragglers from the dining room were filing in, Adolf called lockup. Spanky tried to explain that we were entitled to choose between lockup and one hour in Reception's tiny, walled concrete yard.

"I haven't heard anything about it," screamed Adolf.

"It's right on the schedule on the range bulletin board," Spanky said quietly. "Take a look."

"Don't tell me what to do. I've been here a long time. Since when do inmates decide the schedule? Get out of here."

"But —"

"I'll charge you if you say another word. Get out and tell those idiots to stop staring in here and get in their cells."

Adolf locked everyone up instantly, slamming each door as loudly as he could; the junior guard on duty with him tried to conceal his embarrassment.

The pounding on the cell doors and screaming didn't let up for over an hour. Adolf retaliated, refusing to allow a coffee break and afternoon telephone calls to lawyers, and finally charging the noisiest offenders. But things didn't quieten down until the evening shift reported.

Later in the afternoon, through the crack between the door and the wall, Slinger whispered, "What happened here this afternoon?"

"Adolf was here; otherwise, you know me, I didn't see nothing, didn't hear nothing."

"It only takes one idiot to start a riot."

Apart from taking Slinger's confidence as a compliment, I thought he was right. It did take so little, either Dwayne's way or Adolf's way. Both were exceptions, but thankfully, most staff at Warkworth leaned in Dwayne's direction, tending to humanity. I was glad to see Dwayne promoted within a year; Adolf, considerably senior, remained a two-striper.

In Reception's rigid, maximum-like environs, I worked out a routine to avert boredom. By staying up late and sleeping until noon, I avoided all but three hours of daytime lockup; nighttime's peacefulness coalesced best with confinement, mitigating its effect.

Prison regulations, called the Commissioner's Directives, or CDs, gave me a right of access to the legal materials in the library. In mid-September, I asked Slinger for permission to go to the library.

"Not this afternoon," he said abruptly.

"Well, the Commissioner's Directive …" I started to argue.

"Don't give me that legal crap. You have a right of *reasonable* access. That doesn't mean today. You can go tonight, when it's open to everybody."

"Well, what's the reason?" I demanded.

"No reason. No reason at all. Get back to your cell."

"We'll see about that after I file my grievance," I fumed.

"Inmates have only won two grievances against me in my twenty years here," Slinger boasted. "Now get back to your cell and write your grievance."

I returned to my house, grabbing two complaint forms on the way. I found the CDs I had borrowed from the library and worked out my frustration on the wording of my grievance.

When I finished, I proofread my complaint. I imagined another round of confrontation, fruitlessly recycling my anger.

That evening, I approached Slinger. "Can I talk to you for a minute?" I asked, in a contrite voice.

"That's what they pay me for."

"I'm sorry about this afternoon," I said. "I've been under a lot of stress, and I'm appealing my transfer, so I have a lot of legal work to do."

"You've got a right to go to the library. But so does everybody else. The reason I didn't let you go was because the librarian wouldn't have let you in. We'd already sent three inmates. We try to be fair to everybody."

"I didn't realize that. Sorry for playing lawyer." To this point, I had been acting humbly, substituting masks. Now I felt humble: in my anger at the system, I hadn't stopped to consider the staff's limitations; that realization instantly changed the way I looked at things. Slinger may not have been a diplomat, but then I had tried to bully him.

"That's OK. We all have our bad days," he replied.

"Look," I said, "is it just a matter of asking?"

"Right, as long as you don't push it."

For the rest of my three-month stay in Reception, I made it to the library three to four times a week. There, I used the word processors to continue my correspondence, whose volume was greater than ever.

The run-in with Slinger taught me something of my place in

this new world, and concurrently, I began to appreciate my inflated sense of entitlement in the old one. As I substituted acceptance for control, my relations with others and with the staff lightened; by accepting my place, I was accepting myself, demanding less as I felt less empty; the less inclined I was to push my way in — to force or buy my way into the game — the easier it became for others to accept me. In hindsight, I understood my arrogance, and, as I did so, I looked forward to humility's rewards, balance and rest.

Towards the end of September, I checked out Warkworth's voluntary tutoring program, hoping it would get me out of the cell even more frequently. Unlike Beaver Creek, where tutors were distrusted as privileged, white-collar, know-it-alls, Warkworth's program was inmate-run, low-key, and decentralized: inmates and tutors met as they saw fit, where they saw fit, and the program's voluntary nature obviated class distinctions.

Reception inmates were not permitted to work, go to school, or seek out jobs. The ostensible reason was that inmates required a period of observation and adjustment before they could be trusted in the general population of their new environment. In truth, Warkworth, like Beaver Creek, has an unemployment problem; the institution buries the issue by locking up ten percent of the population in the sixty-six-bed Reception Unit for up to three months and claiming that another three hundred are involved in CSC's education and vocational program. Only half of the latter are actually in class, most on a part-time basis; forty inmates engage in full-time "cell studies," pursuing correspondence courses in their cell, until very recently only superficially monitored by the school. One hundred and twenty others take vocational training in the institution's industrial shops, where outdated techniques are not uncommon and teachers' licences were not required of supervisors until September 1993. In the words of an inmate who was a licensed tradesman, some of Warkworth's training was "ten years behind anything that's happening on the street."

Apart from the volunteer tutor program, only the Adult Basic Education program used tutors. Judd, who ran the program, recognized the need for one-to-one attention for the illiterate or near-illiterate students who made up his class. Beginning in late September, whenever the guards were willing to overlook the rules, I volunteered as a tutor in Judd's class several mornings a week.

By early October, Warkworth was home. One evening, after a noisy communal shower to wash off the perspiration of my nightly tennis game, I watched, with fascination, the encroachment on prison's them-and-us mentality as our community of sports fans cheered the Blue Jays' drive to their first World Series; often, the guards stretched out coffee breaks and rec when they intruded on crucial innings in crucial games, allowing those inmates who had no television to share in the excitement to the end. The uncommon goodwill and light-heartedness culminated on a sunny afternoon when the whole unit — staff and inmates — gathered to watch the Blue Jays' victory parade, routine forgotten in a scene that proved that, even in the dungeons, the keepers and the kept could hold hands, if only for a moment, finding their own hope in the same breath of air.

Unmasking

If you do what I do, you write ...
without hope and without despair.
WILLIAM STYRON

As time went on, a newfound ability to keep to myself hinted at the advantages of self-reliance, allowing me to mould interactions unimpelled by the obsessive, wasteful gregariousness of my past. By shutting myself in, I could look out through my own eyes, and, as my black eyes healed, my lifelong masks faded with them.

As uninvolved as I was with my range mates, Tiny was hard to miss. A giant, six-foot-four, four-hundred-and-twenty pound man, he had earned a fearsome reputation as a drug trade kingpin in his four years at Kingston Penitentiary. Tiny's size, his fabled lifts in the pits, and his on-the-street reputation as an enforcer discouraged hostility of any kind.

Not that any ill will was forthcoming: now that he was off drugs, Tiny's gentle, sensitive nature emerged; its incongruity in his gargantuan physique brought out a remarkable affection among inmates and staff. A round, smooth face worthy of Michelangelo's cherubs, dancing eyes, a worn baseball cap, and a wispy pony tail of stringy light brown hair were the outward confirmations of the boy in the man. Tiny's common sense, prison-wise ways, and refusal to succumb to the pettiness, bitterness, and envy that marked his buddies made him one of a kind in prison: what was said behind his back was said to his face.

Tiny had been in Reception for a month before I arrived, uncommonly unobtrusive for someone so powerful in an environment where prowess is tested by physical strength. But in Reception's close quarters, I observed Tiny's intelligence, his interest in human nature and self-analysis, and his love of computers. In days past, looking for friends and acceptance, I would have approached him; nowadays, I watched.

Three weeks into my stay at Warkworth, Tiny was atypically direct. "You're alone in your cell," he observed. "Must be nice."

"It is."

"You getting a new cell partner?"

"No." That was factually correct: Dino was in the hole, but this was prison and it was none of Tiny's business.

Tiny surprised me by persisting. "When your cell partner's name comes up on the list, you'll get a new partner, even if he's in the hole."

I thought that Dino had lost his position on the transfer list for the Blocks when he went to the hole: that would technically have kept him in Reception and me alone in our cell. Deflated, I lapsed into silence.

"Are you all right?" Tiny's question struck a friendless chord in me.

"No, I'm awful. I got kicked out of the Creek. Some of my stuff still isn't here. My daughter's away. Everybody's still looking at what's left of my black eyes."

"I thought you were kind of depressed. You walk around with your head down all the time. Things'll get better."

"Yeah, I applied for the EMU, but they say it takes a while."

"I noticed you don't smoke. Either do I," Tiny said pointedly. "Does your cell partner smoke?"

"Yes, he does, but mostly when I'm not there. Anyway, he's in the hole most of the time."

"My partner smokes, too."

"Does that bother you?" I asked, continuing the conversation only to avoid rudeness.

"Yeah, it does. It's worse when you've quit smoking, like me."

"How long since you quit?" I asked.

"Almost three years."

"That's great. It's hard to do in here."

"Listen, uh," Tiny asked, "would you, uh, like me to move in when your cell partner leaves? That way you won't have to worry about a smoker."

One month earlier, I would have jumped at the offer, flattered by the attention from one of Warkworth's paragons.

"I'm not sure. Dino might still be here for a while. I don't even know if the guards will let us do it. Who's your LU?"

"Slinger. Same as yours. They'll let us switch if we have the same LU."

"Well, I'll want to stay on the top bunk."

Tiny grinned.

"I know. I heard you telling one of the guards that. Can you imagine me climbing up there?" Tiny's laughter boomed above the noise of the crowded lounge.

I shrugged, unsure.

"I've got a computer," Tiny said. "I see you write a lot of letters."

I brightened, but tried to hide my interest. "I don't know, Tiny. Let's talk about it when it's more of a reality."

"The thing is, the guards will want to know before Dino leaves. After it'll be too late."

"It won't happen for a while," I insisted. "I want to think about it."

When Tiny asked again a week later, I put him off — somewhat less convincingly.

"You look like you need a friend," he said, with unexpected insight. "I'm a good friend."

"Just let me think about it, Tiny." Still cynical, I didn't want to overreact to his empathy, nor pre-empt the chance of getting a cell partner I knew better, someone less hard core, perhaps a white-collar type; but the computer tempted me, and Tiny was very likeable and a good conversationalist and storyteller.

I was still asleep at ten the next morning when Slinger opened my door.

"Lawyer's hours?" he laughed, as my bleary face projected the belligerence of an unwanted awakening. I didn't mind the humour: unlike the staff at Beaver Creek, the guards at Warkworth did their kidding when other inmates weren't around.

"What's up?" I groaned, in my best "it can't be that important" voice.

"Do you want Tiny to move in?"

"What? Now?"

"This afternoon."

"Can't I have some time to think about it?"

"Nope. New load coming in tomorrow. The cells have got to be cleared today."

"What happened to Dino?"

"He's on his way to Ten Block."

"Can I get a nonsmoker?"

"No promises. Do my best. I thought you wanted Tiny in here."

"I haven't made up my mind yet."

"Well, make it up. What should I tell him?"

"Tell him to move his stuff here."

Slinger smiled his wicked smile. "He'll be glad to hear that."

I looked ahead glumly to my prospects: six hundred and forty pounds of humanity sharing fifty-five square feet of space, twelve pounds per square foot.

After lunch, Tiny arrived with an overfilled laundry cart.

"That it?" I asked.

"Just a few more things."

I sat down in the lounge, a book in hand, waiting for Tiny to move in. At the rattle of wheels on linoleum, I looked up to see Tiny pushing the same cart stacked higher than it had been the first time; his computer wasn't in the cart, meaning there was more to come.

"Jesus, Tiny, how are we going to get all this stuff in here?"

"Don't worry. At Kingston, the cells were smaller than this. Once we get it all packed away, it'll be fine."

By afternoon count, packed away it was: boxes piled to the ceiling on top of our locker; boxes piled six feet high at the foot of the bed, leaving just enough room for one of us to squeeze between them and the toilet on the way to the desk and our beds; Tiny's stereo system, TV, and printer piled underneath the window to the sill; his monitor and CPU blanketing the desktop. The two of us standing in that cell at the same time was a tight squeeze; both of us moving simultaneously was a *tour de force*.

But we managed, and we managed well. When the cell doors were locked, one of us stayed on the bed if the other was up or working at the computer, except to use the toilet. I slept late in the morning, giving Tiny, an early riser, some privacy. Limited by his profound respect for the Code, he confined himself to reading, listening to music, or watching TV with his headphones on while I slept. Afternoons, Tiny's preferred computer hours, I was at the library or volunteering in Judd's class. In the evening, I spent the first half of rec exercising; at changeover, Tiny left the cell to play bridge in the lounge, while I showered, dressed, and either watched the baseball game or used the computer. At 9:45, Tiny got ready for bed as I moved to the lounge, lining up at the microwave and toaster with my evening snack of cheese, popcorn, or a plate of gourmet goodies Tiny had scooped from his buddies in the kitchen.

After lockup, we shared a cup of tea, exchanging tales of worlds apart that had converged in this cell. One evening, *Lifestyles of the Rich and Famous* came on TV; Tiny kept laughing at the program.

"What's so funny?" I asked.

"Those are the kind of people you associated with, eh?" he said. "I used to break in and rob their houses."

The stretched skin in the crook of his left elbow bore witness to the hundreds of needles that had driven Tiny's life since he was a teenager. He had tried every drug imaginable, by injection, ingestion, and inhalation: uppers, downers, heroin, Percodan, LSD, Valium, speed, cocaine, and hash, randomly and in combination.

"When I ran out of money or drugs, I just took hundreds of bennies [caffeine pills bought over the counter at any drugstore] at a time."

Tiny's size and strength made violence a natural partner to drugs and trafficking a convenient source of money and supply. When in shape, Tiny boasted two hundred and eighty pounds of hard muscle and a thirty-six-inch waist; with easy access to guns and knives, he had no compunction about using them.

At dinner one evening, Tiny pulled off his T-shirt.

"Here," he said, pointing to a large scar on his left side, "a guy stuck a knife in me so hard it flew up in the air when it hit my rib cage. Look at this scar on my belly, I've got them all over my back and my arms." He leaned towards me, pulling down his lower eyelid. "See the red. I'm partially blind from being clubbed."

Tiny's lifestyle led to numerous convictions, many violent and all involving drugs, either as the crimes' object or their ignition. He had been in prisons throughout Canada for twelve of the last fourteen years, from Oakalla in British Columbia to Dorchester in the Maritimes. Following two years of dead time in the Don Jail, he got twelve years for two violent break-and-enters.

Tiny had come a long way this bit. In May 1992, five years into his sentence, he wrote to one of his victims:

> *I'm having a very hard time trying to write this letter to you. The reason is how do you say your sorry for what I've done to you. Can I say I'm sorry, and will that be good enough. Can I tell you I'm sorry one hundred times, and will that be good enough. Can I tell you I'm sorry until I'm blue in the face and will that be good enough. Can I promise you that I'll be good and never do what I did to you to anyone else, and will that be good enough. Is there anything that I can say or do that will ever be good enough. The answer is THERE IS NOTHING THAT I CAN SAY OR DO THAT WILL EVER BE GOOD ENOUGH FOR THE INJUSTICE THAT I'VE CAUSED AND FORCED UPON YOU.*
>
> *Don't miss understand my intentions about this letter. I'm not asking for you to accept this as an apology, I don't expect it. I'm not asking you to forgive me, I don't deserve it. What I am asking for is for you to understand that I can't change the past as much as I'd like to.... But what I can tell you is that for the first time in my life I'm in control of myself....*
>
> *When I broke into your home and terrorized you I was an empty hating machine. I didn't care about anything or anybody.... And if something did get to me I would cop out and get high ... I didn't even care for my own family, I took from them too.... So what I'm saying to you is that I care for people, all people ... for the first time in my life I feel truly free and ... that ... I'm doing something right.... I hope you can understand that I'm using this time that I have to better myself and become a real person. Thank you for your time.*

The vulnerability that drove Tiny to drugs and a life of crime now heightened his awareness and compassion for others. With a subtle look, he could read my mood swings, knowing when to stay away and when to intervene; in many ways, he was better medicine than the Prozac I was taking.

"I never let myself get down any more," Tiny would say. "I think about the good things. Think about Melissa. She's coming back soon. Think about all the mail you get. I never seen anybody get so much mail in prison. You got education. You got family. Think about it."

I thought about Tiny's fight against substance abuse, carried on for three years without a single visit from the outside, with no telephone calls, and mail perhaps once a month; I thought about the computer he had purchased by saving his seven-dollar-a-day level-five salary, doing without canteen for almost eighteen months; I thought about his good humour and determination as his buddies laughed at him, threatened by his refusal to stay in their world; and I watched the growth of a profound respect for him, for sticking to his guns and achieving what his friends had not the courage to attempt. Most of all, I marvelled at his unflinching honesty, hiding nothing, proudly preferring rejection to deception — things I could learn from him.

To Tiny, I represented the world to which he aspired: I could paint a picture of his goals for him and assure him that he had what it took. I was too dejected and exposed and lacked the energy to interpose my masks in our friendship; our late-evening chats became practical lessons in self-esteem that Tiny led by example.

Within days of Tiny's arrival in my cell, I began to slip out of the gloom that had persisted since I was kicked out of the Creek. I started counting down the days to my parole hearing the next summer.

Counting down invoked the real world. I raised the future in a telephone conversation with Doug, who had provided the bulk of my consulting work at Beaver Creek. His unexpected reserve about hiring me on my release was jolting, stretching the frailty of my new inner resources. Barely able to cope with the present, I had been denying the hardships of the future.

I walked away from the phone call with Doug frightened and upset. But instead of brooding, determination came. A part of me welcomed Doug's rejection. I didn't much like the idea of looking for favours, counting on goodwill rather than ability to sustain me. As a supplicant, I wouldn't function well; there must, I told myself, be a dividing line between defensiveness, humility, and begging.

I had never been one to sit still, a quality that, for most of my life, had translated into a desperate impulse for instant gratification; now, with nothing to hide, the quality became an asset, a cold-headed steadfastness. Over our journeyman's tea for two, Tiny and I sat in the narrow space between our beds and the desk.

"I have to write," I said. Writers were self-employed, without concerns about overhead and the productivity of partners. My work would be judged independently of my past; and it would give me purpose and intellectual stimulation in jail.

That night, I wrote — whatever came to mind. Writing came easily and naturally, my newest escape, a flight of expression. No matter how hopeless I felt, writing brought me back to myself, to self-discovery, to release, to an appreciation that all was not lost.

I had buried myself in correspondence for months, to much the same effect; but letters to others bear shades and shadows of conscious or subconscious impression, laden with the urgency of mailing: that may explain why we will never be happy with Canada Post, the interloper between our words and their immediacy. Writing as an avocation is much more solitary than corresponding — the reason I had avoided it. With luck, I could make my avocation my vocation.

I wrote whenever I had free time. Tiny, who like many experienced cons was not a night person, disinclined to stretch out his time by making his days longer, charitably tolerated my tapping on his keyboard into the early morning hours. He recognized that something special was happening.

Unhappily, Tiny moved to the Blocks at the end of October.

I saw him at meals and whenever I could at rec, but the differing routines in Reception and the Blocks limited our contact. I was healing, but not healed: without Tiny and his computer as an outlet, melancholy set in again.

Despite my inner turmoil, I was comfortable at Warkworth and starting to accept the ups and downs as functions of growth. As prison became a habit, I was able to take a more distanced, analytical look at my surroundings.

Sex, drugs, and gamblers

The armed robbers hate the hounds,
The hounds hate the diddlers,
The diddlers hate the baby killers,
And they all hate Clifford Olson.

PRISON TALK

Among prisoners, Warkworth is known as "Wallyworld," a reflection of the prison's reputation as a warehouse for sexual deviants. And because sexual deviants have traditionally been in protective custody, Warkworth has become known as a PC haven, there for "guys who wouldn't survive anywhere else in the system."

That wasn't the idea when Warkworth opened in 1967. Intended as a "program institution," a model for rehabilitation, a relaxed, medium security institution more along the lines of a mental health facility than a prison, Warkworth housed offenders with substance abuse, anger management, sexual deviance, cognitive, and living skills problems.

Soon, the facility gained worldwide renown for its Sexual Behaviour Clinic; among its patients were lifers whose crime had a sexual component, whose security classification allowed for a transfer to a medium security institution, and who had prospects for release. Although lifers with aggression and drug and alcohol problems are a significant part of Warkworth's population, the prison remains Ontario's chief warehouse for sexual offenders, with a few beds occupied by white-collar types like myself for whom Collins Bay and Joyceville, medium in name but reserved for the hard-core, are inappropriate settings.

Prisoners at Warkworth who are not sexual offenders are quick to distinguish themselves from the "hounds" — rapists and abusers of women — and the "diddlers" — prison vernacular for pae-dophiles or anyone involved in crimes against children. Nowadays, "sexual offenders" cuts a wide swath at CSC: caught up in a wave of public opinion and frightened of its own shadow because of releases gone wrong and the outcry for "predator" legislation, CSC lumps virtually all crimes in which women are victims in the same grab bag.

In doing so, the service often stretches credulity in its assess-ments: witness the gas-bar robber who, in the words of his vic-tim, "brushed the back of his hand against my breast when he was tying me up." The robber's lawyer let the remark go by as part of the Crown's statement of facts at the sentencing, unaware that this offhand remark would label his client a sexual offender and doom his chances of parole. This broad-brush approach, at the expense of prioritization, aggravates CSC's chronic shortage of treatment facilities.

Inmates expend a great deal of their energy explaining why they are at Warkworth. Many lie, out of fear that they will be harmed, ridiculed, or labelled, often by individuals who have committed sim-ilar or worse crimes but are better liars. In fact, there have been no homicides at Warkworth in its twenty-five years of existence, but suicide is a regular occurrence. Fights at Warkworth are not unusual; but fists and boots, for the most part, take the place of shivs and pipes; few disputes result in prolonged hospitalization. Nonetheless, self-consciousness about PC labelling prevails, so much so that inmates post their CSC classification documents on range bulletin boards to prove their place in the hierarchy. Perhaps change is coming, evidenced by the attempt made by a small group of sex offenders to form their own club, Hounds Are Us.

Cop killers are at the top of the social order, the most solid of criminals, followed by lifers whose crimes do not involve women or children; then armed robbers, drug dealers, and other violent non-sexual offenders. Property offenders and white-collar criminals are a class of their own, their standing determined by the nature of the offence: stealing from banks is solid, very solid; stealing from small investors, "widows and children and friends," is not. The white-collar offender's precise status is also affected by his age, his charm, his ability to adapt, his usefulness — as in legal skills — and the size of his perceived stash.

Hounds and diddlers are never solid: as PCs, they are perceived as rats, beholden to the Man to protect them. CSC security, which relies on informers and intimidation to the virtual exclusion of real investigative work, encourages inmates to look to the system for protection in return for information.

Prison's fine social order goes on to divide hounds and diddlers into sub-classes. Hounds are condemned relatively to the social status of their victims: "It's one thing to fuck some whore who's ripped off your dope, and another thing to jump out at women in the dark or beat up your old lady, even if you catch her fucking somebody else, then you put a .357 Magnum to the guy's head." Diddlers rate inversely to the age of their victims: the younger the victim, the more reprehensible the perpetrator.

The futility of all this appears on examination of many convicts' attitudes to the women in their lives — regardless of what they're in for. Simply put, those attitudes hearken to the Dark Ages: the numerous phone calls I overheard on the open ranges, conversations in V & C, and dining-room talk all convinced me that the feminist movement had never reached the majority of inmates. Women were possessions, rights, objects, to be protected and cared for in return for unquestioning fealty.

Vince, a muscle-bound thirty-year-old doing five years for a vicious assault, proudly announced that he had not called his wife and children for four years.

"Why?" asked Hazel, the Anger Management Program's facilitator.

"What am I going to tell her? She knows where I am. And there's nothing I can do in here to help her with her problems out there," Vince replied.

"Maybe she needs your support," Hazel suggested.

Vince, unaccustomed to a female's challenge, sat up, corroborating Hazel's point with his body language. "What support? I ain't got no money and I can't give her what a woman needs. She'll be there when I get out."

"Just waiting with open arms?"

"Yup," replied Vince confidently.

"And the kids too?"

"Yup."

"How old are your kids?" asked Hazel.

"The boy's six and the girl's seven."

"They were very young when you went to jail."

"What's that got to do with it? I'm their dad," Vince argued.

"How do they know that if you don't call them?"

"My old lady tells them. That's her job."

"Why don't you have them visit?"

"They don't need to see their father in jail. What am I gonna tell them?"

"At least they'll know you."

"They know me. I'm their father. That's all there is to it. There's nothing I can give them now."

Hazel drove to the real issue. "What if your wife's changed? She's been making it on her own for four years. Don't you think that might change her?"

"Nope."

"Well, she might be used to doing things without asking your permission."

"Either she does what I say or I'm gone. That's it."

"You might be in for a surprise."

"She's the one who'll get the surprise."

Vince's attitude was typical, demonstrating that the average con's animosity to sex offenders had much more to do with machismo than respect for women. Low on self-esteem, tossed out of society, cons create a ladder so that they have somebody to look down upon. Their ability to distinguish their own crimes surpasses that of the finest legal minds, and the alacrity with which they pass judgement on others would test the reflexes of ping-pong champions.

Fortunately for the psyches of those at the lower end of the ladder, Clifford Olson occupies the bottom rung by himself. Tiny was at Kingston during Olson's stay there.

I remember when they moved Olson into Lower H, "Cliffie's Range." They put a plexiglass barrier around his cell to protect him from the piss and the shit and the food people threw at him and to stop his cell from being set on fire. He had to use a small little security yard. It had an overhead mesh or grill they originally put in so guys couldn't throw contraband drugs from the top range, which was handy because now guys couldn't throw things at Olson. The only time he got out of his cell was for yard or a shower.

Cliffie looks fucked up since he been down there. Last time I saw him, was in July '92, walking down the hall. They actually shut the joint down when they moved him. His eyes are all bugged out, there's a nervousness about him. He comes out, his head's always jerking around like an animal that's been locked up for a long time. He's got a crazed look in his eye, like he's finally losin' it, like the lockup's been getting to him.

Surprisingly, at Warkworth, race does not generally affect the social order. Although Warkworth's large minority population includes blacks and natives — the largest groups — Orientals, East Indians, Jews, Muslims, and even a hard core of Wiccans, racial tension has been almost nonexistent. Native guards are always on duty in the prison; the six or seven black staff represent a two hundred percent increase over the two blacks employed at Warkworth when I first arrived.

The prison is a beehive of cultural activity: native assemblies, black cultural programs, a French club, a Jewish congregation, and an Italian group, all flourish with the administration's encouragement. Cliques are everywhere, but they are mainstays of individual culture, not defensive barriers. The situation is a credit to the professionalism and evenhandedness of Warkworth's staff, from whom I never heard a racial slur or joke directed at inmates, publicly or privately.

Not all minority members at Warkworth would agree with my assessment. Many claim that an insidious, subtle racism pervades Warkworth. And to be fair, those discriminated against are always the first to know.

Cigarettes are the mercantile heartbeat of prison, its currency, its tokens of generosity and hostility and its ultimate tranquillizers. Unenforceable regulations acknowledge cigarettes' power by limiting the number of cigarettes inmates can possess. The incidence of smokers is proportionate to the rigours of confinement: almost all the inmates in the bucket smoked, about ninety percent of the population in Millhaven Reception were smokers, and although the numbers decrease in less restrictive facilities, smokers always made up at least sixty-five percent of the population in the jails I inhabited.

As payday approaches, cons who have run out of cigarettes because of excessive smoking, poor money management, gambling, or drug debts begin their furtive search for smokes. "Juice," premiums on the advances, increases as smokers get more desperate. Payday is every two weeks, and on the weekend prior, a borrowed bale of tobacco ($3.25) returns an additional pack of cigarettes ($1.45) on canteen day. As the week begins and canteen, usually a Wednesday or Thursday, gets closer, juice increases to as much as three for one. Late payment can double or triple the interest.

The creditors, who are either practised usurers or the more successful gamblers or drug dealers, build their stockpiles and trade them for cash, drugs, sex, TVs, stereos, CDs, food, clothes, jewellery, haircuts, and other goods and services. At Collins Bay, which is heavily double-bunked, the Inmate Committee is said to be instrumental in allocating single cells: $500 of cigarettes or drugs will buy privacy.

Much of prison's debt finds its origins in illegal gambling. The eight or so bookies who control Warkworth's gambling get the Vegas betting lines with a phone call to friends on the outside; the *Toronto Star* and the *Toronto Sun,* one bookie told me, "are out of date, for amateurs." The bookies protect themselves by the use of "runners," and the more conservative among them pyramid their trade, using only two or three trusted friends as middlemen.

Gambling's high season coincides with NFL football; on Sunday afternoons and evenings, Monday nights, and American holiday Thursdays, the rec areas are quiet, almost empty, as thousands of years of prison time stay glued to the television. The four bookies I talked to averaged a "take" of $500 weekly during the football season; that translates into $800,000 wagered by Warkworth's seven hundred inmates during the twenty-week football season — more than $50 weekly per inmate, about twice an inmate's salary; bookies' annual incomes average $15,000. Because money, in prison as elsewhere, represents power and prestige, the bookies sit at the top of the heap, regardless of their crime.

With gambling and drug debts accumulating constantly, the market seethes with creditors who discount their claims to musclers and with debtors ready to pay off their debts in the compound's darker shadows. Debt among inmates creates the phenomenon known as "checking in," inmates requesting segregation to get away from their creditors. Even a slight delay in administrative response to this request can bring on a severe beating, making it the moment of greatest opportunity to recruit informants. Unscrupulous guards or IPSOs (Internal Preventive Security Officers), taking advantage of every opportunity to augment their network of informants, may refuse or delay the check-in unless the debtor "rats out"; the unfortunate prisoner's only alternative is to deliberately commit internal offences that will force him to the hole, at the risk of creating a record that will prejudice his release.

Too often in prisons, security and safety are defined in terms of what the authorities know or think they know. For the sake of that information, the system expends a great deal of energy building a network of informants that sets inmate against inmate, all the while using its arbitrary power to intimidate, and to grant and withdraw favour. Ironically, prison security is so dependent on informants that the disappearance of the black market would seriously impair the flow of information to the authorities.

The reliance on informers poisons prison's atmosphere, perpetuating distrust in distrustful men, filling them with anger, causing tension and violence, and heightening the paranoia that implodes on their return to society. Many guards despise the informers they encourage, sending out double messages to their already confused patrons, weakening inmates' capacity for trust, and tragically contradicting the rehabilitative messages that grace CSC's mission statement.

Drugs are prison's prime commodity and the overriding source of violence. This is the free market untrammelled, Ayn Rand's prototype, where value is anything, including the point of a knife, that can make a claim stick; one unfortunate dealer had his rectum carved up by a desperate addict who took the most direct route to further supply.

The fate of Warkworth's most prominent and discreet traffickers illustrates drugs' primacy in prison culture. When Terry announced that he was moving to Beaver Creek, security received a "kyte," an unsigned note, informing them of several grams of hash in the man's jacket. The subsequent denial of Terry's transfer application left his best customers, who had planted the drug, ecstatic.

On canteen night, when inmates have bought the cigarettes that are most commonly traded for drugs, discreet clusters of two or three cons gather, often shielded from prying eyes by a larger, surrounding group. Sunglasses come out even after the sun sets, drag queens barter their services, and impecunious inmates who have used up their credit make loud, ardent promises of repayment. On market nights, Warkworth's compound reminded me of the crowded, mysterious *medinas* that I had toured with Deena and Melissa in ancient Morocco.

Drugs get into jail in various ways. "Hooping" or "suitcasing" is the rectal or vaginal secretion of a condom filled with drugs; the visitor removes the stash in V & C, passing it on to the prisoner, who hides the condom in his own body cavity in the inmate bathroom. The practice is dangerous, because if the condom bursts, absorption is rapid and often fatal.

In Kingston, traffickers tried to get themselves into segregation temporarily; segregation has its own special visiting area, known as "closed visits," where plexiglass separates cons from their visitors, and conversation takes place over a telephone intercom. One of the cubicles hides a tiny hole; guests roll or blow drugs to the inmate through a straw.

Drugs are also imported in the heels and soles of visitors'

footwear, which are exchanged for inmates' shoes in V & C; similarly, clothing lining is a common hiding place. Commerce is particularly brisk following the twice-a-year socials at Warkworth, where hundreds of visitors mix with inmates. Acid can be mailed in as paper blots, undiscovered by staff who are generally prohibited from reading inmates' mail; occasionally, lawyers, guards, and volunteers bring in drugs for motives as various as profit and sex.

In buckets, the traffickers float in and out. After hooping their supply, they have themselves arrested for a minor offence necessitating a night in jail. There, they sell the drugs at premium prices that are, inevitably, an insignificant portion of the next day's fine.

One ingenious trafficker reeled in his cache with a fishing line from a window in the Don Jail, his venture co-ordinated by an accomplice on the range phone connected to the supplier's cellular phone on the street outside. Until a net was put overhead, drugs were simply thrown into the Don Jail yard.

Homemade alcohol, called "brew" or "shine," is another staple; most of the ingredients are secreted from the kitchen. Finding a hiding place for the stills is trickier: Randy and two of his cronies, all lifelong substance abusers, tried to cache their brew in the crawl space between the kitchen's false ceiling and the roof of the building, requiring Randy to manoeuvre the industrial kitchen pot full of brew on narrow two by fours. Unfortunately, Randy had downed a bit too much of his old brew while preparing the new, misstepped, and fell fifteen feet through the false ceiling, brew and all, into the crowded officers' mess. He escaped with severe bruising and a few weeks in the hole, arguably no worse off than the staff whose lunch was rudely interrupted by Randy's peremptory landing.

Sex is as marketable as drugs, and homosexuality's acceptance in a world of self-proclaimed "he-men" is a reflection of prison's power structure. Much of prison's homosexuality is situational, prevalent

among lifers and other long-termers, those near the top of the hierarchy; their way of life becomes the signpost for the rest of the
population. Because drag queens offer a valued, scarce commodity
to the élite, the nature of their crimes is overlooked in the social
order. Jealousy over queens is also a regular source of violence.

The queens, caught up in a system that, like the rest of the
world, is trying to come to grips with the diversity of its population, have won the right to wear makeup, dress in female clothing,
walk hand in hand with their lovers, and embrace and kiss openly. In that way, queens, their partners, and gays can share warmth
and closeness in an environment where affection and love are
never in stock.

Yet prejudices towards gays still exist; at Warkworth, gay magazines and videos are much more heavily censored than corresponding "girlie" rags. At Beaver Creek, Angie, the drag queen, was
relentlessly persecuted.

"How would you feel undressing in the same room as her?" one
Beaver Creek guard asked me.

"I undress with cold-blooded killers, rapists, and paedophiles,"
I replied.

"Kids" are in as much favour as drag queens. Generally, the
term refers to younger men under the protection of older lovers
in return for sexual favours or as part of a lasting relationship. Often
kids, particularly in maximum, have no choice but to seek a protector, reluctantly giving their bodies to one to protect themselves
from ravaging by many. To numerous young men, however, being
someone's kid or everyone's kid is a choice they make to enhance
their life in prison: "dads" supply their kids with drugs, cook for them,
buy their canteen, and clean their cells. Prostitution is rampant,
but many relationships are monogamous, though enforced transfers
and scattered release dates force a practical end to many affairs.

Sex need not be furtive; the courts have declared that homosexuality is not a crime, and the hour-long intervals between guard patrols on the ranges leave ample time for intimacy, as do the floors under the cell beds, the showers, largely unused during the day, and the secluded racquetball courts. On the whole, the relaxed attitude towards homosexuality among the population is a palliative, a humane affect in the midst of inhumane constraints.

Heterosexual attractions between female guards and inmates, of which the most notable example may be the relationship between Patty Hearst and one of her keepers, is a recurring phenomenon in Canadian prisons. There are many reasons for the attractions: the hostage-and-captor "Stockholm syndrome," the emphasis on the physical, the abundance of great bodies, and the everpresent, raw sense of danger with its attendant tension. CSC has documented many instances of relationships between cons and staff; less formally, snide stories of guards and inmates caught in the act abound.

Cam, a notorious druggie, tried to barter information about his affair with a guard for a transfer to camp. The guard "resigned"; Cam spent a month in the hole for his trouble; indignantly, he sued CSC, screaming "rape" as loudly as he could, garnering a front-page headline in Toronto's *Sunday Sun* and a talk-show appearance on *Shirley*. Regardless, because "screwing" a guard is the ultimate degradation of the Man, the legend would follow Cam wherever he went, securing his place in prison's distinctive hierarchy forever.

Inhuman Rights

Freedom is not divisible, it disappears
from a society as soon as it is denied
to any member of that society.

DR. GABOR MATÉ

The civil rights of prisoners are the lowest common denominator of democracy. In jail, correctional supervisors are the judges in internal disciplinary courts where their foot soldiers are the prosecutors (one CS convicted a prisoner in the absence of witnesses because "no guard would take the trouble to write out a charge unless it was true"); permission to telephone a lawyer during business hours hangs on the whim of employees of the State; prisoners do not have access to Bell information or telephone books on their ranges; calls are collect only unless written permission is obtained; and telephone discussions with lawyers transpire in a public place or in a CO's office in the presence of CSC staff.

The apathy of all but a few criminal lawyers as well as the Canadian Civil Liberties Association; the reluctance of a cash-starved Legal Aid system to spend its budget on the convicted; the low levels of education and high levels of illiteracy in the system; and CSC's ignorance and disregard of basic procedural fairness in its day-to-day operations all ensure a trampling of prisoners' rights. Ironically, CSC forbids the use of the Inmate Welfare Fund, inmates' money, for legal assistance.

The protection of our democratic core lies in the hands of a few committed activists like seventy-five-year-old Claire Culhane and her Prisoners' Rights Group, based in Vancouver; Ruth Morris from Toronto; Judges David Cole and Bob Bigelow; a few other practitioners in prison law; and Queen's University's Faculty of Law's Correctional Law Project.

This is not a commentary on the rights prisoners should have: that is for the voters and their elected representatives to decide. Nor is it a denial of the relatively humane conditions under which we warehouse the convicted; rather, it speaks to the disregard of due process that pervades our penal system. As sentences get lengthier, paroles become rarer, and more people spend more time in jail, the prevailing attitude seems to be, "Let's feed them and keep them out of the cold." In a democracy, that will not do; so long as society sees fit to give rights to prisoners, it must protect its values even among its exiles. Our failure to do so says much about our penal system's rehabilitative delinquencies.

CSC's response to the public outcry resulting from my tennis partner Philippe Clement's assault on a Gravenhurst woman after his escape from Beaver Creek was perhaps my starkest experience with civil rights sacrificed on the altar of public opinion and media hype. In the six months following the public outcry, CSC set out to purge the Creek of violent offenders, many of whom were sent to Warkworth, and some of whom opened their files to me. I was appalled at the haste and lack of justification for the majority of the transfers; in no instance was there an immediate threat of escape or violence, yet none of these inmates were given a chance to contact their lawyers before transfer.

My apprehensions about the panic that had set in to Les Judson and his superiors were confirmed orally by some Warkworth COs who were now stuck with these men. One CO put her findings in writing:

> On December 23, 1992, the subject was transferred to higher secu-
> rity (Warkworth Institution) as the staff at Beaver Creek had information
> that the subject, along with other perpetrators, had broken into the inmate
> canteen and stole $3200 worth of merchandise....
>
> These suspicions were never confirmed. No charges, either institutional
> or street, were laid against the subject. There is no evidence which ties
> the subject to this offence. Therefore, there is no valid reason why the
> security classification on the subject should change. He is still classified
> as minimum security.

"The subject" was unusually lucky. He was back in minimum within six months. Had his CO been unsympathetic, it would have taken him from twelve to eighteen months to have his grievance processed. And likely, "the subject," who was barely literate, would have had to do it on his own: Legal Aid refused his application, and for three months his collect calls to lawyers went unanswered.

Apart from "the subject," not a single one of the men summarily ejected from Beaver Creek in the fall of 1992 had made it back to minimum one year later. Even those with lawyers were stymied by the delaying tactics of the Crown in Federal Court and the sluggishness of that court's process.

The greatest price of this arbitrary conduct, apart from the diminution in democratic values, is the cost to society. Many of the cons transferred were the system's successes, the most likely candidates for rehabilitation, men who had spent many years fighting institutionalization and their criminal backgrounds, and who had been adjudged, step by grudging step, to have the best potential for a productive return to society.

Wade, a very young-looking, intelligent and self-educated forty-year-old, with two daughters in their twenties and a son in his teens, had fought his way back from tragic alcoholism and drug abuse that led to conviction for two sexual assaults and a twelve-year sentence.

He had been a model for other prisoners, a star in every therapeutic program he had taken for seven years. At the Creek, he continued his exemplary ways, working in the kitchen, tutoring other inmates, and minding his own business.

The Parole Board, even in the aftermath of the Clement escape, was sufficiently impressed by Wade's record to grant him unescorted three-day passes to a halfway house in Toronto. On his first pass, he dutifully attended the Clarke Institute of Psychiatry for a psychological assessment; there he told the examining psychologist that he had taken one drink almost a year previous, on New Year's Eve.

Wade's honesty was just the excuse Beaver Creek needed to rid itself of another bothersome high-profile case. Wade was summarily advised that the Administration had been "informed" — by parties unmentionable, of course — of "derogatory remarks" Wade had made about the deputy warden. Lacking knowledge of his accusers and without access to counsel, Wade had no opportunity to defend himself and was promptly transferred to Warkworth, where he remained until his statutory release in February 1994.

CSC's extraordinary powers made a strong impression on me when I reported for transportation to a Kingston hospital for medical testing. The escorting officers politely told me to undress.

"Am I under suspicion for anything?" I asked.

"No," was the quick reply.

My question was deliberate. I had researched the new prison legislation as it related to searches, to discover that "routine" strip searches were unlawful in the absence of individualized suspicion, except for some carefully circumscribed exceptions that did not apply here.

"Then you've got no right to search me," I asserted.

The officers resolved their confusion by phoning the security office.

"You can't go if you refuse a search," the senior guard told me as he got off the phone.

"Fine," I replied, "I'll go back to my Block." Visions of medical lawsuits and grievances for damages danced in my head.

"The IPSO says we have to search you anyway."

"You mean that I'm now under suspicion because I insisted on my rights."

"I don't know," said the guard abashedly, "you're the lawyer. I just do what the keeper tells me."

"What are my choices?"

"Go to the hole. They'll strip-search you there." My experience with the deputy warden at the Creek reminded me that a request to call my lawyer would not be well received.

I was in a quandary. If I refused, I'd be in the hole. Mindful of Chandler's report following my expulsion from the Creek, I tried to imagine the write-up on this incident: by the time the IPSO finished, I would doubtlessly be labelled as "under suspicion," CSC's favourite phrase, of trafficking in something or other. I complied, wondering how many thousands of inmates would be searched in ignorance of their rights.

The "cavity search," a fishing expedition through body orifices, is distinguished from assault only by the mandated presence of a doctor and is a more sublime form of intrusion than a strip search. If a tactile proctological examination doesn't reveal anything, the doctor may use an instrument best described as an anal crank to have a better look through a larger opening.

Refusal to submit to a cavity search is, in a system where random urinalysis testing is common, a virtual admission to drug trafficking. Being labelled as a trafficker is, in turn, an invitation to unremitting harassment, restrictions on visits, and a practical bar to early parole.

Cavity searches are, however, expensive, time-consuming, and embarrassing when fruitless. CSC prefers the "dry cell," where the toilet can't be flushed by the inmate. In Kingston Penitentiary, the nine-by-four windowless cell contains a bed, an eating surface, a steel toilet, and a sink. The lights are on all day, and at night, a bulb strong enough to read by intrudes on sleep, but no books are allowed. The cell is video-monitored twenty-four hours daily, and patrolling guards have an unobstructed vista through a plastic plate on the ceiling. The cell design allows the guards to watch the prisoner's excretions, which remain with him in the uncovered toilet, until the guards find time to come around and secure the evidence.

Random urinalysis, recently declared constitutional by the courts, is slowly replacing the cavity search and the dry cell, but the tests are no less intrusive, if somewhat more humane.

To those law-and-order aficionados who cheered their way through the last few paragraphs, I merely point out that these methods are designed to prove guilt. Until and if the shit hits the fan, so to speak, the innocent must pay the price with the guilty. The innocent have no recourse if the suspicions against them prove groundless. The irony is that they therefore have far more incentive than the guilty to submit to these barbaric intrusions.

Occasionally, an activist Inmate Committee chairman tries to help inmates assert their rights. The Inmate Committee exists at the discretion of an institution's warden, but now that CSC is legally required to consult with inmates on all matters affecting them other than security, the Inmate Committee is a handy funnel to the population.

The inmate chairman is elected by the population every six months and appoints his own executive. The chairman's capacity to represent the inmates is severely limited, however, because the chairman is himself a prisoner, whose fate hinges on the whims of his keepers.

While politicization is creeping into institutional politics, wardens tend to deal swiftly and severely with chairmen whom they see as rabble-rousers. Shortly before I got to Warkworth, Greg, a fifty-year-old first-timer serving a fourteen-year sentence for the attempted murder of his wife, was elected chairman. Greying, fatherly, and somehow tweedy in his prison greens, Greg was educated and clever, with a knack for organization.

Greg set out to enforce the Supreme Court of Canada's declaration, in a precedent-setting decision giving prisoners the right to vote, that inmates were entitled to all civil rights other than those that necessarily accompanied the loss of freedom.

To that end, he first presented the Administration with a scheme for effective inmate representation at the grass-roots level. Censorship was his next target: I helped him draw a grievance against the Administration's refusal to allow *Basic Instinct* into Warkworth; after months of enduring explicitly violent martial arts movies on prison video, I laughed at the exclusion. Simultaneously, Greg hotly protested the Administration's control and occasional misuse of the Inmate Welfare Fund. The powers-that-be were most unhappy with him.

"They're going to get me, Julius. They don't want a chairman who does anything," Greg told me.

As the tension rose, Greg desperately tried to get in touch with a lawyer; he wrote both to the Ontario Provincial Criminal Lawyers Association, which continued its historic disregard of those who had already paid their bills, and the Canadian Civil Liberties Association, which must have had more popular fish to fry and didn't bother to answer. I finally called Bob Bigelow, who agreed to see Greg on his next visit to Warkworth.

Before Bob could see Greg, the Administration pounced, blaming him for irregularities in the canteen; without explanation, he was hauled out of a visit with his wife and sent to the hole. Soon afterwards, Greg resigned, a non-presence in short order.

Inmate Committee chairmen are not the only targets of the kind of intimidation Greg experienced. Grant, convicted by an internal disciplinary court of possession of a joint after eight offence-free years in the pen, objected to the severity of the penalties for his minor offence. On the street, he would have been fined lightly, at worst; in prison, he lost his cell in the EMU, was transferred back to double-bunked Reception, had his pay cut by four levels, lost his job, and spent a week in the hole awaiting Disciplinary Court.

With the law clerk's certificate he had earned in prison from the American Trial Lawyers Association in hand, and with some guidance from me, Grant filed a claim in the Federal Court challenging the severity and multiplicity of his punishments. The attorney general applied to quash Grant's claim, but failed in its summary motion. Grant, who worked in the kitchen, thanked me for my help with a plate of delicately cooked fresh crabmeat that a friendly guard had smuggled in for him.

For a few months I heard nothing more about his case, attributing Grant's silence to the long delays in Federal Court.

"I shut it down," he said six months later, in a hush, averting his eyes.

"Why?" I was sincerely dismayed.

"I've got to do what's right for me. My wife wants me out of here, or at least in camp. I'm on a life beef — they call the shots."

Not yet dislodged from the insulated naïveté of my street days, I had no idea what Grant was talking about.

"They called me in, the unit manager," he went on. "He told me that even if I win, I lose. If I forget it, maybe I get to camp soon."

The threat was not an idle one. And if the unit manager chose to forget his promise once Grant dropped his claim, he could always find new facts to support his change of heart; CSC's power to affect the man's freedom would be as useful in the breaking of the promise as it was in its making.

As I chafed at the injustices, the feelings that drove me as a criminal lawyer came back in spades. In January 1993, I wrote to Claire Culhane, whose books I had been reading, offering to help in her cause of prisoners' rights. Though my ability to assist was limited by the inaccessibility of research materials, our correspondence continued throughout my incarceration.

CSC's licence to trample human rights stems from its lack of accountability. Politically, the human rights of convicts is hardly an issue with which to blaze to power; an unsympathetic media and public ensure that accountability, where it exists, operates only to inmates' detriment.

Wardens have some discretion in granting passes, escorted and unescorted, as well as work releases; release in serious cases, the ones in the headlines, are the province of the National Parole Board. CSC, through its case management teams and therapeutic staff, makes highly influential recommendations to the board. Wisdom and insight into the human psyche sprout from the mouths of twenty-three-year-old COs barely out of community college, secretarial school graduates who have won the CSC promotion competition, or MA students suddenly become "therapists." Their power is frightening and unchecked, often subjective and arbitrary; if quality control or any serious effort at consistency in release decisions and recommendations existed, I couldn't find it in the files I reviewed.

There is little risk for CSC in urging the Parole Board to detain an inmate, but a wrong call for release can have disastrous public relations fallout; thus, it is not surprising that case management teams lean against release. As Jeremiah's CO told him, "Personally, I don't think you should be in here, but I don't want to be the one kicking my lunch bucket down the street." Reid, who had spent seventeen years in prison, observed, "When I got in the system, COs tried to help you. Now, they try to find obstacles to keep you in so they can cover their ass."

CSC's materials are essentially unchallengeable before the Parole Board, a body that the late Chief Justice of Canada's Supreme

Court, Bora Laskin, called Draconian. The hearings consist of a presentation by the CO, followed by thirty minutes to five hours of untrammelled inmate grilling by at least a two-member board, many of whom are trained only in the fruits of political loyalty and start with the assumption that credibility is not in a criminal's repertoire.

Anything in a CSC report passes for evidence: fact, opinion, hearsay, innuendo, and suspicion — even philosophical musings; reports are in writing, there is no in-person evidence and no opportunity to cross-examine in the quest for liberty. The inmate's lawyer is reduced to an "assistant," usually sitting by without objection, involved only in procedural matters and ten minutes of final arguments. Where evidence favouring release exists, the Parole Board is notorious for capriciously ignoring it, going so far as to reject, without reasons, recommendations from CSC's own professionals. Homespun psychology is regularly expounded as definitive gospel by politically appointed board members, many of them part-time, with little experience and less training: "The offender's response to our questions shows that he has not fully appreciated the consequences of his actions and is not ready for release" are the board's favourite buzzwords.

Always, the spectre of public opinion hangs over the proceedings, twisting the issue of "risk to society," the fundamental question the Parole Board is empowered to decide, into considerations of "how will it look?" Thus, by ignoring the law, the Parole Board assumes the role of lawmaker, affecting a demagogic juggernaut that tramples on concepts of fundamental justice. These concepts are democracy's triggers of accountability, ever so slight a curtsy to an inalienable right — not to freedom, but to the right to fight for it on even ground.

Rehabilitation?

No one is born a rapist or a paedophile.
DR. W. L. MARSHALL AND SYLVIA BARRETT

Prison is a growth industry: two and a half million Canadians have criminal records, thirty thousand Canadians are incarcerated, and one hundred thousand Canadians are on probation, parole, or statutory release. In 1992–93, transfers to federal penitentiaries increased by fifteen percent over the previous year; by the turn of the century, there will be at least eight hundred lifers in the system; and CSC is the fourth-largest custodian of property in the federal government, in charge of nine hundred thousand square metres of space with a replacement value of $1.8 billion.

With the call for longer prison terms, predator laws, and harsher limitations on parole and even its abolition, CSC, while hailing to a mission statement that lists rehabilitation and reintegration as primary objectives, is preparing for the onslaught — and doing so despite costs of $200,000 per cell to build new prisons and $50,000 to maintain an inmate yearly.

CSC's mindset is evident in the expansion of CORCAN, CSC's industrial arm, which provides decently paying jobs for prisoners; the growth of CORCAN will eventually turn many of Canada's prisons into giant fenced factories, ghettos for lawbreakers; new commissioner's directives even lay out guidelines for the establishment of inmate-owned businesses, some of them employing other inmates. Reflecting this trend, CSC is spending millions to replace greens with blue jeans, bomber jackets, and white, red, and blue golf shirts, sturdier outfits better suited to industrial work and more reflective of normal wear on the street. A Warkworth escapee need only rip off his name tags to make himself sartorially indistinguishable from the vacationers he will encounter on his exit route from the Kawarthas.

The legislation that keeps inmates in jail longer also grants them broader rights during their stay; the courts, while reflecting society's demands to keep criminals off the street longer, are becoming proportionately more liberal in their interpretation of prisoners' rights in those cases that do manage to reach them. Yet the courts can do nothing about the overcrowding, dehumanization, and violence that comes with the territory.

Michel, an astute thirty-five-year-old, served his entire eight years for a violent attack on his homosexual lover.

> It's the disregard for life that hardens you. Look at what they do here in Warkworth. That guy that died of a heart attack in the kitchen last month, did you see what the coppers did to the dead body? They chained it to the stretcher, because he still might be alive. They're supposed to rehabilitate you, teach you respect for life, and here they are, coppers, regular guys, guys who go home every night, making a spectacle out of a dead body. How are we supposed to learn respect for others? In Kingston, the guy in the cell next to me hung himself. He was so dead, his hands were black, they still chained him. Give me a break. We don't need rehabilitation. We need respect.

If the American experience is indicative, society will no more tolerate the high cost of maintaining a huge prison population humanely than it tolerates the convicts themselves. Consider, for example, the following memorandum dated June 21, 1993, from the Inmate Committee chairman to Warkworth's population, giving new pace to the term "emergency":

> It has come to the Inmate Committee's attention that a lot of guys are unaware of how to use these Emergency buttons beside your sink.
>
> In case of an emergency you must:
>
> 1. push and hold your button for at least 5 to 7 seconds.
>
> 2. push your button at least 2 to 3 times in succession for immediate response.

The memo brought to mind two scenarios: both assumed that God was familiar with CSC buttons and allowed a grace period during emergencies. In the first scene, I was having a stroke in my cell in the middle of the night; one hand was on the emergency button and the other was holding a watch with a second hand — presciently brought to jail by inmates for just such an eventuality.

The second scenario envisaged three doped-up freaks come to wreak vengeance against me, a representative of the "dump truck" profession that had sold them out in court.

"Excuse me, gentlemen, could you hold on for just ten to twenty-one seconds while I push this little button here two or three times? It won't be long."

Only in the abstract, through the Charter of Rights and the rule of law, are inmates considered citizens or people. Cruelty, rather than toughness, will eventually be the rule. Unless we do something about it, or put everyone away for life, the ones with three-year sentences will attack us, the ones with ten-year sentences will attack our children, and the ones with thirty-year sentences will attack our grandchildren.

Yet there is a compelling case for long prison sentences. Most convicts, as most people, mellow with age. My unscientific observation was that the prisoners who "burned out," who got sick of being in jail and of their own senselessness, were the most likely candidates for rehabilitation; the extent to which this reflects insufficient and ineffective rehabilitative facilities is for the academics to examine. From my viewpoint, Stony's story was typical.

By the time I was twelve, I was into big trouble. Raids with street gangs, drugs, robberies, that sort of thing. When I was twelve, they put me in training school. I was in a group there with fifteen other kids, and they asked us if we could see ourselves in the penitentiary. Just me and another guy said yes.... I hated myself and everybody else. I got into dangerous situations all the time. I don't know how many times cops drew their guns on me. By the time I was seventeen, I'd done everything, including sexual assaults. Then I killed somebody in 1972. Jail saved me. I'd be dead if I hadn't gone to jail. Some cop would have shot me.

I met this woman eight or nine years ago. I'm thirty-seven now, she's seven or eight years older. We got married. She's got a kid — we've got a kid — I'm the stepfather — who's sixteen now. That's all I live for, for my family.... I'm also close with a niece. She keeps asking me when I get out.... One day, I'm going to show up on her doorstep for her birthday.

You know, when you start thinking about someone else, it isn't long till you start thinking about your victims. They have families too, don't they? I never thought about my victims before. It was over for me, but not for them. I know that now. But you know, when I was a kid, they never made me clean up my own shit. The victims weren't real; the cops or someone else dealt with the victims. I never heard about them or saw them again....

... I change faster the older I get. I'm tired of the shit and the fighting.

To be sure, some prisoners don't want to be rehabilitated; but surely that speaks to the need for greater emphasis on rehabilitation; if we impose sentences that keep people in jail until they are responsive to rehabilitation, we must have a system that attempts to rehabilitate them effectively and releases them as soon as they are ready. As Dr. W. L. Marshall, the father of CSC's sexual behaviour treatment program, and his associate, Sylvia Barrett, point out in their landmark work, *Criminal Neglect*:

> *Treatment should be provided to all incarcerated rapists and pae-*
> *dophiles early in their sentences, when the motivation to change is the*
> *highest. When sex offenders are forced to wait years for treatment ...*
> *their hope and enthusiasm dissolve into cynicism and despair.*

We are working ass backwards. Early treatment rarely happens in our system, but it is not CSC's fault, and certainly not that of its frontline staff, its overburdened LUs, COs, and therapists. Bound up in a huge case load and overwhelming paperwork — as cigarettes are the currency of prison's guests, paper, it seems, is the life-blood of its hosts — COs have little time for people. The high-water mark of neglect may have been reached when an inmate, after years of pleading, was finally scheduled to attend a Community Reintegration Program in Warkworth that, unfortunately, commenced two weeks *after* his release date.

Although media-induced hysteria points the finger for the correctional system's failures at CSC and the Parole Board, the truth is that the federal government refuses to provide adequate funds for facilities or training that will enable CSC to carry out its mandate. COs cannot recommend treatment for those who require it because the waiting list is too long; they cannot prioritize treatment for the most motivated inmates because the few places available are taken by cons who have been in the longest, who are closest to statutory release or warrant expiry, and who are the least likely candidates for success.

One of my neighbours in Ten Block was Dustin, a forty-three-year-old wife beater grown into self-awareness after spending ten of the last twenty-five years behind bars. His story, documented in the CSC files that he showed me, reminded me of Philippe Clement's haunting remark that many of society's criminals are "victims too."

It started when I was eight. Two of my aunts abused me. Two of my cousins who were abused by the same aunts drowned themselves. I was gang-raped in reformatory when I was eighteen. This is my second pen bit. My first was in Joyceville, for three years. I was there for beating up a woman who loved me, my common-law wife. She bought me a farm and a herd and gave me all the money I wanted. But when things went bad, I thought she was blaming me, I felt belittled, so I tried to show her love by forcing her to have sex. They did nothing for me in Joyceville. They let me out with no money, I couldn't get any welfare, I slept in an abandoned car.

It's just since the last time I've been in jail that I realize sex and love and aggressiveness aren't the same thing. But it's not thanks to Warkworth. I've been at Warkworth for two years and they've done nothing for me again.

For almost a year at Warkworth, I taught Dustin computers and helped him with some of the fifteen diploma courses in farm management that he had taken and passed with honours, a result made possible by long days of hard work at his books and computer. His relationship with his long-time girlfriend, Bonnie, which preceded his immediate sentence, had deepened in jail as he had come to understand loving and being loved. When Bonnie, despairing at the unhelpfulness of the authorities, sought solace in a three-month affair, which she ultimately confessed to Dustin in January

1993, this man with a history of violence towards women worked it out rationally and lovingly with his mate. By summer, their relationship was stronger than ever.

But Dustin was getting bitter, his motivation to improve himself becoming harder to sustain. Things didn't get better when he was told, the day before his brother's funeral, that CSC was asking the Parole Board to gate him. That meant that he could attend the funeral only if he went in handcuffs and shackles. "Have you tried hugging somebody when you're cuffed?" he asked me when he returned.

CSC would try to help Dustin only before his release, when he was least motivated to seek it. The result, I guessed, would be the release of an angry man just a few years after the system might have freed a rehabilitated one. I believed that if Bonnie stuck it out, Dustin would make it, no thanks to CSC; if he reoffended, CSC could point to Dustin's passage through the program motions just before his release, confirming Marshall and Barrett's opinion that "the primary purpose of existing treatment is to appease the public in the wake of controversy."

Warkworth's untargeted, release-date approach to rehabilitation with little regard for cost-benefit analysis touched on the ludicrous when Whiff, a lifer, complained to me about his program.

"This program's a waste of time," he moaned. "For the last three weeks, all we've been talking about is the past. Why do they bring up the past? It's all over and forgiven. What's the point?"

"Whiff," I explained patiently, "maybe they think that by looking into your past, you can understand your feelings today."

"I know how I feel today."

"The idea is for you to understand why you feel that way. What's it all about, anyway? What program are you taking? Anger Management, Coping Skills, Substance Abuse?" I prompted.

"How am I supposed to know? Nobody ever told me."

Similarly, other courses require literacy, writing, and comprehension skills that much of the prison population lacks; these people would be better off in school. I spent many hours assisting inmates who could not cope with their programs intellectually, their frustration turning to the anger many of the courses were aimed at mitigating.

More and more inmates are refusing treatment. Those who have been "gated" — detained until warrant expiry — have nothing to gain; those who are approaching parole or statutory release dates have no faith that their participation will facilitate their release; the word is out that the Parole Board has succumbed to public pressure and that program participation doesn't make a difference. Like it or not, human beings need incentive, and for the jailed, release is the greatest incentive. The benefits to society of rehabilitation should be enough incentive for the government and the Parole Board, but they seem to be missing the point — often lawlessly so.

Just as often, the laziness of the indolent, the cynical, and the uncaring frustrates both their well-intentioned competent co-workers and the prisoners who do cry out for help.

Louis, just turned thirty, had an ugly history of violence and drug trafficking but had managed to stay out of the penitentiary until his current three-year sentence for drug possession and possession of a dangerous weapon, a sawed-off shotgun. Louis was exceptionally bright but emotionally ravaged, so much so that he had set his cell on fire in a suicide attempt while in the hole in maximum.

I met Louis in Warkworth Reception, where he took as much of my time as he could. His questions were mostly about what he could do to help himself; he had been distressed since his suicide attempt, having received no help in maximum. In October, several months before his statutory release date, his CO presented him with a gating notice. Soon afterwards, his mother died; he attended her funeral, chained. The prospect of another year in jail and the death of his mother, as well as his wife's determination not to let him see his son when he was released, grated on him.

Louis became more and more irritable, to the point that he himself sensed an explosion nearby. He asked me to talk to the guards to get him some help: "They'll listen to you, they won't listen to me. I'm just a piece of shit to them."

Although I was wary of breaking the Code's strict rules against discussing other prisoners with staff, I thought Louis was sincere. In a brief, ten-minute conversation, I told one of the guards of Louis's fears about his emotional state, offering my own opinion that Louis needed help badly and immediately. Nothing was done.

Two weeks later, Louis snapped, tearing up the Reception lounge, destroying the toaster and fridge and throwing the microwave through the glass surrounding the bubble. I never saw him again after a dozen guards took him to the hole; from there, Louis went back to max. He was released, his pleas for help ignored, sometime in late 1993. I doubt that he will seek help on the street; so they will send him back and probably let him out again. If he hurts someone badly enough, someone may find time to listen — or maybe they'll just throw away the key.

Many convicts I encountered had a less situational, more long-term desire for rehabilitation than Louis. Most of them, however, swore the system was of little help in their efforts. That was Tiny's opinion:

> They were suspicious when I told them I'd changed. When I gave up smoking, I took back control. It was the first day of my life. But they didn't care. They only trust you if you change because of their programs. They got no fucking respect for anything you do for yourself. But I'm not waiting for them. They're just gonna store me away until my statutory and six months before that try to change me. What's the point

of trying to change you and then send you right out? They should get at you early in your sentence and see if you can live with the changes you say you've made.

When Tiny first became my cell partner, I could see him struggling, on his bad days, to turn down the drugs he was continually offered, but he never faltered. That made me wonder about a system that tries to rehabilitate people by forcing them into close quarters with the very influences that have induced and sustained their criminality. If those coming out are more prone to antisocial conduct than when they went in, the argument that "at least we're keeping them away from potential victims" is faulty: the separation is temporary and the relief illusory.

Apart from seeking my company, Tiny avoided the prison subculture by participating in Narcotics Anonymous and Alternatives to Violence programs; he was instrumental in building NA's membership, eventually becoming its chairperson. A natural marketer, he talked up the benefits of substance-free living whenever he went; his polite ways and the respect he engendered inspired other inmates. Our conversations about lifestyles and drugs and victims convinced me that something special was happening to this man who had spent his last fifteen birthdays in prison and known nothing but substance abuse and violence since he was a teenager.

Winston, jailed for abusing his thirteen-year-old stepdaughter, was at the other end of the spectrum. He was in denial until he was released in early 1993. He had refused to take any programs and spent his entire sentence aggravating his bitterness by protesting his innocence and blaming his ex-wife for the "conspiracy" that landed him in jail. Winston vented his case in an exculpatory manuscript that was his unintended confession.

As soon as we got home I set up the camera and asked Linda if she was ready to pose.... **I had to get her to pose so that I could use the pictures to keep her from my bed. This not getting any sleep was killing me and I wanted to show her the consequences of her action should she pose like that when she got older.** *She said that she wasn't going to pose until I said that I would pose with her.... Then she went to her room and came back with a ... book.... She said that we could pose like the people in the book.... Which we did as the pictures will show. There is no picture which shows us having intercourse.*

Unrepentant, Winston laughed at the system.

I was arrested in 1987 and charged with molesting my stepdaughter.... To date it has cost you, the taxpayer over $381,000 to keep me here, feed me, clothe me, educate me and to house me, and what for? Lets suppose I had touched my stepdaughter. Now if I had, $1/10$ of the amount of the money spent would have been more than enough to cover therapy for both her and I, she wouldn't have been put through the guilt of feeling she broke her mother and I up, she would not feel guilty about me going to prison, and her mother would not be doing on one pay cheque what took two to do before. They are now sitting down to kraft dinner while I'm sitting back resting, being educated, fed steaks, chops, roasts, and relaxing like I have never been able to before, because I had them to feed, clothe, and educate etc.

Winston's attitude makes the best type of argument for the enactment of "predator legislation." The outcry for a Sexual Predator Act, which would keep offenders in jail indefinitely beyond the end of their sentence, did not arise because our law has inadequate mechanisms to keep incorrigible sexual criminals off the street under a system of law that befits a democracy: life sentences and indefinite sentences under our Dangerous Offenders Act could do the trick quite nicely. It arose because our system and the people in it have failed to assess properly whether and when those sentences should be imposed and how they should be carried out. If we are not equipped to decide when to release, how can we decide whom to detain, without the risk of a grave injustice? Fortunately, the Liberal attorney general, Alan Rock, has rightly concluded that predator legislation would be contrary to the Charter of Rights.

There is, of course, also considerable doubt as to the effectiveness of treatment; Marshall and Barrett note, with disapproval, the Ontario Ministry of Health's conclusion that sex offending is not a mental health problem. I had an opportunity to assess one of CSC's programs in April 1993. Warkworth, desperate for space, had been trying to send me back to minimum since early that year, but, content with the anonymity and my routine and delighted with the way the staff treated me, I refused to go. Since Warkworth is a treatment facility, I couldn't stay without taking a course; my fight with Nick qualified me for the Anger Management Program.

At first, I resented being forced to take a course with ten hardened criminals. But my course mates changed as they learned; some of them would not act on what they learned once the pressures of life overtook them, but for many of them, the program was their first hint that there was another way of looking at what was bothering them, what made them act as they did, and what brought them to prison.

That we do nothing is not true; that we could do much more is true: the right answers are "not enough" and "not intelligently enough."

"White-collar criminals," the expression the élite uses to voice its disgust that one of "us" has gone bad, are in a different position as far as rehabilitation goes. Their crimes are not violent, their recidivism rate is low, and generally, there are no realistic concerns about their reintegration into the community.

Many criminologists, sociologists, and lawyers opine that it is a waste of taxpayers' money to warehouse white-collar criminals at horrendous cost; put people like Melnitzer to work, the argument goes, doing community service, using their capabilities to make restitution and do some good for the segments of society who could use the help. There is no need, these professionals say, for "specific deterrence" for white-collar criminals; in my case, the collapse of an entire life as I had known it is sufficient punishment, as well as restraint on my future conduct. Spend the money on the high-risk and the violent.

Opponents of this philosophy speak of "general deterrence," which suggests that only the prospect of incarceration will discourage others from behaving in the same way. Mr. Justice Maloney invoked this principle as justification for my nine-year sentence.

With the distinct advantage of actually spending time in prison, I agree, to my own fascination, with the advocates of jail time for white-collar criminals who have committed crimes of the magnitude of my own, but I do so for different reasons.

Society at large and crime's victims in particular have a need for revenge. That need is satisfied by shaming, the disgrace that comes with eviction from mainstream society into a community of pariahs with whom we are forever associated.

Shaming is not so much imprisonment. In my case, and that of others like me, shaming is the ignominy of being led to a doctor's office in the Belleville Mall in handcuffs and shackles, sitting bound in the waiting room, and having the cuffs, but not the shackles, removed, at the insistence of the outraged physician.

This type of shaming is society's true revenge, for it does not leave the psyche easily; I refused to leave Warkworth again for the CAT scan recommended by the doctor, because the memories of the Belleville Mall were too vivid. They still are.

And that's fine with my victims — and with many observers. For my victims take no comfort in my rehabilitation if it means that I am being readied to live among them again.

For recidivists, for people who have known no other life, and perhaps for those whose crimes are not of sufficient scope to invoke a public outcry, shaming does not serve the same function. In the case of the criminal subculture, society cannot satisfy its need for revenge by casting its outcasts to their own kind. Here society takes precautions, not revenge, by denying freedom, by separating offenders so they can do no harm.

Convicts who have changed their ways are welcomed back to the fold, because their rehabilitation speaks formidably to the mainstream's social conscience. No such welcome awaits the mainstream's own who have strayed; society, ashamed of its wayward members, rarely wants them back.

The call for community service as the appropriate penal disposition for white-collar criminals misses these impulses. If people like me were ushered into community service, we might re-establish ourselves through the exercise of the same talents that allowed us to commit our crimes, this time channelling them to the public good. Community service for us would be an invitation to ingratiate ourselves with the very society we harmed, rebuilding our reputations by benefiting the community; those members of society who were not our victims might well climb on the bandwagon of our new achievements. Shame would be diluted in favour of reconstruction. Philosophically, there is much to be said for that approach, but it is an unrealistic reflection of society's visceral needs.

Speaking personally, jail offered me an opportunity for happiness that would not have arisen had I remained in the community. Community service at the time of my sentencing could have reignited the need for recognition that destroyed me. I would have pursued that path legally and decently, glorying in the wonder at my rehabilitation — but with no more happiness than turning to crime gave me; for while my path to recognition may have changed, my drive to it would not have diminished.

In jail, I learned that rehabilitation is a quiet thing — to enjoy, not to display.

Reprieves and reminders

As commendable as remorse may be,
it does not suffice ... anymore than merely
regretting a fire will prevent a recurrence.
DR. ABRAHAM TWERSKI

Most of Warkworth's population resides in four living units located on the corners of a rectangular compound. A broad walkway divides these buildings from a central square awash, in the summer and fall, with a thousand plantings of bright flowers and bushes, the blooming a tribute to Warkworth's inmate gardeners.

Rarely is more than one guard on duty in the compound, and he or she is usually occupied in the innocuous concrete block hut that blends into Nine Block in the northeast corner. On summer evenings and weekends, the compound fills with cons in leisurewear, some half-naked, tanning, playing cards, strumming guitars, talking, chatting, smoking, and dealing.

There is something restrained, almost lazy, about the compound, and but for the preponderance of young men, its deceptive ease gives off the air of a seniors' complex in Miami. On canteen nights or when a large shipment of drugs has arrived, the hum of trade takes over, not as peaceful, yet soothing in its cadence. Whatever the night, the compound comes off like a well-worn neighbourhood, where all is as it should be.

At the end of November, I moved from Reception to Ten Block.

Pushing my belongings past the EMU down the breezeway to the compound prompted memories of other hurried moves in the system, all memories of helplessness and of rupture, where the decision to move wasn't mine.

The main landing in Ten Block accommodates the bubble, a card room, and two TV rooms outfitted with fridges, microwaves, toasters, and a hot-water sink. Six yellowish ranges are grouped in three pairs, three above and three below the bubble; twenty-one inmates live in seventeen cells on each range; all the ranges have a collect telephone and an enormous shower room for individual use.

Cell D17 was spotless, reeking of occupancy by obsessive-compulsive twenty-year-old Jeff, my new cellmate. A few weeks after I moved in, Jeff confided that he had lived in terror until he was convinced that I had no sexual interest in him; his cell partner in Millhaven had sodomized him. In defiance of the Code, Jeff reported the incident to the Ontario Provincial Police, who laid sexual assault charges against his tormentor. As the trial approached, Jeff was repeatedly threatened, unsafe even at Warkworth; at his request, he was transferred to western Canada.

In the past, I would have taken an interest, tried to open Jeff up and do what I could to help. Now, withdrawal kept pace with solitude; ten months in prison had taught me that low profile was a combination of silence, ego control, and distrust. A wholesome selfishness was eroding my contrived and controlling mask of charitability, as I continued my search for an identity based on fusion rather than seduction.

The unit manager called for me on my third day in Ten Block. Behind a desk, next to a large window overlooking the compound, sat a fleshy, bearded, middle-aged man; a tattoo on his right wrist hinted at a naval background. Beside him sat a tall brunette in her mid-thirties.

"I'm Rex," said the man. *No kidding. And I'm Gene Autry. What's your horse's name?* "And this is June, your CO."

I nodded at June.

"So you're a lawyer," Rex went on.

"Was," I replied without hesitation.

"Still picking on words, though," Rex taunted. "Did you know Peter Demeter and Joe Pomerant, the lawyer?"

"I knew of them."

"Well, I got along with Joe. He did pretty well in prison. Used the time to lose thirty pounds. Peter thought he owned the place."

"I remember reading something about the warden here inviting Demeter to a party at her house," I said.

"Yes," said Rex, looking at June, "we don't do that any more. Well, how do you like it here?"

"I like it. It's the best prison I've been in."

Rex's deep eyes magnified behind his glasses. "How about this unit?"

"So far everything's good. I've only been here two days."

"We'd like to keep it that way." Rex picked up a brown file in front of him. "What are all these grievances about?"

Although I had abandoned my efforts to return to Beaver Creek, I had maintained grievances seeking rescission of my disciplinary status, reinstatement of my pay level, and back pay for my three months in Reception.

Rex opened the file, picking up my back-pay grievance. "This is five pages long. There isn't anybody in Warkworth who understands it. We'll have to bring the lawyers down from Ottawa."

I had made the grievances as technical and difficult as I could. From the corner of my eye, I saw June shaking her head ever so slightly, her bemusement betraying her insight.

"This will cost thousands of dollars to process. I haven't got enough money in my budget," Rex complained. "How much money is involved?"

"A few hundred bucks," I answered.

"Is it worth it?" Rex asked.

"It is to me. I'm furious at Beaver Creek. I'm not complaining about Warkworth."

"They do screw things up over there. Mind you, I know Les Judson is a good man. Have you tried to talk to him?"

"Not civilly," I joked. "Take my word, I'm not on his appointment schedule.... They never charged me with anything."

Rex looked at June, unbelievingly. "Is that right?"

June nodded and shrugged affirmatively; Rex tapped his fingers on his desktop.

"I'll tell you what. I'll see if I can get the grievances allowed, but I want a promise from you."

"What's that?" I expected another request to join the rat patrol.

"Promise me that if you have any problems, you'll talk to me and June before filing any grievances."

"I'd be delighted." I *was* delighted, knowing I functioned best with direct access to the top. "I promise."

"Good."

I was genuinely taken with the man's reasonableness. I decided to take him at his word. If he wouldn't play games, I wouldn't.

For months, I took my problems and complaints directly to Rex and June; without exception, our differences were resolved quickly and fairly, so much so that I refused the comforts of the EMU when my turn came up in February 1993.

There was much more freedom in the Blocks than in Reception. The cell doors, locked overnight, opened at seven for breakfast. We could do as we chose until 8 A.M., when work, school, or CSC programs started. Shift workers, like kitchen, library, and canteen staff, had the run of the prison during the day; cell students, supposedly locked in their rooms during working hours apart from two ten-minute coffee breaks, often wandered to the library, their friends' cells, or on personal business around the prison, depending on how well they got along with the guards.

At 11:30, everyone returned to their cells for a forty-five-minute lockup count; at lunch hour, we were on our own. Afternoon working hours ran from one to four, with half an hour to pick up the mail before the supper count at 4:30; five to six for dinner was followed by four and a half hours of uninterrupted leisure.

Inmates could choose among a myriad of activities: canteen, hobbycraft, the gym or the yard, cultural groups, chess club, computer club, weight club, Toastmasters club, JayCees, AA, or NA; they could read in the library, wander around the prison gossiping, make out in their cells, watch television, play cards in the common rooms, work on their computers, play pool on any of the four tables in the lounge above the gym, get high unless they got caught, or telephone their friends and loved ones. Cons went to inmate purchasing for mail-order goods, everything from manila envelopes to CDs to TVs to computers; recreation purchasing sold sweatsuits, shorts, T-shirts, running shoes, tennis racquets, and other sports equipment; prisoners pursued glass painting, leatherwork, woodcarving, and a host of other interests in the hobbycraft shop; chose from a selection of greeting cards in the card shop; and arranged for photographs of their activities and visits in the camera shop. These amenities, and others, have led to the popular, but misplaced, arguments regarding the connection between Canadian prisons' comforts and the system's rehabilitative failures.

Apart from the clubs and cultural activities, Warkworth had an organized sports program that was the envy of the penitentiary system. The weight area in the large gymnasium was badly overcrowded and the machines in poor shape, but the pits were moved outside during the summer, solving the space problem for almost half the year. The gymnasium itself was large and functional, including two weight pits, two racquetball courts, and two squash courts. All year round, the Inmate Committee and JayCees organized heavily competitive leagues and tournaments; basketball, floor hockey, indoor soccer, badminton, volleyball, and racquet sports flourished in the winter, with baseball, soccer, and tennis leagues in warmer weather.

The scenic track around the yard brought out the walkers and runners daily in the spring, summer, and fall, and on winter weekends the cross-country skiers glided by my window on their way across the sports field. Less active inmates played miniature golf and participated in pool and card tournaments on long weekends. Transferees to Beaver Creek complained, justifiably, about the relative lack of organized activity at the camp.

When the yard closed, I turned from tennis back to the pit and temporarily rediscovered my boyhood passion for snooker, but soon missed the aerobic exercise and learned to play racquetball. My knees ached, but I learned moderation, to quit while I was ahead of the pain; I also learned to play for fun, to lose without *Angst,* to enjoy the sweat for its release and the game for its play.

Warkworth's generous visiting hours helped pass the time. Visitors were welcome from one to four each weekday afternoon and six to nine on Tuesday and Wednesday evenings; on weekends and holidays, V & C was open from nine to four. There were no limits on the number of visits; some of Warkworth's residents serve practically their entire sentence in V & C; these were the "locals," cons whose wives and families followed them from prison to prison, moving to the closest town. The locals' wives formed their own community, sharing the same problems, taking turns driving one another to the prison, and delivering one another's kids to hubby at the jail for the afternoon or evening when Mom couldn't make it.

The visiting room, though overcrowded and noisy at times, was pleasant, with glassed-in windows and doors opening to a patio garden surrounded by the handiwork of the same gardeners who planted the compound's flowers. Cheery lawn furniture and umbrellas, a large sandpit and slide, green grass and trees all around, and the sounds of children playing gave V & C an unlikely festive air in the warmer months. Yet the condescension of a few guards was almost always inescapable, leaving visitors with the unmistakable message that they were doing something wrong by visiting a criminal.

Occasionally, heartbreaking partings left me with a detached dullness when my visits ended, as did the Orwellian sound of my name over the loudspeaker from time to time, but, for the most part, the dedicated trips of Melissa, my mother, my brother, and my loyal friends and clients stood for warmth and life at the end of the line.

Now that I was in the Blocks, I was allowed to work. Unlike many of the inmates, who remained in their cells because they couldn't find a job, I had four offers of employment.

Tutoring was low-profile and comfortable because of the easy relationship I had formed with Judd. And I liked working in out-of-the way Eighteen Building, which housed the Adult Basic Education (ABE) classroom.

A short, slim, dark-haired man of fifty, Judd had started as a guard in the Maritimes twenty years earlier, moved to Warkworth in the mid-seventies, upgraded his education, and turned to teaching. Although, technically, Judd reported to the head of education, the ABE program and classroom were his fiefdom; he proudly referred to both as "mine," using the power of his tenure effectively.

Unlike many of his contemporaries at CSC, Judd had come to terms with himself; he had no need for naked power as self-enrichment, resorting to his authority only as a last resort. His credo was that inmates were people, not robots. Judd understood the limited intelligence, impaired cognition, and deprived background of the vast majority of his students, handling their tantrums with an equanimity remarkable in the penal system. He ignored harmless shoving matches, preferring to let inmates work things out on their own; anywhere else in the system, the same behaviour would have drawn a charge and hole time. Judd tolerated inmates who called him names, but only once, gently drawing them aside to warn them; a second outburst was an intolerable challenge, but Judd quietly waited until the end of the class to give the inmate his termination notice. His offhand ways were matched by a scrupulous evenhandedness that avoided charges of favouritism.

Above all, Judd was an effective teacher. His methods depended on the give-and-take jocularity of his relationship with the students: he prodded them, goaded them, and made them laugh, but never embarrassed them. Virtually every student who could progressed, and some made enormous strides, graduating from illiteracy to the regular school in Twelve Building. Judd worked hard at instilling pride and self-confidence in his charges, doing more for their rehabilitation than any number of Warkworth's touted programs.

Judd's class worked partly because his tutors were self-motivated types: at one point, the group included a lawyer, a doctor, an architect, and a civil engineer; Judd took full advantage of their backgrounds, allowing them as much independence as he could, brokering an unusual tension-free togetherness in the class.

I was comfortable here, among the unlikely group who constituted prison's underprivileged. I bristled at cons who, on hearing where I was working, laughed at the "dummies" and "retards" in the class. Most of the students were trying and learning, overcoming prison's restraints in their creeping, honest way; that was more than I could say for many of the better-educated or smarter cons, whose manipulative, parasitic ways doomed them to a life of feigned smugness. I was proud to be in Judd's class, taking a quiet satisfaction even in the progress of students in which I had played no part, relieved to be in one of prison's sanctuaries.

As Christmas 1992 neared, I lost myself in my writing and in my workouts, pouring out years with my words and anger with my perspiration. It was not enough to offset the melancholy pall that the holiday season cast over the prison. December is very quiet in the penitentiary, a time of year when cons drop their guard and admit to themselves how much of the world they cannot share; most of them bear their pangs alone, for the Code does not change with the seasons and emotions remain bolted.

A harsh winter made country roads dangerous, and Melissa, a regular visitor since her return from Israel in mid-October, came less frequently; others delayed their trips. The mail slowed down, and December's Christmas parties made it difficult to reach my friends on the telephone. My first illness in prison, a painful ear infection, dampened my spirits.

Tiny, ever alert to my moods, took to bringing me evening snacks, heaping platters of his delicious culinary concoctions. The sight of Tiny's beatific, smiling face at the bottom of the stairs to Ten Block's landing was the day's moment of sunshine. My friend supplemented his generosity with his never-ending positivism, which he dispensed on our habitual walks around the compound, often in inclement weather.

"The thing is this, you gotta look at the perspective," he reminded me. "I only spent two Christmases on the street in the last fourteen years."

"I'm not used to it, that's all," I said.

"Shit happens! Look at the bright side, you'll be out this time next year."

On our walks, Tiny told me more about himself. He resented his mother for leaving his father when he was a teenager; despite his father's harshness in Tiny's youth, the old man meant a lot to Tiny. They stayed in touch with the occasional letter, and his father sent cash gifts at Christmas and on Tiny's birthday.

"Remember I was telling you about that job I had in microfilm at KP?" Tiny asked one night as Christmas drew near. "You saw that letter my boss gave me saying what a good job I did. Well, I sent it to my father, and he called my boss to see how I was doing."

I thought I saw The Small Man, as I had come to call him, choke up through the snowflakes. "When you were still in Kingston?" I asked.

"No, I sent him the letter after I made it to Warkworth. My buddy, who used to work in microfilm too, got shipped here today and told me about it."

"That's great. Didn't your father ever say anything to you?"

"Nah, he wouldn't say that kind of thing."

"Don't you guys write? Have you got any letters here at Warkworth?"

"Yeah, I got one, but he didn't say nuthin'."

"It means a lot to you, doesn't it?"

"I guess so. It's nice to know he's interested in me."

"You should be proud of yourself, Tiny."

"Maybe he'll say something when he sends me my Christmas present."

"Well," I said impulsively, "I'm going to give you a Christmas present. I'm going to write your father and tell him how much that phone call means to you. I'm also going to tell him how well you're doing staying off the dope, and how important his support is."

"Nah," Tiny protested. "You're kidding." But his eyes lit up.

The gentle giant grew misty when I handed him a copy of my letter the following week. And his father wrote back to Tiny, acknowledging my note and saying things he might never have said otherwise. Tiny didn't show me the letter, but he talked about it, one firm step farther away from his outlaw past.

I learned how much it all meant to Tiny when he polished up his treasured Toronto Maple Leaf mug, a priceless prize in prison, and made his oldest, most cherished memento his Christmas gift to me.

Christmas Eve and Christmas Day are the only times the joint and the Code break down openly. Buffet tables dress up the ranges on Christmas Eve, and the Salvation Army and Inmate Committee provide gift bags for all. The prison becomes still, the swearing decreases, counts are short, even the most hardened guards look the other way at minor transgressions, and meals are served on white tablecloths in the decorated dining hall. On Christmas morning, some of the early risers shake hands sheepishly with their jailers, equals for a moment. For a few short hours, anger goes into remission, giving way to the warmth of smiles and good wishes, even the odd "Happy Chanukah." Near the end of my first year in prison, the true spirit of Christmas prevailed, in the last place I expected to find it.

Perhaps it was the season, or the passage of time, but my silent tirades against the warden and Deena quelled somewhat. Contrasted against Warkworth's sudden peacefulness, however, my anger was still too intrusive, and I searched for ways to belay it. I wrote a lengthy letter to the solicitor general, Doug Lewis, regarding my knowledge of the Clement escape and the lax security at Beaver Creek; on December 23, I mailed the letter, and as I dropped it in the inmate mailbox at Two Control, I felt the first real dilution of rage.

My feelings for Deena were another matter. There was nothing I could write to her, or about her, that constructively vented my emotions. Yet somehow all my writing seemed incomplete, as if I was writing in the third person about myself, depersonalizing the events of my life in prison — and outside it — by excluding their pain.

To pass the time while I solved my dilemma, I began a short story about my relationship with a woman with whom I had had a brief affair. I started on Christmas Eve and wrote for three days.

On December 27, when I was halfway through the story, Deena called. As soon as I heard her voice, I knew I had come a long way from our phone call in September: then, I would have given anything to have her back; now, I wasn't sure — not at all.

Later, with help from Hans, I realized that the woman I had written about was Deena. Our marriage had been an affair. With that realization, I let go.

At the turn of the year, I applied for day parole. The Parole Board scheduled my hearing for July. A preoccupation with release unsettled the hard-earned stability that had come with my belated adjustment to incarceration. But it was an equivocal preoccupation: jail wasn't a bad place to hide, I thought, and, more than once, I wondered whether re-entry into society was the real *coup de grâce* of punishment. As if to emphasize that point, the *Globe and Mail*'s *Report on Business* featured a cover story on my case, and within weeks, a hardcover book about me made it to the *Toronto Star*'s best-seller lists.

Inside Warkworth, the effects were minimal; the staff who knew of the publications were discreet in their remarks, unlike the catty personnel at Beaver Creek. Warkworth's alert librarian took the *Report on Business* piece out of circulation, a decision ratified by security. My gratefulness eluded my distaste for censorship: I rationalized that the withdrawal was not my idea.

Still I despaired at the effect of the publicity on my family, especially on Melissa and my mother. This gut reaction, a sincere regret for the pain I had caused them, was the first real jump from self-pity to remorse.

Soon, visions of my victims kept me awake: their lives, their savings, their kids, their homes, their jobs, our good times together, their respect, their blind belief in me. My mind's eye travelled through their days whenever remembrances of me came into their lives, along the fleeting shafts that passed through their decisions and their happiest, brightest moments as memories of what I had done to them put stoppers on their trust. I pictured them lying on their beds, late at night, unable to sleep, angry, hating, silently cursing, blaming themselves — uncannily like myself. But they were innocent. And I knew that made it worse for them, much worse than it was for me. Punishment was having to make the best of my life, knowing I could never change that.

Betimes, I came to terms with myself. I could not undo what I had done, but neither could I live forever by the opinions of others: that was too much like my old life. *Anyway, there's something ludicrous about "showing" remorse. What does remorse look like? Since when is a show, an obvious display, proof of the existence or intensity of any emotion?*

Melissa's three-day family visit in early February dissolved our mutual anxiety over the publicity. We were both sure the worst was over. February 10, the last day of our visit, marked the first anniversary of my incarceration; over a simple dinner in the darkened CSC cottage, by the peaceful glow of the kitchen stove's lamp, we celebrated survival.

Part Six

REJUVENATION

*I think somehow, we learn who we really are
and then live with that decision.*

ELEANOR ROOSEVELT

Reorientation

He never grew up; but he never stopped growing.
ARTHUR C. CLARKE

Prison wasn't so bad, and getting better all the time. When Jeff moved to a single cell in the middle of February, my new roommate, Sandy, Warkworth's "Merchant Prince," spent most of the next two months in the hole, leaving me single-bunked again for most of March and April. I stepped up my writing at the computer my mother gave me in December 1992; Judd conferred greater responsibility at work and time passed effortlessly.

After a year in jail, I was as comfortable as I had been anywhere, inside or out. I had learned to fit in, in a system where compromise was concession and frustration was the norm. When some of my friends suggested that I was getting "institutionalized," I took it as a compliment. As time passed, my profile rose as more inmates and staff came to know me, but I had mastered the art of keeping a high profile at a low level, and I encountered little of the envy that dogged me at Millhaven and Beaver Creek.

To be sure, not all of that was my doing; the passage of time, the decreasing publicity, the large population, and the staff's sensitivity all played their part, as did Hans's continuing devotion, the Prozac, and, of course, Melissa. My greatest contribution to my own peace of mind came from my contentment, which kept me apart without being aloof, and my relinquishment of ingratiation as a tool of integration and control. With the masks disappearing, the things I liked about myself were the things that showed, and, to my surprise, they showed well.

I traded quietly in prison's markets, making life for myself as good as it could be without scattering my resources. My wages were more than enough to provide for my needs: juice, extra food, extra cereal and desserts from the kitchen, haircuts from a qualified barber, cell-cleaning and personalized daily laundry services, preferential court time from the inmates who worked in recreation, underpriced gifts from inmates who worked in hobbycraft, and daily newspapers from inmates with access to them.

From the outset, I approached the staff in Ten Block cautiously, letting them engage me at their own pace; I had learned the hard way not to volunteer information or advice. Careful not to seek indulgences until the staff made it clear that they trusted me, I thanked them profusely when they did, letting them know that I appreciated the leeway. I took "no" in silence, whether I thought it was right or wrong. Custodial minds are more interested in deference than rules, and the staff at Warkworth was no exception, more than happy to make life as pleasant and humane as possible for trustworthy inmates. Mindful of my need to stay productive and that I could help other inmates, the staff permitted students in my cell during lockups and looked the other way on the slow days when the lessons turned into social gatherings.

I refused opportunities to take charge, begging off requests to speak at the prison's clubs, turning down a petition to be Ten Block's representative on the Inmate Committee, and even rejecting Rabbi Schneider's request that I lead a Jewish study group, though I conducted the Passover Seders in his absence. At school, I ensured that Judd openly sanctioned my educational initiatives, having learned to keep my personal agendas to myself.

Professionally, I volunteered no information, joking my way out of most inquiries.

"You a lawyer?"

"Used to be."

"What kind of lawyer?"

"Courts."

"Could you help m——-"

"Sorry, I'd get fifty guys at my door every night." Respect for privacy, "quiet time," was inherent in the Code. When that didn't work, I asked for an inmate's file, telling him I couldn't help him unless I got both sides of the story; or I asked for a bale of tobacco as payment for my time. Almost invariably, the conditions ended the conversation.

At the same time, I didn't have it in me to refuse, or charge for, simple requests to draft complaints, letters, or parole applications for the illiterates or nearly illiterate who had nowhere else to turn; I referred the serious legal problems to lawyers.

At times, I wondered, as I had in Millhaven, whether my search for the best of everything was only being slowed by my circumstances; after all, things were as convenient as they could possibly be. I still worked the system well. But there was a difference: now I worked within the system, not obsessively against it.

It was a question of degree. I had no aspiration to monkishness or the ethereal reaches of a purely spiritual existence. I still had ideas, many of them pragmatic in an earthly sense, but that was OK too; a thoughtful sense of proportion was replacing my corrosive insatiability.

Though I still endured the cycle of anger, depression, confusion, and progress, the phases in the cycle became less extreme as time went on. Satisfaction in each step forward solidified and defined my growing sense of self-esteem; I began to see disappointment as a part of life, a guide to the future, not merely a repository of humiliation. In that frame of mind, I made a proposal to my creditors; my heart and hopes sank at their rejection of my offer without discussion, but the disappointment didn't detract from my feeling that I had done the right thing.

Melissa, my family, my capabilities, and my new sense of self were the building blocks of a new life, but they were fragile, needing focus and exploration. I would have to narrow my world further, continuing the stabilizing process by which the territorial boundaries of prison were leading me to inner shape.

Self-evolution of that kind cannot be forced or hurried. It is a process of recognition, of finding lenses for our insides that one day permit us to recognize the glosses on life, the steps to fulfilment, the conditions by which we seize all the things we can't control and make them meaningful. So it was with the aftermath of the public's reawakening to my case through the cover story in the *Globe*'s *Report on Business* and the book about me that followed.

My friend Doug, my consulting client, had visited at Christmas and our friendship had grown. But after reading the book about me, his tone seemed to change. I wrote him about my feelings, knowing that I was trashing my best opportunity for financial security when I got out. But I didn't want to pretend any more.

In the next few months, more friends drifted away, as if the prospect of my release made them realize they would have to meet me on the street; others, without saying so, patted me on the head gently, as if to say, "Yes, yes, Julius, all this philosophy is great now, but you'll want all the things we want when you get back out — and we know you have what it takes." To these people, I found myself defending my emerging views of what life should be; soon I recognized that by embracing a different, not better or worse, value system, I was threatening them.

In jail, though, my enhanced ability to get along made life better for me than for many of the inmates at Warkworth. Conditions deteriorated as longer prison terms and the Parole Board's blatantly political exercise of their mandate forced more double-bunking; simultaneously, a deficit-reducing government capitalized on the popularity of cutting back services to convicts.

The degenerating atmosphere contributed mightily to the drug-assisted violence that invaded Warkworth in June 1993. Despite tight security at V & C, described by my mother and Melissa as "tougher and more thorough than Millhaven," the drug trade got the upper hand.

Within a few days, Rosie, who had followed Tiny as my room-mate in Reception, literally had his head kicked in by a strung-out kitchen co-worker, necessitating four weeks in the hospital; my range mate John, deeply in debt, expressed his frustration by spitting in the face of three of his supervisors, which got him a trip back to Kingston Penitentiary, a street charge of assault, and another nine months in jail; Geri, one of several resident drag queens, likely loaded on Percodan, chased her most recent patron around the baseball field with a putter from the miniature-golf course, decrying his lousy business ethics; and three hoods, desperate for a fifty-five-year-old inmate's two cases of pop that could be bartered for drugs, beat him unconscious.

The senselessness, fed by rumours of more double-bunking, put Warkworth at the edge. Communication between guards and inmates became clipped; inmates kept their distance from one another, hearing nothing, seeing nothing; tempers flared over the use of the phone; and prison's banter disappeared. For two weeks, Warkworth felt more like maximum than Millhaven, and never in prison did I fear more for my safety.

In Millhaven and at the Creek, I had sensed the hostility — I could imagine an angry attack by a con with a real or imagined grudge against me — but the drug-related tension at Warkworth induced a fear of the unknown, the notion that I could be an incidental victim, a bystander, injured or dead at the hand of someone who had no purpose in his attack, and no idea who I was or that I was.

In June 1993, an inmate attacked one of the institution's female psychologists, shortly after an unpopular copper was punched out when he accidentally wandered in on a pill party. Warkworth security cracked down. Unlike the feeble and disorganized *ad hoc* security efforts at Beaver Creek, the IPSO's plan at Warkworth made it clear that trafficking would be tough on the innocent as well as the traffickers.

With a single request for a strip search of the wife of a prime suspect, whose visiting rights were cut off when she refused, Warkworth served notice that all visitors were under scrutiny; inside, inmates were randomly strip-searched on their way back from their visits; security posted guards at the dining hall exit, forcing inmates to disgorge their extras; even kitchen workers, traditionally entitled to goodies as the perks of their job, were not excluded from the new measures.

The discovery of drugs or an outbreak of violence brought lengthy lockdowns, often during visiting hours: on Canada Day, 1993, I awoke to a darkened range and no response to my buzzer. I was expecting three visitors arriving separately, all from the Toronto area; I had no idea whether they would be turned away at the gate or how long they would have to wait before I could see them. I contented myself by writing until the cell door opened at mid-morning, comfortable with the tranquillity I had learned.

The harsh measures made informers of many of the innocent, incensed by punishment for crimes to which they were not a party. As drugs' availability grew scarcer, the ringleaders took more chances and their drug-starved clients grew bolder, facilitating apprehension. By the end of June, the main players were in Kingston or

Collins Bay. Things went back to normal — at least until a new drug hierarchy emerged in the constantly changing population.

Apart from my unease at the outbreak of violence, the spring and early summer were good times for me. The only serious disruption arose when CSC tried to send me back to camp, after June classified me as a minimum security inmate. With June's passive cooperation and Bob Bigelow's intervention, I successfully resisted the attempt, confounding many staff and inmates who couldn't understand the notion of happiness, or at least contentment, in jail.

My new roommate, Josef, a physician, was a welcome surprise. As former professionals who led respectable and successful lives, we related well intellectually and emotionally: arrested at the pinnacle of our careers, we both suffered the ravages of unrelenting publicity and broken marriages; on the bright side, we retained a surfeit of love and friendship from our children, our family, and loyal friends, old and new.

When Judd gave Josef a job in the school, he and I became inseparable. Soon Josef was joining Tiny and me at mealtimes, their separate friendship fostered when Josef, an expert gardener, offered to help Tiny with his vegetable plot. Tiny relished the broadening of his mainstream associations, and his common sense, good humour, and hard-core knowledge of prison life helped Josef adjust to his new realities.

Shared anxieties about our upcoming day-parole hearings in July preoccupied both Josef and me: in his bad moments, Josef feasted on my understanding of the system and its legalities; at the same time, his steady, sensible approach to life was a tranquillizer to my own anxieties.

In April, I put to rest other vestiges. In response to my December letter to the solicitor general, CSC had promised an investigation into my allegations about Beaver Creek, but retracted the promise

two months later. I resolved to go to the press, hesitating, however, to consider whether my outrage was just another burst of
attention-seeking.

At Melissa's suggestion, I sent my material to the *Gravenhurst
Banner,* on condition that they respect my anonymity and return my
originals. The ease with which I adopted my daughter's idea assured
me that my motives were not masks. The *Banner* didn't act on the
story or respond in any way. I let the matter drop; I had done the
best I could.

At the beginning of May, I made a list of employment contacts
and potentials, keeping them in the perspective of the writing career
that was my primary goal. In order to write and make a living at it,
I would have to keep life simple and overhead minimal. I wanted my
own place and I wanted a car and I wanted to write; I could shoot for
everything — but that would be approaching life as I had approached
it before. I applied the lessons of jail and opted for simplicity.

Life was as good as it had ever been. The anger against Deena
and Les Judson had disappeared. On the Friday evening of Victoria
Day weekend, I wandered down D range's hallway, looking to borrow a stapler and a few manila envelopes. The music from Detroit's
cell caught my attention. Music had not distracted me since Sister
Margaret took me to her chapel, but now, the occasional object of
my range mates' quizzical stares, I sat on the cement floor for an
hour listening to the tunes. *Escape. Not like before. Not to retreat. To
rapture. Hans, I've learned to smell the roses. You'd be proud of me. I'm
proud of me.*

False start

You lied. Only your facts were correct.
JANE L. GLASSCO

Josef and I were both optimistic about day parole. June, our competent and caring CO, readied the paperwork for our hearings early. The halfway house had accepted me, the parole office was willing to undertake my supervision, and June's recommendation to the Parole Board urged that I had garnered the "maximum benefit from incarceration." The letters from the Crown and the RCMP recommending early day parole were before the board, and Hans reported that I was an "extremely low risk" to reoffend.

In the spring, Bob Bigelow had expressed his first reservation about my chances for release, discouraged at the Parole Board's adherence to an internal policy against day paroles longer than twelve months — a policy that, on its face, was in violation of the governing legislation. As I read through the strong case Bob had put together for me, I thought little of his reservations.

In Josef's case, the merry-go-round of CSC buck-passing reached new heights. Josef was a sex offender, serving five years for fondling a patient ten years before his conviction. Before his sentencing, Josef took intensive sexual behaviour counselling from a Clarke Institute psychologist who is one of Warkworth's consultants. Both the Clarke

Institute psychologist and the senior psychologist at Warkworth concluded that Josef, having lost his licence to practise medicine, was no threat to anyone; Josef's case management team agreed, as did the halfway house that accepted him. The Warkworth psychologist, however, felt that it would be prudent for Josef to undergo phallometric testing for deviancy at the Regional Treatment Centre (RTC) in Kingston to corroborate the testing at the Clarke.

At RTC, Josef fell into the hands of a young Master's student in psychology, who took an immediate dislike to him. The phallometric reports were consistent with the earlier results, showing no evidence of sexual deviancy, but the psychology student recommended continued treatment in a prison setting. The head psychologist at RTC, who had never interviewed Josef, signed the report.

The report's conclusions astonished Warkworth's senior psychologist; he concluded that many of Josef's answers were taken out of context, as Josef claimed, and opined that the student's bias was so strong as to suggest that he was himself a victim of abuse. Josef's lawyer recommended an adjournment of the parole hearing; without the opportunity to subpoena the signatory to the report and without the right of cross-examination, the lawyer was helpless. I suggested to Josef that he commission a rebuttal from an independent psychologist; his lawyer agreed, but observed that the Parole Board was sceptical of professionals who were not "CSC sanctioned."

Josef now faced sure failure at the Parole Board or a wait of several years to get into CSC's backlogged treatment programs. He could easily spend an extra two and a half years in jail based on a jaundiced opinion from a junior staff member. Luckily, the sympathetic staff at Warkworth arranged for his prompt transfer to Bath, where hopefully, his participation in a ten-week program for sexual offenders would clear up the treatment issue for the Parole Board. At best, Josef would be out six months later than he should have been; other, less marketable offenders, non–white-collar types without Josef's resources, charm, and *savoir-faire* would have been in for years. In his case, CSC used up a valuable spot in a treatment program for a man who didn't need it, spending scarce funds in doing so.

Josef's trials gave me some pause about my own chances, but a move to a single cell on F range, a visit from Hans, and another three-day family visit with Melissa on the weekend of June 18 kept me at ease. The Parole Board scheduled my hearing for July 22.

Thursday, July 6, was the tail end of a heat wave. Our class poured onto the lawn outside Eighteen Building to escape the humidity indoors. I was lying on the grass with my eyes closed, trying to catch up on the sleep I had missed by staying up to write until five in the morning, when Judd poked his head out the window.

"Julius, they want you back at Ten Block."

I walked back leisurely. June met me at Ten Block's door, frazzled.

"Your parole hearing's on this morning," she said.

"What? Is my lawyer here?"

"I'm sorry. I had no idea either. They called me twenty minutes ago. I haven't had a chance to prepare my presentation. You can probably get an adjournment."

Time and time again, I had seen what happened to inmates who adjourned or waived anything at the Parole Board; it took months for their hearings to be rescheduled, as if their consent to a postponement encouraged CSC and the Parole Board to treat their freedom casually.

"No way, June. I'm going ahead." She didn't try to dissuade me.

I hadn't shaved in three days; my white T-shirt was full of grass stains and streaked with sweat. Perspiration poured down my face and through my clothes as we double-timed to the main building. June seemed more upset than I was, concerned about performing her duties off the cuff and miffed at the Parole Board's bungling,

about which she had often complained to me. I didn't really mind:
I could take care of myself.

The two members of the Parole Board sat behind a conference
table in a meeting room dominated by a structural pillar awkwardly
placed in the middle of the room. The chairman, a pleasant-faced
fellow in his mid-fifties, oozed redneck from the cut of his hair to
the knot of his necktie. He would not have stood out anywhere,
but almost certainly would have hung around long enough, devot-
edly dutiful, to be remembered by his local MP when he'd had
enough of working for a living.

The woman to his right was a long-haired brunette in her late
thirties, sufficiently fashionable in her bright business suit to offset
the fuddiness of her male counterpart. She generated an air of intellectual respectability with her careful choice of scholarly spectacles,
a model I would have chosen if I was trying to explain the meaning
of "Ms." to the uninitiated.

The chairperson read the formalities, asking if I wanted to pro-
ceed without my lawyer. His tone encouraged an adjournment; I
reconsidered briefly, but declined. At the back of my mind was the
absence of the media; it hadn't occurred to a sloppy *London Free
Press* that my hearing might precede my August eligibility date; a
one-month adjournment would let the newspaper correct its mistake. With a look of serious distrust, Ms. carefully grilled me. "Don't
try to set up an appeal at my expense," she seemed to be saying.

June summarized her report, concluding that I was an "assumable
risk" for day parole. When the chairperson opened his questioning by
observing that my hearing was "right on time," well in advance of
my full parole eligibility date, I suspected my freedom was in trouble.

"How do you think the public will react to your release after
only eighteen months?"

It didn't matter that I was a low risk to reoffend; it didn't matter that there was no evidence to suggest that I was anything other

than a low risk; it didn't matter that I had unanimous support for release. Parole Board decisions, as I had long observed — and subliminally feared — had little connection to law and logic. What I had either overlooked or denied was the impact of releasing, only eighteen months into a nine-year sentence, a man who had stolen millions of dollars and whose close friends were among his victims. It simply wasn't enough punishment, and the fact that the Parole Board's job wasn't to assess punishment stood for nothing.

"Sir," I answered, "I think that some members of the public will be very upset if I'm released, but you know as well as I do that that's got nothing to do with this hearing."

The chairperson shrugged off my remark; Ms. didn't like it.

Thirty minutes later, having heard about the hearing by chance, Bob Bigelow arrived. During a fifteen-minute adjournment, he tried to calm me, but it was too late; I had put on my lawyer's robes and, despite the silent discouragement of Bob and June, continued my aggressive remonstrances.

Ms. could barely contain herself when the chairperson finished. She warned me that a negative public reaction to my release could impair my reintegration and therefore was a component of risk. *As if the bankers and lawyers are going to demonstrate in front of the halfway house.*

Ms. went on to compare my psyche to that of the sexual deviants whom she routinely gated. When I wouldn't given in to her Psych 101 lecture, she asked me to shorten my answers. By this time, Bob and June were beside themselves. I wasn't hopeful when the board retired.

The board was divided on whether to release me, without revealing how each member voted. That meant another hearing in August before a different panel.

In failing to consider the political and emotional forces at work, I had ignored my own lessons to my advocacy students, to whom

I had always emphasized the importance of differentiating merit and impact in presenting a case. While the bizarre circumstances of this hearing were unlikely to be repeated in August, I now estimated my chances of release at no better than fifty-fifty. I felt little anger, however, a bonus for which I was thankful.

A capacity to accept disappointment without humiliation was not the only indication of how far I had journeyed in a year; another week went by before I realized that July 13, my wedding anniversary, had come and gone, disappearing with the bad dreams and the anger; twelve months earlier, I was agonizing over the conciliatory letter I hadn't mailed to Deena.

Soon after my hearing, June was promoted and replaced by Kim, an inexperienced CO who was unfamiliar with my file. I had barely come to grips with June's departure when Bob Bigelow called to tell me of his appointment as a provincial criminal court judge. I congratulated him.

"To tell you the truth, Julius, I'm going to miss you," Bob said. The spontaneous admission from a man of few words and fewer overt emotions heartened me beyond words. Bob recommended that I hire Sandra Leonard; considerably junior to Bob, Sandra had worked closely with him and with David Cole. I followed Bob's last bit of advice, as confident in it as I had been in his careful, caring guidance throughout.

I began ticking off each of the thirty-eight days between July 6 and August 13, my new hearing date, on my calendar.

On Friday, August 13, I woke early, easing my nerves with a long shower. I distracted myself at my computer until the PA summoned me to the administration building at 10:30. I slipped on my jeans, running shoes, and short-sleeved prisoner's golf shirt; I had saved the new shirt for this occasion, even had it pressed by the Block laundry man (for a pack of cigarettes, naturally). As I made a final

check of my grooming in the mirror, "MELNITZER" in black capitalized lettering announced me severely from the one-by-three white
label just above my breast pocket.

On my way to the hearing, I practised deep breathing exercises,
promising myself to restrain my aggressiveness. Melissa had arrived
an hour before I showed up, awaiting my arrival impatiently in the
main building. Sandra Leonard came shortly after Melissa, consci-
entiously prepared.

Two senior board members, Mr. Stienburg and Mr. Macdonald,
would hear my case: Stienburg was the chairperson who had turned
down my application for parole by exception at the Creek, but he
had been scrupulously fair and by-the-book in his decision. The
bad news was that the *London Free Press* was in attendance. I had a
disquieting sense of futility, even as Melissa and I infused each other
with alternate doses of hopefulness and comfort.

As the hearing began in the same room where the July hearing had been conducted, Stienburg noted — ominously, as if he
had been there the first time — that was I eighteen months from
my full parole eligibility date.

The board's questioning was much more to the point than it had
been at the last hearing. The panel was sceptical of the sincerity
of my therapy with Hans, my financial status, and even the motivation behind my tutoring. Two of the questions indicated that the
board was relying, improperly, on information the members could
have obtained only from the *Report on Business* piece and the best sell-
er about my case; I glanced over at the tape recorder to make sure
it was running, aware that good grounds of appeal had just arisen.

Stienburg shamefully took every opportunity he could to char-
acterize the entirety of the legal profession as disreputable, a stand
he had been taking for his more than twenty years on the Parole
Board, without rebuke or objection from any professional association. I held my temper, the lawyer in me, and my sarcasm in check,

seriously strained though it was when Stienburg asked Melissa whether she wanted to say anything. In the midst of her remarks, Melissa, reflective, emotional, tearful, and holding my hand, asked for a moment to collect her thoughts. Stienburg observed, cruelly, that she was "[her] father's daughter"; perhaps he was referring to my habit of pausing and thinking before I answered his questions, but, in the context, it was an undeserved and mean slight. For Melissa's sake more than for my own, I kept my mouth shut.

It didn't make any difference; nor did my scorpion, which I had clenched in my fist for two hours. After a short recess, the board denied my parole: the decision emphasized the enormity of my crime, the issue of my emotional stability, and my greed; the board conceded that "institutional reports are favourable, all noting your efforts, your progress and even the contribution you have made in specific areas," but lamely concluded that release on day parole could "act as a destructive move" and "could result in increased risk." The board did not directly address the question of the "risk of reoffending," cowed, no doubt, by the unanimous favourable reports and CSC's point system that put me in the lowest category of risk. Sending me back to jail, the board concluded, exercising its capacity as God, was not "additional punishment" but an opportunity for the continuation of a "growth process."

Throughout the hearing, I sat directly opposite the chair across the narrow width of the conference table that separated us. As Stienburg read the decision, I stared straight ahead at him, unblinkingly, sending the silent message that his transparency was inescapable. When he finished, Stienburg asked if I had any questions. I said no, got up, and left.

But my anger didn't last long. The board's dishonesty was their problem, not mine. Even the realization that my careful management of my guilty plea had not expedited my freedom was liberating; months earlier, I had lost my desire to survive by conscious imperative alone.

Sandra, Melissa, and Kim were all supportive, agreeing, without prompting from me, that the board's decision was political. Despite Sandra's gentle urging, I had no desire to focus my energies on the anger I knew would come with an appeal. I would apply for a new hearing in six months, and in the meantime, spend the time that had become so precious to me peacefully and productively.

When I left the main building, there was no crowd and no questions. Only Tiny and Josef, among the inmates, knew of the hearing; the few Block staff who knew and Judd, whom I told, were sympathetic and discreet. The Toronto papers didn't bother with the story.

Melissa stayed for three days, and friends followed her, visiting for another three days after she left. I had people I loved around me. I had no secrets. I had learned to accept myself and the things I couldn't control. A year wasn't a big price to pay to find out I wasn't angry any more; time anywhere was precious to me, so I was much better off than I had ever been. These were all prison's gifts.

That evening, I went to an anniversary party at Narcotics Anonymous: Tiny was celebrating his first drug-free year. He would make it. So, I was sure, would I.

Exit

Our life's work is to use what we
have been given to wake up.
PEMA CHODRON

I resigned myself to remaining in prison until my full parole date, leaving hopes of earlier release to the realm of pleasant surprises. But whenever that release came, I would build for it now. Even the warden's initial rejection, in November, of the unescorted passes recommended by the Parole Board in its August decision barely intruded on my resolve. I had learned to live in the present, feeling my way around myself a little better every day.

Sick of hiding, I started writing with publication in mind. My first effort was a piece about the untimely heroin-induced death of my roommate, George Chuvalo, Jr., son of Canada's best-known heavyweight boxer, within days of his release from Warkworth. The *Toronto Star* featured the article on its front page. Within six months, the *Globe and Mail,* the *Toronto Sun,* and the *London Free Press* had published my work. I offered a critical piece on the role of lawyers in the prison system to *Canadian Lawyer,* but it was turned down as "inappropriate" — not for its content, but because I was its author.

At Warkworth, I resisted renewed hints that I transfer to minimum, encouraged by a change of CO from the inexperienced, defensive Kim to a seasoned and intelligent woman named Marla. As word of my computer skills and legal background spread, I was called on by many of the teachers, the shop bosses, and the librarian to maintain their computers, install software, and write data bases; the Education Department looked to me for surveys of the inmate population, research, and general advice. Throughout, I continued tutoring in Judd's class, now confining my teaching to one-on-one lessons with the neediest students.

Socially, I remained in my comfortable niche, spending most of my time with Tiny, otherwise confining my leisure hours to my cell, apart from trips to the racquetball court in winter and the weight pit in spring and summer. Tiny continued to mature despite a debilitating bout with cellulitis; the heartbreaking and untimely death of his dear friend and inspiration, the Reverend Donna Easter, founder of the Unity Church in Mississauga and a devoted volunteer at Warkworth; paralysing injuries to his brother resulting from a car accident; and his seventy-nine-year-old father's battle with cancer. To help Tiny through the hard times, I suggested he join the Warkworth Jewish Congregation as an observer; there, inspired by Rabbi Schneider (whose jurisdiction included both Warkworth and Beaver Creek), he became a moving force in the group, developing a genuine interest in Judaism. When Reverend Easter died, we sat on a compound bench reciting the *Kaddish,* the Jewish prayer for the dead, he in English, I in Hebrew.

Apart from Tiny, rehabilitative reviews were mixed, for I had now been at Warkworth long enough to catch the failures on their trips back to the joint. The biggest shocker was Mickey, my pal from Beaver Creek; after his release on parole, he was arrested on numerous rape charges occurring between 1978 and 1982, and was eventually sent to Kingston Penitentiary on an indeterminate life sentence as a dangerous sexual offender.

My first Warkworth roommate, Dino, got out in the summer

of 1993 and was back before a year was up, along with countless others too numerous to mention. Jason, the gym enforcer from Millhaven Reception, was released from Bath at the end of 1993, breached his parole, and was returned to Millhaven following a man-hunt in eastern Canada. Philippe Clement, the escapee from Beaver Creek, got two additional life sentences for his attack on a Gravenhurst woman and is doing his time, likely forever, in a maximum security institution. His victim sued CSC for allowing Clement's escape; at the trial, in September 1994, I testified before Madame Justice Susan Lang about the security conditions at Beaver Creek and about Clement's state of mind in the weeks preceding the escape.

But it wasn't all doom and gloom: Kevin, my first friend on the Grey Goose, contacted me at Warkworth in the summer of 1994. He had stayed at Beaver Creek as long as he could, as promised, finished up a number of university computer science credits at the government's expense, and was now attending the University of Waterloo full time. Undiscouraged by his marital failures, he was about to wed a young coed he had met on campus.

Wade, the man transferred from Beaver Creek to Warkworth because he admitted, during a therapy session, to having a solitary drink one year previous, left on statutory release in early 1994. He's still out, employed, and putting the lie to his past.

Aaron was eventually released on day parole. I never heard from him again. Plug was investigated and eventually transferred to anoth-er penitentiary in British Columbia. Beaver Creek now houses two hundred inmates — and things are much stricter there. Les Judson is still the warden. Josef, my physician friend, was turned down for parole and is still in jail. Nick, my fellow pugilist, is on parole, working and rebuilding his life.

While I couldn't have been happier, considering my circum-stances, the general conditions at Warkworth took a steady turn for the worse. An upturn in drug-related violence robbed the Christmas season of its unique mellowness, kick-starting 1994 with a heightened bitterness in the population. CSC's new fiscal year, beginning April 1, brought rumours of further overcrowding, cutbacks in food services, and belt-tightening for inmates' education, programs, and activities. Within weeks, triple-bunking began, and before my eyes, Warkworth changed — forever, I suspect.

In my *Globe* article, I had predicted that Warkworth, now twenty-seven years old, would soon experience its first homicide: a changing population, a quarter of whom were now coming from hard-core Collins Bay and Joyceville; escalating drug trafficking; stepped-up cell searches and strip searches before and after conjugal visits; frustration over deteriorating living conditions; anger over inaccessibility to overcrowded programs that were preconditions to parole; and a frustrated staff who were becoming more and more alienated from the prison's management, all promised spiralling violence.

In the summer of 1994, two stabbing incidents and an attack on a guard, previously rare at Warkworth, led to maximum-style lockdowns: twenty-three-and-a-half-hour lockup, meals shoved under cell doors, and cancelled visits without notice to visitors. By mid-July, I had decided to transfer to minimum if my upcoming parole hearing was unsuccessful.

Racial overtones started to creep into the violence, but as of August 1994, the Administration had done an admirable job of keeping the lines of communication open with the black inmate community, constantly adding black staff. Paradoxically, Warkworth elected its first black Inmate Committee chairperson that summer. Early in its mandate, the new Inmate Committee was the subject of sabotage attempts by hard-core druggies angry at being ousted from power and the trafficking opportunities that power presented.

Apart from my success at having my writing published, my personal life had stabilized: by agreement, Deena served me with divorce papers in June; Melissa and I were closer than ever; a growing rapprochement with Cathy, to Melissa's delight, began with my letter to her, thirteen years late, apologizing for my callousness; my sister, whom I had neither seen nor spoken to for almost eighteen months, came to visit, fostering a new, warm relationship; I grew closer with my mother and brother. When I left jail, I would have a family.

Leaving jail became a reality in February 1994, when the warden approved two escorted passes, allowing me to visit Hans. My escort was Judd, with whom I had now been working for almost eighteen months, to an ever-deepening friendship. Two unescorted weekend passes to Toronto followed; I spent them with Melissa celebrating, among other things, her admission to medical school.

As my parole hearing, scheduled for July 21, approached, fear did not, as it had the previous year, intrude on my desire for release. The attitude of both staff and inmates, all of whom wished me well, reflected the changes in me: somehow, I had learned to live with others and still be myself.

With that strength, a start in a new career, the capacity to feel and give love, and the peace of mind that came from knowing that Melissa's future was secure, I feared nothing and had nothing to hide — for the first time in my life. I glossed over the vagaries of making a living, confident that even if my writing didn't sustain me, my abilities and my core happiness would find a way. My growing security coincided with a burgeoning desire to do what I could to undo the harm I had wrought and compensate my creditors — within the parameters of my psychological and financial survival, heeding Hans's advice to avoid new obsessions in the guise of remorse. I had learned enough about life to make a start on living.

On July 18, three days before my parole hearing, the *Ottawa Citizen* published my criticisms of the Parole Board in an article entitled "Parole Board Hog-tied by Its Own Procedures." Don Clark, the chairperson, began my hearing by asking: "I hear you don't like us?" I agreed, but, to the board's credit, my published critiques did not seem to influence them. Clark's questioning was thorough and relevant. At one point, he asked how I thought the victims would feel if I was released after two and a half years.

"Victims aren't above the law," I responded. "If they think I should do the whole nine years, let them elect somebody who'll make that the law. But it's not. I don't want to be treated better or worse than anyone else. Just according to the law."

Later on in the hearing, at which I represented myself, board member Gayle Puddicombe wanted to know if I thought I "owed society something." That made me think.

"No," I finally answered. "Society has chosen its punishment and should be satisfied with it. But I'd like to do something, on my own, without feeling I have to. Both for the people I hurt and the people in here. I think, you know, I have a unique perspective on the penal system — I've seen it from all sides."

The board didn't take long in deciding to release me to a halfway house for six months of day parole pending full parole. My mother, who had attended her first hearing, Melissa, and I celebrated with an afternoon visit. Our mood was confident, not jubilant; Melissa's prediction, over two years ago, was right: jail had really been the beginning, not the end. Tiny, honest to the end, had mixed feelings — as I had about leaving him behind; but I promised him — and myself — that Warkworth's gates would not break our bond.

One month later, a bed opened up at a halfway house in Toronto. On August 17, Marla told me I would be leaving on Wednesday, August 24; the news was a pleasant surprise, cutting two months from the three-month wait I anticipated. In the thirty days since my parole hearing, I had continued my routine with little change; living in the present had become instinctive. On Tuesday, the day before my departure, I packed up and moved my possessions to A & D.

In late summer's evening light, I sat in my stripped-down cell, wallowing in an unreality I couldn't define. Prison's end, yet so much like its beginning: alone, in a bare cell, with an uncertain future. But I had me, and I liked myself. Somewhere between the beginning and the end, the trappings had lost their hold.

On Wednesday morning, Tiny walked me to A & D. By coincidence, he would be honoured for another drug-free year at the NA meeting that evening. I saved the homemade card I designed on my computer until the last.

"Thought I forgot because I was leaving, didn't you?" I joked.

"Nah," Tiny replied unconvincingly, just as unsuccessful in containing the solid con's forbidden blush. "You didn't have to," he said, barely getting the words out. "Thanks, thanks — thanks for everything, buddy."

"No, Tiny, thank you. I won't forget you. I promise. Make sure you call."

Melissa waited outside V & C, where she had resolutely lined up for two years. We hugged until the guard urged us on.

"Don't hang around. We might change our mind."

With my daughter in the driver's seat, I stood by her car, turned around, and took one last look, reminding myself never to forget the lessons of freedom I had learned in jail.